Scouts Out!
The Development of Reconnaissance Units in Modern Armies

John J. McGrath

Combat Studies Institute Press
US Army Combined Arms Center
Fort Leavenworth, Kansas

Library of Congress Cataloging-in-Publication Data

McGrath, John J., 1956–
 Scouts out! : the development of reconnaissance units in modern armies / John J. McGrath.
   p. cm.
 Includes bibliographical references and index.
 ISBN 978-0-9801236-1-6
 1. Scouting (Reconnaissance)--History--20th century. 2. Military reconnaissance--History--20th century. I. Title.

U220.M433 2008
355.4'130904--dc22

2008006375

CSI Press publications cover a variety of military history topics. The views expressed in this CSI Press publication are those of the author(s) and not necessarily those of the Department of the Army or the Department of Defense. A full list of CSI Press publications, many of them available for downloading, can be found at http://www.usacac.army.mil/csi/RandP/CSIpubs.asp.

The seal of the Combat Studies Institute authenticates this document as an official publication of the CSI. It is prohibited to use CSI's official seal on any republication of this material without the written permission of the Director of CSI.

Foreword

The Combat Studies Institute is pleased to present *Scouts Out! The Development of Reconnaissance Units in Modern Armies* by CSI historian John J. McGrath. *Scouts Out* is a wide-ranging historical survey of the theory, doctrine, organization, and employment of reconnaissance units since the era of mechanization in the early 20th century.

Reconnaissance and counterreconnaissance are battlefield missions as old as military history itself and missions for which many armies have created specialized units to perform. In most cases, these units were trained, equipped, and used differently from the majority of an army's fighting units. Horse cavalry performed these missions for centuries, for it had speed and mobility far in excess of main battle units. Once the horse was replaced by mechanization, however, the mobility advantage once enjoyed by the horse cavalry disappeared. Since the early 20th century, the search for the proper mix of equipment, the proper organization, and the proper employment of reconnaissance units has bedeviled armies around the world. This survey uses a diverse variety of historical cases to illustrate the enduring issues that surround the equipping, organizing, and employment of reconnaissance units.

It seems that these specialized units are either too heavily or too lightly equipped and too narrowly specialized or too conventionally organized. Prewar reconnaissance doctrines tend to undergo significant change once fighting begins, leading to postconflict analysis that reconnaissance units were "misused" in one way or another. McGrath ends his study with an intriguing conclusion about the role that specialized reconnaissance units should have in the future that may surprise many readers.

Scouts Out is a thought-provoking historical study that we believe will contribute to the Army's current and future transformation efforts. If this study of the past stimulates thought among today's professionals, it will have achieved its purpose. *CSI—The Past Is Prologue!*

Timothy R. Reese
Colonel, Armor
Director, Combat Studies Institute
US Army Combined Arms Center

Acknowledgments

My previous several works were quantitative ones. I'm proud to say I did not turn on a calculator once while completing this project. The work is the completion of a long process that began several years ago as a project assigned to another historian. When circumstances prevented its completion by that person, it was reassigned to me. However, the needs of the service diverted me to other projects before I could return to complete the research and writing in the fall of 2007. This is an important subject. I have felt a historical study of reconnaissance units was long overdue since it seemed in the US Army that such units frequently fluctuated organizationally between wheeled and armored vehicles on a regular basis. At the same time, commanders in the field often used such units as regular combat units rather than specialized reconnaissance elements. However, despite this trend, when the Army devised its new modular structure starting in 2003, it added a cavalry squadron to each brigade while removing a line maneuver battalion. Since no historical works existed analyzing the light-heavy debate while looking at operational employment of reconnaissance units, the modular decision was not made based on historical precedent. Although this work cannot assist, in retrospect, the formulation of the modular construct, it should provide background for future decisionmakers if and when the issue of the "misuse" of cavalry units reappears.

A graphics-intensive work such as this taxes the limits of the editorial and layout staff. Their efforts were extraordinary and produced an excellent product. Mrs. Marilyn Edwards provided yeoman service as editor and layout specialist. Ms. Robin Kern, who has edited or done graphics on most of my previous works, again played a key role in this product. CSI staff management personnel, Mr. Kendall Gott, Dr. W. Glenn Robertson, and CSI Director Colonel Timothy Reese also played key roles in the creation, revision, and production.

Several other individuals require acknowledgment. Mr. David Goldman of the US Army Center of Military History provided key research materials. Ms. Sharon Strein of the Combined Arms Research Library greatly assisted with several important interlibrary loans. Finally, Dr. Alexander Bielakowski, Department of Military History, US Army Command and General Staff College, began this project, providing a draft document that proved helpful in the early stages.

The soldiers of the United States Army and the other armed services, as well as all the civilian and family support components, require specific acknowledgment. As with all the works of the Combat Studies Institute Press in general and my works in particular, it is hoped that in some small way this work will augment the efforts of the troops in the field.

                                          John J. McGrath
                                          Combat Studies Institute
                                          US Army Combined Arms Center
                                          Fort Leavenworth, Kansas

Contents

Page

Foreword iii
Acknowledgments v
Figures ix
Key to Symbols Used in This Work xiii
Introduction and Background 1
    Definitions 1
    Pre-1914 Background 2
    Summary 4
Chapter 1. The Death of Cavalry: Reconnaissance Units and World
             War I 7
    Prewar Organization and Theory 7
        Equipment 8
        Organization 9
        Tactical Employment 12
        Tactical Reconnaissance 13
        Operational Reconnaissance 14
    The Opening Campaign, August 1914 14
    Combat Case Study: The Battle of Hamipré, 20 August 1914 ... 16
        Prelude to the Battle: Cavalry Operations in Early and Mid-
            August 1914 17
        The Advance on Hamipré and the Opposing Forces 22
        The Battle of Hamipré 29
    Insights From the Opening Battles 36
    Reconnaissance Operations in World War I After August 1914 37
    US Army Reconnaissance Units in World War I 40
    Summary 42
Chapter 2. Reconnaissance Theory and Organization in the
             Interwar Period 49
    Introduction 49
    The American Experience 49
         The Air Force as the Army's Reconnaissance Element 49
        The Development of Mechanized Cavalry 51
        Divisional Reconnaissance Elements 55
    The German Experience 56
        Doctrine and Theory 56
        Reconnaissance and the Development of Panzer and
            Motorized Forces 60

	Page
Reconnaissance Troops in Other Armies in the Interwar Period	64
The British	64
The French	67
The Soviets	69
Summary	70
Chapter 3. Reconnaissance Units in World War II	77
Introduction	77
The German Experience in World War II	77
General German Theory, Doctrine, and Organization	77
The Polish and French Campaigns—Ardennes Redux	78
Later German Organizational Developments	88
North Africa and Russia	90
Fusilier Battalions and the Last Years of the War	94
Summary	96
The American Experience in World War II	96
General	96
The Mechanized Cavalry Group	98
The Armored Division	104
The Infantry Division, Regimental, and Separate Battalion Reconnaissance Units	106
Marine Corps Reconnaissance Units	108
Summary	109
The Experiences of Other Armies	111
The French	111
The British	111
The Soviets	112
Summary	113
Chapter 4. Reconnaissance Units and Operations, 1945–2005	123
Introduction	123
Reconnaissance and the Israeli Defense Force	123
Reconnaissance Unit Organization to 1973	123
The IDF 1973 Armored Reconnaissance Battalion and Company	129
Since 1973	133
The Soviet Experience	133
Organizational Structure	133
Operational Employment	136
Summary	138

		Page
Reconnaissance Units in European Armies		138
The British Army		138
The French Army		141
The German Army		142
Operational Reconnaissance Units		145
The American Experience, 1945–2005		145
Postwar to Vietnam, 1945–63		145
The Armored Division, 1945–63		147
The Pentomic Division		148
Battalion-Level Reconnaissance Units		149
The Armored Cavalry Regiment, 1948–63		149
US Army Reconnaissance Units, 1964–2003		151
Modular Army		177
Summary		182
Conclusions		197
Overview		197
The Light Versus Heavy Debate		198
The Availability of Forces		200
Hybrid Units		201
Echelonment		201
Conclusion		202
The Nature of Reconnaissance		203
Glossary		207
Selected Bibliography		215
Primary Sources		215
Secondary Sources		217
Appendix. Selective Comparative Reconnaissance Platforms		233
Index		235
About the Author		253

Figures

Figure 1.	The echeloning of French and German reconnaissance units, 1914	10
Figure 2.	French cuirassiers	15
Figure 3.	French and German cavalry maneuvers, 1–19 August 1914	19

Page

Figure 4. Situation in the Ardennes, 19–20 August 1914 23

Figure 5. German infantry on the march 24

Figure 6. Organization of the French 9th Cavalry Division, August 1914 26

Figure 7. German organization, Battle of Hamipré, 20 August 1914 28

Figure 8. Battle of Hamipré, 0900, 20 August 1914 29

Figure 9. Battle of Hamipré, 1100, 20 August 1914 30

Figure 10. Battle of Hamipré, 1230, 20 August 1914 31

Figure 11. Battle of Hamipré, 1530, 20 August 1914 33

Figure 12. Battle of Hamipré, Dusk, 20 August 1914 34

Figure 13. Typical air observation group, AEF, 1918 41

Figure 14. M1 (T4) medium armored car 53

Figure 15. Proposed German infantry division reconnaissance battalion, 1923 57

Figure 16. German light division, 1939 59

Figure 17. German infantry division reconnaissance battalion, 1939 61

Figure 18. The *SdKfz 221* light armored car 62

Figure 19. German armored reconnaissance battalion, 1939 63

Figure 20. British divisional mechanized cavalry regiment, 1939 67

Figure 21. The echeloning of German and French reconnaissance units, 1940 79

Figure 22. Operations in southern Belgium, 1940 82

Figure 23. Guderian (center) and the staff of the 4th Armored Reconnaissance Battalion (Lieutenants Voss and Munck in black panzer uniforms standing behind Guderian and battalion commander Major Alexander von Scheele to his left) at Bouillon, Belgium, 12 May 1940 86

Figure 24. The German armored reconnaissance battalion, 1944 89

Figure 25. German infantry division fusilier battalion, 1944 95

Page

Figure 26. The echeloning of German and American reconnaissance units, 1944 97

Figure 27. US Army mechanized cavalry group in World War II 99

Figure 28. 14th Cavalry Group in the Losheim Gap, morning, 16 December 1944 102

Figure 29. 14th Cavalry Group situation, afternoon, 16 December 1944 104

Figure 30. US Army armored division mechanized cavalry reconnaissance squadron, 1944 105

Figure 31. US Army infantry division mechanized cavalry reconnaissance troop, 1942 107

Figure 32. An M8 armored car in Paris, August 1944 110

Figure 33. The Sinai theater of operations, 1956 and 1967 124

Figure 34. Israeli AMX-13 light tank 126

Figure 35. IDF 643d Reconnaissance Company, 5 June 1967 128

Figure 36. IDF armored reconnaissance battalion, 1973 130

Figure 37. IDF 87th Armored Reconnaissance Battalion in the 1973 Yom Kippur War 131

Figure 38. Soviet divisional reconnaissance battalion 134

Figure 39. Soviet regimental reconnaissance company 135

Figure 40. Soviet reconnaissance vehicles: the PT-76 light tank (left), BRDM-22 (right) 136

Figure 41. British first-line armored reconnaissance regiment, 1983 139

Figure 42. British reconnaissance vehicles: Scimitar (left), Scorpion (right) 140

Figure 43. French reconnaissance vehicles: AMX-10 (left), Panard ERC-90 (right) 141

Figure 44. German reconnaissance vehicles: Fuchs (left), Luchs (right) 142

Figure 45. West German panzer reconnaissance battalion, 1985 143

Figure 46. US Army light tanks: M3/M5 Stuart (left), M41 Walker (right) 146

Page

Figure 47. US Army armored division reconnaissance battalion, 1948 148

Figure 48. US Army armored cavalry regiment, 1948 150

Figure 49. US Army ROAD divisional armored cavalry squadron, 1968 153

Figure 50. An M114 vehicle in Vietnam showing its difficulty with cross-country mobility 155

Figure 51. M551 Sheridan firing a Shillelagh missile 156

Figure 52. A troop of M48 tanks and ACAVs in Vietnam 157

Figure 53. US Army AOE armored cavalry regiment, 1988 161

Figure 54. American reconnaissance vehicles: M3 CFV (left), HMMWV (right) 162

Figure 55. US Army light cavalry regiment, 1997 164

Figure 56. J-series divisional cavalry squadron, armored and mechanized division, 1987 165

Figure 57. L-series divisional cavalry squadron, armored and mechanized division, 2003 167

Figure 58. AOE light infantry division cavalry squadron, 1997 168

Figure 59. Cavalry forces in Operation DESERT STORM, 1991 172

Figure 60. Cavalry units in Iraq, March–April 2003 176

Figure 61. SBCT RSTA squadron, 2003 179

Figure 62. Modular brigade RSTA squadron 181

Figure 63. The reconnaissance paradox 199

Figure 64. A new paradigm 204

Key to Symbols Used in This Work

Unit Type Symbols

	Reconnaissance/Cavalry		Helicopter
	Armored Cavalry		Aerorifle
	Infantry		Attack Helicopter
	Mechanized Infantry		Aeroscout
	Tank/Armor		Fixed-Wing Aviation
	Stryker Reconnaissance		UAV
	Armored Car		Surveillance
	Machine Gun		Signal
	Field Artillery		Air Defense Artillery
	Antitank/Tank Destroyer		Supply
	Mortar		Medical
	Engineer		Maintenance
	Radar/Sensors		Combined Arms

Combined With Other Symbols

	Headquarters
	Miscellaneous
	Motorized
	Motorcycle/Bicycle
	Airborne/Paratrooper
	Air Assault
	Armored/Self-Propelled

Unit Size Symbols

Squad	•
Section	••
Platoon	•••
Troop/Company	I
Squadron/Battalion	II
Regiment/Group	III
Brigade	X
Division	XX
Corps	XXX

Introduction and Background

This special study examines the development, role, and employment of units in modern armies designed specifically to perform reconnaissance and security (counterreconnaissance) missions. The analysis discerns common threads from the past. Conclusions are drawn from historical trends that may apply to future force development planning and unit operational employment.

In the past, dedicated reconnaissance units were unique in their organization and capabilities due to the presence of the horse. This provided cavalry with a marked mobility differential over infantry and artillery. In the mechanized age, this monopoly on mobility vanished. Nonreconnaissance mechanized and motorized forces were equipped with similar weapons and vehicles. Reconnaissance units then became distinctive primarily by their organizational structure and specialized mission rather than by their equipment.

This conceptual transformation has created a great dichotomy for modern reconnaissance forces. Should such forces be light or heavy? A lighter force might be able to conduct reconnaissance operations, at least theoretically, in a more nimble fashion, while a heavier force could defend itself when conducting reconnaissance and security operations. An additional consideration is the question as to what organizational level should dedicated reconnaissance forces be provided and used. This work examines these two major threads from a historical perspective since World War I.

Definitions

Following the development of gunpowder, but before the development of industrial age weaponry, reconnaissance and security activities at the operational and strategic levels were primarily the responsibility of horse cavalry forces. At the tactical level, such reconnaissance was generally a unit responsibility. After the development of industrial age technology and the decline of horse cavalry, modern armies have deployed various units configured and dedicated to conducting reconnaissance and security missions at both the operational and tactical levels. Apart from this, many other former roles of horse cavalry (and some infantry) have been taken over by mechanized combined arms teams built around the tank. Particular among these are offensive combat, pursuit, and exploitation.[1]

The World War II US Army defined reconnaissance as "the directed effort in the field to gather the information of the enemy, terrain or resources [to] gain the information upon which to base tactical or strategic operations."[2] In turn, counterreconnaissance was defined in the same period as the measures "to screen a command from hostile observation."[3] Before the end of World War II, the term "cavalry" used in this work refers to horse cavalry; during World War II, the term "mechanized cavalry" is used for US Army reconnaissance units; and after World War II, the terms "armored cavalry" and "air cavalry" are most commonly used in the US Army. However, since the adoption of the Army of Excellence organizational structure in the mid-1980s, the unmodified term cavalry has reappeared to designate the division reconnaissance unit that consisted of a combination or variation of ground helicopter units and the ground units equipped with armored or wheeled vehicles. Therefore, the use of the term cavalry in that context does not refer to a unit equipped with horses.

Various armies have echeloned the conduct of reconnaissance into several levels. In this special study, ground reconnaissance operations are divided into two levels, operational and tactical. Operational reconnaissance, sometimes referred to as strategic reconnaissance in older works, is that information developed by large units at corps level and above, operating at a distance from the supported force about the dispositions and movements of the enemy's large units. Tactical reconnaissance, sometimes divided into tactical and close or combat intelligence in older works, is that reconnaissance conducted by lower units to identify the enemy forces arrayed against them, either in contact or close enough to be in contact on short notice. For each historical era examined in this work, both operational and tactical levels are examined by organization and employment of dedicated reconnaissance organizations at each level.

Pre-1914 Background

Before World War I, horse cavalry, along with artillery and infantry, was one of the three basic combat arms found in land forces. Cavalry's role in this triad was the lightly equipped but highly mobile portion of the combined arms force. It was basically an "all purpose, mobile combat force."[4] While considered as such, cavalry generally was used for certain specific roles at the operational level. It guarded the flanks of advancing and retreating forces and generally provided reconnaissance and security for brigade-sized forces or larger. Cavalry also kept the enemy cavalry at bay and provided army commanders with a mobile reserve with which they could present the shock action of a mounted attack as a coup de grace against a shattered enemy army and exploitation of operational success in pursuit of retreating enemy forces.

Horse cavalry forces had specific characteristics that shaped their role and employment. Such units required more logistical support than infantry forces, including the need for forage for the animals and replacement animals as necessary. In most armies, such assets were limited, and commanders husbanded them accordingly, often retaining the cavalry at higher levels in consolidated units.

Before the mid-1800s, horse units typically fought mounted using sabers, pikes, lances, and rapid-firing carbines. Units so equipped could mount a charge faster than defending infantry could fire enough volleys at the advancing cavalry to weaken it to the point where the shock effect of the charge would be neutralized. In such cases, infantry had to use a maneuver in which it formed a complete square formation with a row of riflemen crouched with bayonets sticking up in the air. The bayonets had the effect of stopping the advance of the horses. The utility of the square meant cavalry was usually not used against line infantry unless the latter had already been broken and was in retreat.

Technology, in the form of rifled muskets with faster rates of fire, meant that, by the time of the American Civil War, mounted cavalry could not face the firepower of line infantry under almost every circumstance. Consequently, commanders rarely placed their cavalry in a position where it had to attack line infantry. On the defensive, cavalry fighting dismounted was often used temporarily against advancing infantry to provide security for a main defending force to cover a flank or to delay an enemy advance until the arrival of infantry. In such instances, the horsemen had several distinct disadvantages. A certain number of men had to be retained to hold the reins of the horses, making units proportionally smaller. Additionally, firearms used by the cavalry, while capable of relatively rapid fire, were also short ranged. Except in unusual circumstances, dismounted cavalry could not stand up to line infantry and was not expected to do so.

Horse cavalry possessed a mobility not found in infantry and artillery units. This mobility allowed cavalry forces to move operationally and tactically around the battlefield and area of operations to gather information on enemy dispositions and the terrain. Cavalry also had the responsibility of denying such information to the enemy. Therefore, with the cavalry on both sides being similarly ill-equipped to face infantry, the cavalry forces of opposing sides often ended up fighting each other. Neutralizing the enemy cavalry, therefore, became the de facto main mission for cavalry forces.

Cavalry organization was somewhat more flexible in the Civil War era US Army than was that of the infantry. Unlike the infantry regiment, which was subdivided into companies all directly controlled by the regimental commander, cavalry regiments were typically divided into squadrons of 4 companies each, giving the cavalry regimental commander 3 relatively large subunits to maneuver instead of the 10 companies an infantry regimental commander was expected to control.

Apart from cavalry, which was generally found only at the brigade level in small numbers and larger numbers at higher levels, there were no dedicated reconnaissance elements at the tactical level per se. However, after 1756, the British, in particular, developed specialized light infantry companies in each regiment that served the functions of reconnaissance and security in tactical operations. Eventually, these light companies were grouped together separate from their parent unit and given specialized missions. The role of tactical reconnaissance and security fell to detachments from the line units themselves, organized on a mission-by-mission basis.[5]

In the age of massed infantry, foot soldiers marched in columns and fought in lines shoulder to shoulder armed with rifled muskets fired in volleys. Local reconnaissance and security below the brigade level were a unit responsibility. To conduct these missions, commanders took forces out of hide. Depending on the level directing the mission, part or whole units could be devoted to these tasks. Offensively, these reconnaissance elements were known as skirmishers. Skirmishers advanced in front of the infantry line, found the enemy position, and defeated the enemy advance elements (that is, pickets) before falling back to the main infantry line as the opposing forces closed with each other. Skirmishers were spread thinner than the main infantry line and used cover and concealment to aid in completing their mission.

Pickets were the defensive equivalent of skirmishers. They spread out similar to skirmishers, but the forces they were protecting were usually stationary and either on the defensive or encamped. The picket force provided early warning for its parent unit of any enemy actions on the unit's front. This role was most important at nighttime. As with skirmishers, pickets were assembled from within the unit itself.

Summary

Before World War I, operational-level reconnaissance and security missions were the role of horse cavalry. Tactical-level reconnaissance missions were assumed by the unit itself. World War I, with its massive fortifications, firepower, and eventual rise of air power and mechanization, changed all this. From 1918 to the present, various ground forces at both the operational and tactical levels have designed reconnaissance units using different combinations of weaponry and mechanized and motorized vehicles. This special study examines these developments chronologically, analyzes trends, and develops logical conclusions about the utility and composition of reconnaissance forces based on the historical experience.

The two threads of echelonment and equipment weave through the history of reconnaissance units in modern armies. The classic debate on reconnaissance unit equipment contrasts the fielding of lightly equipped reconnaissance units versus units with heavier vehicles and more firepower. If units are lightly equipped, the historical tendency, as will be seen, is to either not use the units for fear of their destruction or reinforce them, making them heavier units unable to be nimble and stealthy. Field commanders have, in contrast, tended to use heavier units in nonreconnaissance roles. In the past, military observers have considered both of these tendencies to be misuses of reconnaissance assets and have typically proposed a solution that resulted in the opposite extreme, creating a cyclic pattern—the light-heavy debate.

This work proposes a more discerning solution than getting caught in the reconnaissance unit misuse cycle. The frequently cited misuse may, in fact, be an indicator of something more than inappropriate equipment. That field commanders readily forego using reconnaissance specialists for reconnaissance questions the very nature of reconnaissance as a specialized mission conducted by dedicated units.

The echelonment of reconnaissance units also plays an important part in such an analysis. Specialized reconnaissance units may be more important at some levels than at others. Their historical absence at certain levels may be just as significant as their perceived misuse at particular levels.

Modern reconnaissance units developed after World War I. However, the model of these units and their missions were the horse cavalry forces of that war. The next chapter examines the role and operations of such units while focusing on the opening campaign in Belgium and France in August 1914.

Notes

1. Matthew D. Morton, "Men on 'Iron Ponies': The Death and Rebirth of the Modern US Cavalry" (PhD diss., Florida State University, 2004), 2–3.
2. US War Department, FM 100-5, *Field Service Regulations, Operations* (Washington, DC: US War Deparment, 1944), 51.
3. US War Department, FM 100-5, *Field Service Regulations, Operations* (Washington, DC: US War Deparment, 1941), 55.
4. Major Louis A. DiMarco, "The U.S. Army's Mechanized Cavalry in World War II" (Master of Military Art and Science (MMAS) thesis, US Army Command and General Staff College, 1995), 1.
5. R. Ernest Dupuy and Trevor N. Dupuy, *The Encyclopedia of Military History From 3500 B.C. to the Present*, Rev. ed. (New York: Harper & Row, 1977), 665.

Chapter 1

The Death of Cavalry: Reconnaissance Units and World War I

Prewar Organization and Theory

This chapter focuses on the main combatants in the west in August 1914, the French and Germans, and their use of cavalry in that campaign as an example of reconnaissance theory and practice at the end of the horse era. All armies entered the war with large bodies of cavalry. In 1914, reconnaissance was exclusively the realm of the horsemen, although cavalry had additional missions related to being a mobile strike force.

In the opening campaigns, all sides made extensive use of cavalry as forward reconnaissance elements and flank security and counterreconnaisance forces. In Belgium and France, the Germans weighed the largest portion of their horse soldiers to the large German flanking maneuver in Belgium. In spite of the employment of these units, both sides entered battle with a dearth of information about the dispositions of the opposing forces. While the German cavalry was successful in counterreconnaissance, advancing infantry forces often found themselves suddenly opposed by unexpected Belgian or French resistance. On the other hand, defeating the German cavalry consumed the French cavalry to the extent that it was ineffective in both reconnaissance and counterreconnaissance roles.

After August 1914, the use of cavalry as a reconnaissance force atrophied with the onset of trench warfare. Over time, the airplane or the infantry patrol replaced the horseman in this role. In the few places where cavalry was still used later in the war, it was treated as mounted infantry more than as the reconnaissance force, prized primarily for its operational mobility. Cavalry was so irrelevant by 1918 that US forces fielded only one small cavalry unit in the two major campaigns in which the American Expeditionary Force participated.

In 1914, cavalry equipment and organization remained tied to concepts of shock action and mounted combat. Despite this emphasis, most combatants attached infantry units to their cavalry, either mounted in trucks or on bicycles. The German cavalry remained partially effective because the larger cavalry units contained large infantry components. Also in 1914, while cavalry retained several traditional missions, its main role was that of reconnaissance. Reconnaissance was, therefore, tied directly to the saddle at the start of World War I.

Equipment

Cavalry entered World War I with bits of both the new and the old. For various reasons, European armies ignored or deemphasized lessons from the American Civil War in equipping their cavalry. Both the French and Germans retained cavalry armed principally with edged weapons (sabers and lances) useful only in a shock action role. The French retained specialized heavy body armor for the portion of its cavalry called cuirassiers and lances for those called dragoons, while almost all German cavalry carried lances. The overall effect of these then unknown anachronisms was cavalry with less firepower in relation to the other arms in 1914 and limitations on mobility because of the bulky weapons and armor.

Despite a limited adoption of machine guns in the German cavalry division, the cavalry arm was still primarily equipped in 1914 with lances. Between 1870 and 1914, there had been a great debate in European armies over whether cavalry should be equipped with lances or sabers. Both the Germans and French ignored the American solution from 1861 to 1865 of equipping cavalry with rapid-firing carbines as its primary weapon and carrying sabers as a secondary weapon.[1] In the German forces, the original lancer regiments, called *Uhlan*s, were later augmented when almost all cavalry units, including hussars, cuirassiers, and dragoons, were also equipped with lances. Secondary weapons were swords, pistols, and carbines. The lance was 10.5 feet long and weighed slightly less than 4 pounds. It was attached to the trooper's shoulder by a sling. When not charging, the German cavalryman carried his lance across his chest pointing up over his left shoulder.

While one contemporary source claimed that the German cavalry was trained to rely more on the use of machine guns, carbines, and artillery instead of massed shock tactics, the bulk issue of lances dispels this notion. The similar extensive use of the lance in the French service implied that they, too, saw cavalry as first a force of shock action rather than one of reconnaissance and security. From organization, doctrine, and equipment, it was obvious that both the French and Germans believed that shock action used against enemy cavalry and, to a lesser extent, against retreating infantry was considered the first mission of cavalry. Reconnaissance and security operations followed after in importance.[2]

In cavalry equipment and organization, as in most military matters before August 1914, the Germans led the way and everyone else followed. The concept of the continued utility of the lance and its obvious corollary of the importance of the cavalry-versus-cavalry fight was a German one. While one British observer noted that, in the Boer and Russo-Japanese

Wars, the lance and sword were "innocuous weapons," the majority of mounted soldiers in the major European armies were equipped with such weapons in 1914. German prewar doctrine and training clearly stressed the use of cavalry in mounted combat where lances or sabers were the principal weapons.[3]

German cavalry training considered dismounted action to be only a minor temporary expedient conducted by smaller units. During annual divisional maneuvers, German horsemen rarely, if ever, dismounted. In the opening campaigns of the war, at first, all dismounted actions in cavalry units were conducted by attached light infantry (*Jäger*) units, while the cavalrymen continued to sharpen the points on their lances, some of which having been dulled by enemy uniform fabric in the few occasions in which they had been used.[4]

Organization

In the prewar period, the French organizationally structured their 81 home-based cavalry regiments into 10 divisions, each with 3 brigades of 3 regiments apiece. In this way, the French organization contrasted with the German model in which the highest peacetime unit was the brigade. The French Army had organized permanent cavalry divisions only in 1913, but the discussion on such a formation extended at least back to 1901. Paris did not want to go to war having to improvise the largest units in its cavalry.[5]

For use in war, the third regiment in each brigade, which was always a light cavalry unit, was detached to provide the cavalry contingent for a predesignated infantry corps. The divisions were a mix of brigades formed from the four types of cavalry then found in the French Army: heavy cavalry, called cuirassiers (equipped with body armor and heavy straight sabers, forming 15 percent of the cavalry) and dragoons (armed with lances and heavy sabers, composing 40 percent of French horsemen) and light cavalry, consisting of hussars (equipped with lances and light sabers, forming 17 percent of the cavalry) and horse *chasseurs* (equipped with light sabers, making up 28 percent of French horsemen). Its combination of brigades determined whether a division was considered heavy, light, or mixed. Of the 10 divisions, only the 1 located in the garrison of Paris was heavy. Four of the remaining divisions were light, and five were mixed.[6]

However, organizationally, both the Germans and French augmented their cavalry. (See figure 1.) In each French cavalry division, there was also a company of light infantry (*chasseurs à pied*), known as *groupe cycliste*, which was mounted on collapsible, portable bicycles. Additionally, a

Level	French	German
Operational		
Army	XX ▨ Several provisional corps were also organized	XXX ▨ Cavalry brigade was the highest peacetime unit
Primary Equipment	Horses, lances, body armor, 12 75-mm guns, bicyclist company	Horses, lances, 36 artillery cannons, 42 or 63 machine guns
Reinforced With	typically attached ⊠ ⊠ (corps) (division) (bus) (foot)	assigned ⊠ 2-4 Jäger (truck)
Corps	▨ LT	Provided from army assets as necessary
Primary Equipment	Horses, lances	NA
Tactical		
Division	▨ LT Provided by corps assets	▨ or 1/2 Assets taken from broken-up peacetime cavalry brigades
Below Division	None	None

Figure 1. The echeloning of French and German reconnaissance units, 1914.

French cavalry division contained a *groupe* (battalion equivalent) of horse artillery consisting of three batteries, each with four 75-mm guns.[7]

Similarly, German cavalry divisions contained an artillery battalion (*Abteilung*), consisting of three batteries. Apart from the artillery, however, the Germans augmented their cavalry divisions in a different way than the French. After mobilization, each division was provided a machine-gun battalion. This battalion was set up like a German Army artillery battalion, even using that arm's term for such a unit, *Abteilung*. It was organized with three machine-gun companies, one for each brigade in the division. The companies were equipped with seven (including one spare) 7.9-mm Maxim MG 08 machine guns mounted on large sleds. The machine gun and sled together weighed almost 140 pounds. Below division level, French cavalry units were pure horse-and-rider organizations. The Germans were similarly organized except they attached a machine-gun company from the division to each brigade, as mentioned previously. Berlin did not make the distinction between light and heavy cavalry as did the French. Their distinctions were more honorific than real. In mobilization plans and in later employment, the Germans seemingly used their cavalry regardless of type.[8]

Both the French and Germans augmented their cavalry corps and divisions with infantry forces if possible. The one corps the French planned to organize when they mobilized had an infantry brigade of two regiments designated to be attached to it.[9] In war, when the cavalry made long-ranging moves, this infantry followed along in buses. In August 1914, French field commanders usually attached an infantry battalion to the cavalry divisions assigned to their commands.[10]

The Germans assigned infantry to the four cavalry corps they planned to form in wartime. Although it proved to be quite effective, the concept was an accidental development. The German Army in 1914 contained 18 elite nondivisional light infantry (*Jäger*) battalions that were designed to fight in special terrain such as mountains. But in the German operational plan (Schlieffen Plan), there was no place for such specialized troops. So the *Jäger*s were attached to the cavalry, with up to four battalions being assigned to each cavalry corps. *Jäger* battalions were organized similar to regular infantry battalions with the addition of a machine-gun company and additional ammunition wagons. For service with the cavalry, they were reorganized to include an additional *Jäger* company mounted on bicycles and 10 trucks to carry the rest of the *Jäger* infantry. So modified, these battalions provided the cavalry corps with battalions with twice the firepower of regular infantry battalions and mobility comparable to the horse soldiers. The *Jäger*s gave the German cavalry a definite dragoon or mounted infantry tint that was not reflected in prewar doctrine. However, in practice, the German cavalry ended up depending on the firepower of the *Jäger*s.[11]

The French and Germans used their reservists, soldiers who had recently finished their term of conscription, differently. The French slated their reservists to fill out their cavalry forces and primarily provide the manpower for the cavalry squadron designated to support each infantry division. The Germans integrated their reservists completely into their cavalry forces, organizing whole regiments of reservists, most supporting reserve infantry corps.[12]

Tactical Employment

French employment of its cavalry divisions in time of war was flexible. In peacetime, the divisions had been attached to specific infantry corps. However, when mobilized, each infantry corps received a cavalry regiment that in peacetime had formed the third regiment of divisional brigades. Above corps level, the French planned on fielding five infantry armies, theoretically allowing each army to possess a cavalry corps of two divisions. But the French High Command intended to retain flexibility in using its cavalry, giving some armies only a single division and forming cavalry corps only "under certain conditions and on certain terrain."[13] Centralization of cavalry employment at higher levels was a basic tenet of the French Army in 1914. Paris wanted to ensure its cavalry was adequate in numbers to both provide reconnaissance and defeat the German cavalry. Therefore, the high command intended to control and deploy most of the cavalry divisions as it saw fit in accordance with the overall situation.[14]

Before World War I, the German Army's cavalry, except the Guards Cavalry Division, was not organized above brigade level. Each corps area had 2 or 3 cavalry brigades, formed from a total of 146 cavalry regiments (equivalent to US Army cavalry squadrons), which together totaled 55. In wartime, 22 of the brigades were dissolved, and their regiments were divided to provide cavalry for the infantry divisions. The remaining brigades (each of 2 regiments) formed 10 cavalry divisions (each of 3 brigades). The mobilization plan called for combining these divisions and the Guards Cavalry Division into four provisional cavalry corps consisting of two or three cavalry divisions. Some prewar brigades were dissolved as their regiments were parceled out among the infantry divisions to form divisional cavalry forces consisting of two or three squadrons (equivalent to US Army cavalry troops) per division.[15]

German plans called for the formation of four cavalry corps in the west. These corps, although commanded by *Generalleutnant*s just like infantry corps, were technically not considered the command equivalent of the preexisting corps.[16] The number of cavalry corps, half the number of armies in the field (four versus eight), indicated a general intention to provide a corps for every two armies. With no command headquarters above the army except for the overall high command, this arrangement proved to be somewhat unwieldy. Cavalry corps would either have to be attached to an army, depriving another army of operational-level reconnaissance forces, or report directly to the high command. Additionally, the army in the east (the Eighth) was provided with an independent cavalry division, and the role of the four corps to be used in the west was weighted to support the Schlieffen Plan's flanking maneuver through Belgium. The four German armies on the right (northern) flank had in support three cavalry corps with seven cavalry divisions, while the center two armies had the remaining cavalry corps with two divisions. The cavalry corps were to precede the marching infantry armies and cover the movement from the enemy cavalry while discovering the location of the enemy cavalry and infantry. On the right flank, the cavalry also had to cover the army's northern flank as the Schlieffen wheel took effect.[17]

While the Germans planned to use their cavalry corps operationally as part of their prewar planning, French preparations were far less exact. The French Commander in Chief, General Joseph Joffre, planned to concentrate five armies in the northeast, placing the bulk of his forces in a central position from which he could move them anywhere along the front. The plan was decidedly flexible, designed to provide Joffre with the flexibility to shift forces to where he could best attack the Germans. Unlike the Germans, the French believed that large-scale wartime maneuvers could not be set far in advance, requiring situational awareness at the time of the outbreak of war not available in peacetime. As part of this initial deployment, Joffre divided the 10 French cavalry divisions as follows: 5 divisions (with 3 under a provisional cavalry corps) to his right flank in Lorraine and 5 divisions (again with 3 under a provisional cavalry corps) supporting his main maneuver force in the center.[18]

Tactical Reconnaissance

At the start of hostilities, as mentioned earlier, the French command detached the third regiment in each cavalry brigade to provide support to specific infantry corps. This regiment was always made up of light cavalry (hussars or *chasseurs*). The parent brigade maintained control of these forces in peacetime rather than the infantry corps to facilitate training. Each regiment was then, in turn, to provide a squadron to each of the corps' two infantry divisions. When the Army was mobilized, the cavalry regiments each received two extra squadrons of reservists specifically to provide divisional cavalry forces. While the French generally gave their reservists decidedly secondary roles in their mobilization plans, the army considered that reservists could be used in divisional cavalry because, unlike the troopers in larger cavalry units (brigades and divisions), the divisional horsemen would have some preparation time before entering battle. Likewise, the exclusive use of light cavalry in the infantry division reflected a French belief that there was no need for more powerful cavalry in the division. The primary missions of the horse soldiers in the infantry divisions were small-scale patrolling, performing outpost duty, and setting up minor ambushes. Additionally, in theory, such operations would take a greater toll on the horses, making the weight of equipment carried by the rider, by necessity, as light as possible. Overall, therefore, the French planned to execute tactical reconnaissance with a light cavalry squadron (equivalent to a US cavalry troop) at the division level and a light cavalry regiment (equivalent to a US cavalry squadron) at the corps level.[19]

Similar to the French, the Germans only provided their infantry divisions with a cavalry component in wartime. The Germans broke up 22 peacetime cavalry brigades and distributed their regiments among the mobilized army's infantry divisions, with each division receiving either a full cavalry regiment (86 percent) or a half-regiment (14 percent). Divisional cavalry in the German service could be of any type. Corps received no separate allocation. At the tactical level, under the operational-level corps, the Germans fielded between one and two regiments of cavalry with all the cavalry at division level, while the French deployed one cavalry regiment in each corps and a squadron with each division.

Operational Reconnaissance

At the operational level, both the Germans and French used separate cavalry divisions usually, but not always, organized under a corps headquarters. These large cavalry units were supposed to move in advance of any infantry forces, and both prevented the enemy cavalry from determining friendly dispositions and defeating the enemy cavalry. Much attention was devoted to the enemy cavalry, less to determining the location of enemy forces, at least until the press of battle forced such concerns to the forefront.

The Opening Campaign, August 1914

Even before the end of the war, British observers criticized the performance of the German cavalry in the opening campaign.[20] These analysts saw the German cavalry as lacking in initiative, depending on passive reconnaissance. Supporting this criticism, there were frequent disconnects between the cavalry and the infantry in the German sweep across Belgium and northern France where the Germans placed the bulk of their cavalry. For example, while at the operational level the German cavalry cleared the way for the infantry, it often did so too far in advance of the marching columns. In August 1914, Allied forces often slipped into the

Figure 2. French cuirassiers.

space between the German cavalry and infantry and surprised the German infantry by their presence in areas considered to be previously cleared of enemy forces. Additionally, the German cavalry thought its main mission was to defeat the enemy cavalry. However, in the opening campaign, while at times German cavalry commanders attempted, unsuccessfully, to fight French cavalry mounted, the German command generally wanted its cavalry to systematically avoid combat with the enemy cavalry.[21]

French cavalry performance, particularly in the early weeks of the war, at times similarly failed to provide adequate reconnaissance for the following infantry. The French cavalry, although not fixed in its employment to supporting a detailed, prewar plan, was designated to advance forward of the French infantry. This, too, placed the cavalry at the operational level into a situation where it was reconnoitering too far in advance to the infantry, both in time and in space. This problem was exacerbated when Joffre delayed movements and advances based on revisions of the German situation, usually developed through the presence of German infantry discovered at certain points by civilian contacts or aerial reconnaissance. Unlike the German cavalry, however, and probably more as a consequence of the French being placed in the position of responding to German movements, their horsemen returned to previously cleared areas for second and third looks in the days between 6 and 19 August 1914. However, the French gained little knowledge of general German troop movements.[22]

Plan XVII, the French operational plan adopted in February 1914, accounted for the creation of a single cavalry corps. This command's temporary nature was clear from the small staff that it had, the bulk of which only arrived when hostilities began. The corps mission was to cover the left (northern) flank during and after mobilization in case the Germans violated Belgian neutrality, something the French, by February 1914, presumed to be a certainty. Therefore, the corps supported the Fifth Army, the French left (northernmost) flank infantry command.[23]

In August 1914, both the French and Germans used their cavalry to screen the movements of their infantry forces and to discover the movements and dispositions of the enemy forces. The initial deployment of the French cavalry reflected this. On the Lorraine (southern) front, which directly faced the German frontier and where the French deployed 3 armies, Joffre deployed 5 of the 10 cavalry divisions. Three were organized under a newly created cavalry corps (II or Corps Conneau). In the center and north, where there were three French armies, five cavalry divisions were in support, including three under the I or Cavalry Corps Sordet, the corps authorized by Plan XVII.[24]

The Germans deployed four cavalry corps on the Western Front in 1914. Of these, two corps consisting of five divisions were in place supporting the right or northern wing; a third, with two divisions, was in the center able to support either wing; and the fourth, also with two divisions, was on the left (south). While the siege of Liege continued and the infantry of the opposing armies mobilized and moved to their positions, the two corps on the left initially were passive. The II Cavalry Corps deployed to support and screen the German siege of Liege along the west bank of the Meuse River, while the I Cavalry Corps remained on the western edge of the Ardennes Forest in Luxembourg, which the Germans had occupied on the first day of the war. German plans designated the II Cavalry Corps to cross the Meuse River once Liege fell and advance in front of the two rightmost armies (First and Second) across central Belgium, covering their front and the First Army's right and reconnoitering forward to discover the positions of enemy forces. Similarly, to the south (left), the I Cavalry Corps planned to advance in front of the other two right flank armies (Third and Fourth), clearing the Ardennes Forest in front of the Fourth Army and shifting to the north in front of the Third Army.[25]

Combat Case Study: The Battle of Hamipré, 20 August 1914

A good example of the clash between prewar expectations and real-war realities took place on 20 August 1914 at the village of Hamipré near the town of Neufchâteau in the Belgian Ardennes. There, reconnaissance elements of the French Fourth Army ran into the main body of the advancing German Fourth Army whose supporting reconnaissance elements had previously passed through the area without encountering any

French forces. The gap between the German cavalry and infantry at this point had reached 5 days. While the Germans were surprised to encounter French cavalry, they soon overwhelmed it and continued their advance. The French cavalry, too, was surprised to encounter a corps of German infantry and only extracted itself from Hamipré with difficulty. However, the action provided the French command with the vague location of the German forces. A day later, the main elements of both armies met in pitched battle nearby at Bertrix in a battle the French lost at the operational level because their forces were outflanked.

Prelude to the Battle: Cavalry Operations in Early and Mid-August 1914

The Battle of Hamipré was the culmination of a series of maneuvers and smaller operations in the first 3 weeks of August 1914 as both sides mobilized and positioned their troops. German operations depended on the scheme outlined in its detailed prewar plan, usually called the Schlieffen Plan, after the plan's original proponent, the former, now-deceased, German chief of staff. Under its provisions, the Germans planned to spend the first few weeks of the war besieging the Belgian fortress of Liege with a special group of regular army troops. While this took place, the rest of their forces would mobilize and deploy to their start positions, covered by several cavalry corps.

French General Joffre responded to the German invasion of Belgium by realigning his main effort to shift to attacking what he saw as the German main advance. French planners had underestimated the size of the German main effort, however, and it took weeks before he realized the mass of the German movement against his northern flank.[26] Joffre did not expect the Germans to make anything but a shallow outflanking maneuver, and only the movement of the German forces themselves, not information provided by his cavalry, dissuaded him of this mistaken belief.

While specially prepared German forces advanced immediately into Belgium and besieged the fortress of Liege, the bulk of the German forces, as with those of the French, had to mobilize. These forces did not begin their advance into Belgium until Liege was neutralized, starting on 9 August 1914. The Germans staggered their advance, with the infantry in the north beginning its march several days before the infantry in the Ardennes, all forming part of the massive wheel that was the heart of the Schlieffen Plan.

To counter the enemy move into Belgium, once his forces were in place, Joffre intended to attack these German forces with his Fourth Army, executing the main effort against what he perceived as the left flank of the

German forces in Belgium.[27] While Liege was under siege, the German cavalry remained, for the most part, east of the Meuse River. Aside from the operation in Belgium, three of the four German cavalry corps were deployed on the Western Front.

The German cavalry forces in Belgium in August 1914 were operating in accordance with their army's overall war plan. The cavalry had the general mission of providing security for the assembly and movements of the German forces while conducting reconnaissance to discover the French and Belgian (and later British) dispositions. (Figure 3 shows the French and German cavalry maneuvers from 1 to 19 August 1914.)

The II Cavalry Corps, with three cavalry divisions, moved into Belgium on 4 August and supported the forces investing the fortress of Liege by covering the besiegers' northern and western flanks. As part of this mission, once bridging equipment arrived on the 8th, the corps crossed to the west bank of the Meuse River, south of the fortress, and advanced to the west and northwest to reconnoiter and screen the Liege force. In this process, the German cavalry encountered a mixture of Belgian infantry and cavalry forces. On 12 August, the German horsemen of the 4th Cavalry Division, II Cavalry Corps, attempted to force a crossing over the Gette River at a bridge in the town of Haelen. The Belgians resisted aggressively. While elsewhere in August 1914 the German cavalry usually depended on its attached *Jäger* infantry battalions to fight mixed forces of defending enemy infantry and cavalry, this was not the case at Haelen. A German cavalry regiment (equivalent to a US Army cavalry squadron in size) from the 4th Cavalry Division attacked a Belgian artillery position on horseback in a column formation. The Belgian artillery was supported by entrenched dismounted cavalry and infantry. The German attack was, predictably, repulsed with heavy losses, placing the II Cavalry Corps on the defensive until after the fall of Liege on the 16th, following which the German First and Second Armies began their advance through the areas as the extreme right wing of the Schlieffen Plan.[28]

To the south of where the II Cavalry Corps was operating, the German I Cavalry Corps, commanded by *Generalleutnant* Baron Manfred von Richthofen, positioned itself in Luxembourg in early August to support the projected German infantry wheel into Belgium.[29] This advance would start once the forces were assembled and after Liege fell. For the most part, the corps remained in place until 10 August when Richthofen began shifting reconnaissance elements into the Belgian Ardennes. That same day, one reconnaissance unit met and repulsed elements of the French 5th Cavalry Division, French I Cavalry Corps, south of Bastogne and

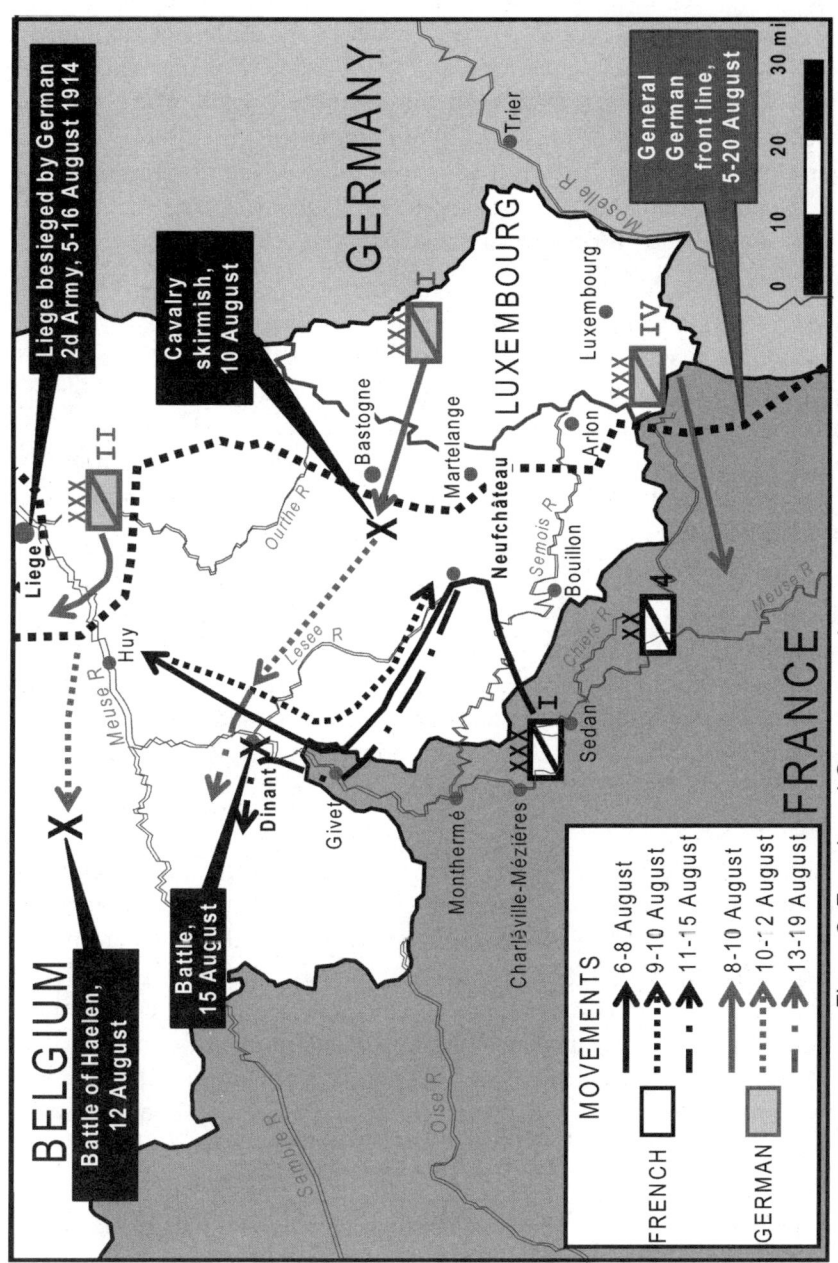

Figure 3. French and German cavalry maneuvers, 1–19 August 1914.

northeast of Neufchâteau, in the first major Franco-German clash in the Ardennes. While the French expected a German cavalry advance directly to the west, Richthofen's initial mission was to secure the area around the Meuse River crossings at Dinant, north of the Ardennes, to support the projected advance of the German Third Army. For that reason, the cavalry in the Ardennes shifted to the northwest, leaving the forested area centered on Neufchâteau devoid of German cavalry after 12 August. When the German Fourth Army advanced toward Neufchâteau, it would have to depend on the cavalry regiments (US squadron-sized) attached to its infantry divisions for reconnaissance support.[30]

The German IV Cavalry Corps was south of the Ardennes. The corps started the war in southern Luxembourg and northern Lorraine, supporting the eventual advance of the German Fifth Army in the general direction of Verdun. On the day of the Battle of Hamipré, the northernmost positions of this corps were only a few miles south of the battlefield, and although these horse soldiers observed the French advance, the information was not passed to the forces of the German Fourth Army advancing directly toward the French.[31]

In the opening weeks of the campaign, the German cavalry quickly discovered that mounted attacks against entrenched enemy forces were unsuccessful. This resulted in operational-level intelligence consisting only of the results of such actions.[32] However, despite these deficiencies, the Germans successfully screened their infantry's advance from the French. Before 20 August, the French identified only the two divisions of the German I Cavalry Corps as being opposite their forces in southern Belgium.[33]

Unlike the Germans, whose operational-level cavalry was functioning in accordance with a detailed plan, French cavalry operations in Belgium in the first half of August 1914 were far more flexible in their execution. The French I Cavalry Corps, sometimes called Cavalry Corps Sordet after its commander, *Général de Division* Jean-François Sordet, and consisting of the 1st, 3d, and 5th Cavalry Divisions, began operating in Belgian territory on 6 August. Sordet's original missions were to determine the scope of any German movements into Belgium, sweep away any enemy cavalry encountered, and, if necessary, delay any German infantry columns.[34]

After moving the corps forward to the Neufchâteau area on the 6th, Sordet advanced eastward the next day, almost to the Belgian-Luxembourg and Belgian-German frontiers, with the 5th Cavalry Division riding through Neufchâteau. The French encountered no major German forces.

Sordet had advanced before the German I Cavalry Corps had made any move in the Ardennes sector. Mindful of his overall mission to determine the scope of German deployments, Sordet immediately decided to shift northward toward Liege where he knew there were Germans.[35]

On the afternoon of the 7th, the French cavalry corps shifted to the northeast to the line of the Lesse River southwest of Dinant, advancing northeast toward Liege the next morning. Sordet intended either to raid the German infantry besieging Liege or to find and fight the German cavalry expected to be massed south of the fortress. However, the movement proved to be slower than expected. The day was extremely hot, and the heat slowed the cavalry's pace. The infantry could not keep up. The buses carrying the regiment could not transport the whole force at once and had to shuttle them by battalion. Additionally, the infantry movement was slowed by a bottleneck at the Lesse River crossing site. The corps supply trains similarly could not keep up. Realizing he could not attack before darkness, Sordet stopped his advance for the night before his cavalry got too close to the German infantry near Liege. The next morning, with the element of surprise now lost, the French corps commander withdrew behind the Lesse, reorienting once again on the Ardennes sector east to the German border.[36]

After the unsuccessful movement on Liege, Sordet's 3d Cavalry Division retired to Neufchâteau on the 9th. The rest of the corps consolidated near the town on the 11th after elements of the corps' 5th Cavalry Division had encountered German cavalry from Richthofen's I Cavalry Corps northeast of Neufchâteau on the 10th. While both sides claimed victory in the small skirmish, which partially continued on the 11th, Sordet consolidated his command west of Neufchâteau, expecting the Germans to advance on that crossroads the next day. The French commander intended to attack. However, on the morning of the 12th, the Germans had vanished from the area. Richthofen's cavalry had moved off to the northwest. On discovering this development, Sordet shifted to follow the next morning, leaving the Ardennes sector, centered on Neufchâteau, devoid of large cavalry units.[37]

The effect of the German and French cavalry maneuvers of the first few weeks of August 1914, aside from wearing out their horses, particularly those of the French, was the movement of these forces away from the Neufchâteau sector. And it was into this sector that French Commander in Chief Joffre intended to attack and into which the bulk of two German armies were preparing to advance.

The Advance on Hamipré and the Opposing Forces

Joffre's strike force for the Ardennes was his Fourth Army. By 14 August, he had finally realized the magnitude of the German movements in central Belgium where the First and Second Armies had begun advancing on both sides of Liege.[38] He planned to have the French Fourth Army advance onto what he perceived as the left flank of these German forces into the void Sordet had discovered and abandoned the previous day. The French commander originally intended to begin this operation on 16 August, but he feared the fog of war. A combination of the uncertainty over German movements (which seemed to extend farther and farther to the north) and a lack of understanding of known German troop movements compelled Joffre to delay the Fourth Army's advance. He did not want to send his strike force into a trap. Additionally, he hoped the delay would exaggerate the effect of the shock effect of the French attack with the sudden appearance of the Fourth Army on the German flank, surprising the enemy.[39]

With Sordet's cavalry corps now operating farther to the north with the French Fifth Army, on 18 August, the French Fourth Army commander, *Général* Ferdinand Louis Armand de Langle de Cary, created a new cavalry corps from the two cavalry divisions recently assigned to support his army (4th and 9th) under the commander of the head of the 4th Cavalry Division, *Général de Division* Pierre Abonneau. De Langle gave Abonneau the mission of shielding from the Germans the presence of the Fourth Army along the Meuse River, west of the Neufchâteau-Ardennes region. The provisional cavalry corps was then to proceed to the attack by moving into the Ardennes in advance of the Fourth Army and clearing any enemy cavalry from the front of the army while discovering enemy infantry dispositions.[40]

Unknown to Joffre and De Langle, while the Neufchâteau region no longer contained any major troop units from either side with the departure of Sordet on the 13th, the German Fourth Army, now assembled in western Germany and Luxembourg, was preparing to advance into the region beginning on 17 August as part of the Schlieffen Plan's wheel through Belgium. Joffre had underestimated the overall size of the available German forces, expecting the German forces in the forest to be weak covering forces. The German forces had been ready on the Belgian frontier since 10 August. The German Fourth Army was only waiting until the three German armies to the north, with farther to march, had advanced on line with its start point. This army formed the southern hinge of the large German turning maneuver that was the Schlieffen Plan (see figure 4). The German advance in this sector finally began on the morning of the

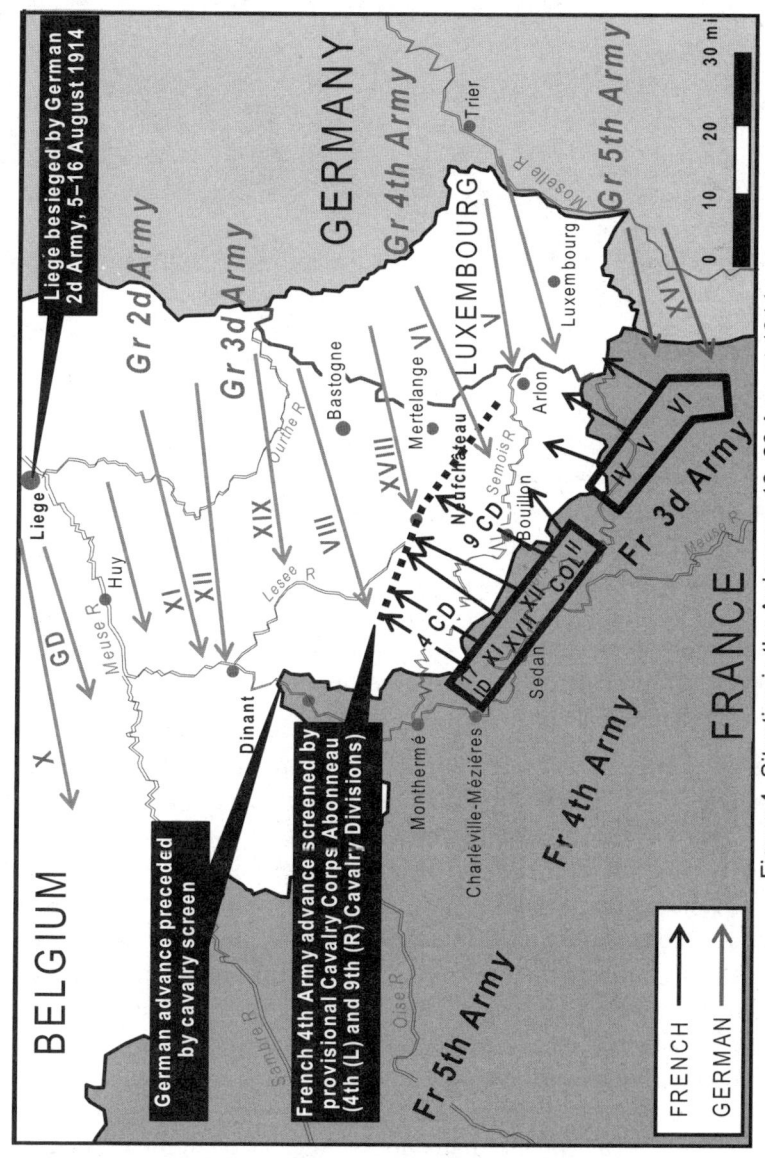

Figure 4. Situation in the Ardennes, 19–20 August 1914.

Figure 5. German infantry on the march.

17th. With temperatures high and with Richthofen's cavalry corps now in the sector of the neighboring German Third Army to the north, the initial advance was slow and cautious in columns by brigade along the main roads of the region. Divisional cavalry reconnoitered to the direct front and sides of the advancing units, but what was beyond the immediate position of these small cavalry elements was unknown. After 3 days of preliminary marches, the Germans halted on the evening of the 19th, less than a day's march from Neufchâteau.[41]

In the center of the German Fourth Army advance, moving slowly toward that important crossroads at Neufchâteau, was the Frankfurt-based XVIII Corps. The corps commander, *General der Infanterie* Freiherr von Schenck, thought the area to his front was clear of enemy forces. With a corps advancing on parallel routes to both his north and south, Schenck felt comfortable that his two infantry divisions could handle any enemy encountered. At this point, the Germans only expected to meet pugnacious Belgian civilians.[42] The bulk of the French forces had not crossed into Belgium, so the cavalry had assured the German command. A misreading of aerial intelligence information also led the Germans to believe that French forces to the west of the Ardennes were shifting to the north away from the area. The Germans hoped to clear the tight confines of the Ardennes before fighting any major battles. But the cavalry had left the sector prematurely. The Germans were blind to any developments after 11 August, except those on their immediate front.[43]

Schenck's command consisted of the 21st Division, advancing on the corps' left (south) and the 25th Division on the right (north). On 20 August, the 21st Division's march objectives included passing through Neufchâteau and continuing to the west. Road space in the Ardennes was so tight that each German division generally advanced along a single road in a long column. The 21st Division's two infantry brigades advanced in succession along the road running from the northeast at the town of Martelange near the Luxembourg frontier to the southwest to Neufchâteau.[44]

On the other side of the Ardennes, Joffre canceled the Fourth Army's advance into the Ardennes on the 17th, forcing De Langle to withdraw his advance guard from the region back to its positions along the Meuse River in French territory. Over the next several days, the French sought to determine the exact enemy situation in front of the Fourth Army. Aerial and human intelligence sources soon detected the preliminary movements of the German Fourth Army but could not determine the German objectives— to move to the northwest toward the Meuse River north of Dinant or to move toward Neufchâteau and the French Fourth and Third Armies. In any event, Joffre decided to attack in the Ardennes on the 21st with the Fourth Army moving on Neufchâteau as its objective.[45]

De Langle had formed Cavalry Corps Abonneau in response to Joffre's query for reconnaissance information about the southern Ardennes on 18 August. While the corps rested on the 19th, De Langle gave the new corps the mission of finding the enemy in the Ardennes on the 20th while screening the army's movement beginning the day after. To fulfill this mission, Abonneau intended to advance to the northeast from screening positions near the Meuse with his 4th Cavalry Division on the left and the 9th Cavalry Division on the right. The 9th Cavalry Division's initial objective was to secure the crossroads at Neufchâteau while screening farther forward to the northeast and east.[46]

The French 9th Cavalry Division, commanded by *Général de Division* Jean-Francois de L'Espée, had previously been engaged to the south of the Neufchâteau sector against elements of the German IV Cavalry Corps. The division had been formed in September 1913. On 20 August, the division had two brigades of dragoons and one of cuirassiers, making it a mixed division in the French categorization of cavalry divisions (figure 6). After giving up a regiment each to various infantry corps when mobilized, each brigade had two (US squadron-sized) cavalry regiments, each with four (US troop-sized) subordinate squadrons. The heavy cuirassier brigade was reserved for use in shock action, while the dragoons were typically deployed operationally into squadron or smaller sized reconnaissance

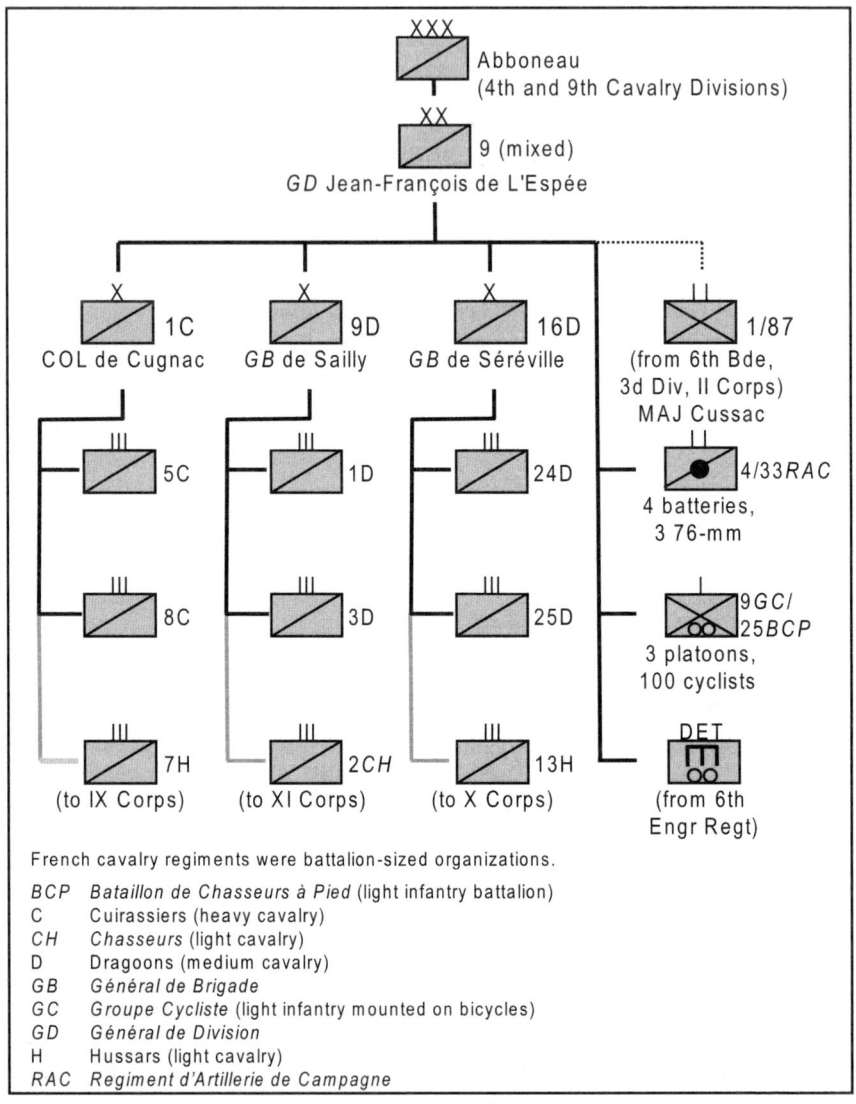

Figure 6. Organization of the French 9th Cavalry Division, August 1914.

parties. Divisional support elements included a battalion (*groupe*) of 12 75-mm field artillery guns and a company-sized group of light infantry mounted on bicycles (*groupe cycliste*) and a detachment of engineers. Since 16 August, a regular infantry battalion, the 1st Battalion, 87th Infantry Regiment, from one of the infantry divisions in the Fourth Army, was attached to the cavalry division. The battalion, commanded by *Commandant* (Major) Antoine Cussac, consisting of four infantry companies, moved by foot march.[47]

General de L'Espée received more specific orders in the predawn hours of 20 August to march directly on Neufchâteau along the main road from the southwest. The division began its movement promptly, leaving behind the 24th Dragoon Regiment from its 16th Dragoon Brigade facing to the southwest to cover the division's flank as it moved. As the division advanced in the early morning, French aviation provided updated intelligence indicating the discovery of several long German infantry columns advancing in the eastern Ardennes. However, the objectives of these columns were still unclear to the French. L'Espée led his advance with a dragoon squadron. Halfway along the roughly 10-mile march to Neufchâteau, half of the lead squadron, commanded by Lieutenant Pastouiel, peeled off to the right to advance across a parallel route. This half-squadron's mission was to reconnoiter the road from Neufchâteau to Martelange, the very thoroughfare on which the German 21st Division was marching down in the opposite direction. The other half of the squadron, commanded by *Capitaine* Bossut, led the bulk of the division directly toward Neufchâteau, with the attached infantry battalion marching along a parallel route just to the east of the cavalry elements. The half-squadron in front of the main body was to advance through the crossroads at Neufchâteau and then to reconnoiter to the northwest along the road to Bastogne. Both half-squadrons were advancing directly into the march column of the German 21st Division.[48]

The 21st Infantry Division was the right march column of Schenck's XVIII Corps. Two brigades of that division marched side by side along the road from Martelange to Neufchâteau. As observed by French aviators, the column was almost 7 miles long. The fragmentation of the German reconnaissance effort on 20 August is glaringly obvious in that elements of the German 3d Cavalry Division, IV Cavalry Corps, had observed the beginning of the advance of the L'Espée Division to the northeast. But word of this movement never reached the German forces marching in the opposite direction toward the French.[49]

The 21st Division, commanded by *Generalmajor* Ernst von Oven, had two infantry brigades, each composed of two infantry regiments, with three subordinate infantry battalions (figure 7). The battalions fielded six machine guns apiece. The division's artillery consisted of 28 cannons.

The divisional cavalry contingent had four (US platoon-sized) troops under a regimental headquarters. This cavalry contingent sent out scouts in

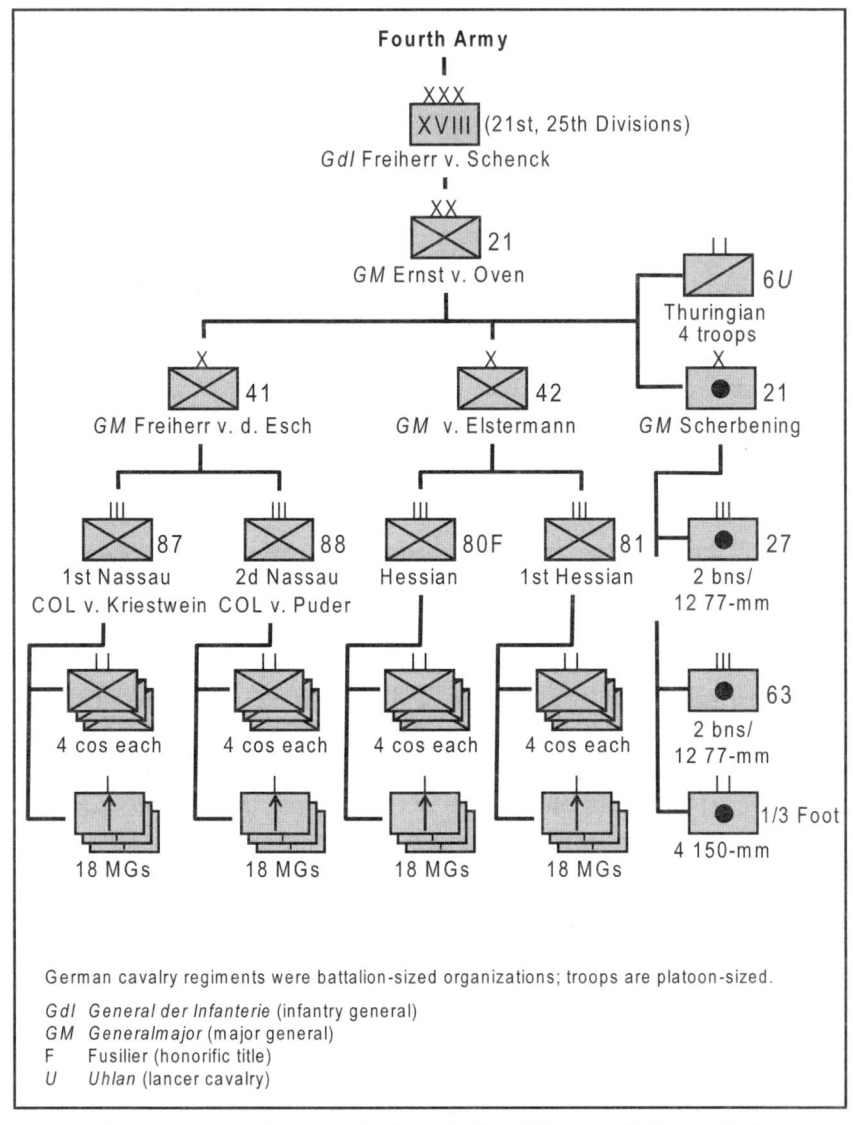

Figure 7. German organization, Battle of Hamipré, 20 August 1914.

front of the divisional column and maintained contact with the 25th Division to the north and the 12th Division of the VI Corps to the south. Although the enemy situation to the front of the division was almost completely unknown, these scouts preceded the infantry column by only about a half a mile. Therefore, the Germans were unaware of the approaching French cavalry division. The French were equally unaware of the proximity of the enemy as the morning progressed.[50]

The Battle of Hamipré

By 0900, the French advance guard half-squadrons had reached Neufchâteau and the village of Léglise on the Neufchâteau-Arlon Road south of the main road to Neufchâteau-Martelange Road (figure 8).[51] The main body of the division and the infantry battalion followed at about 3 miles. On reaching Neufchâteau, Bossut observed German soldiers advancing along the Neufchâteau-Martelange Road near the village of Namoussart, less than 3 miles to the east and German cavalry scouts in the village of Longlier, about a mile to the northeast on the road to Bastogne. Both French half-squadrons stopped to await the arrival of the bulk of the division.[52]

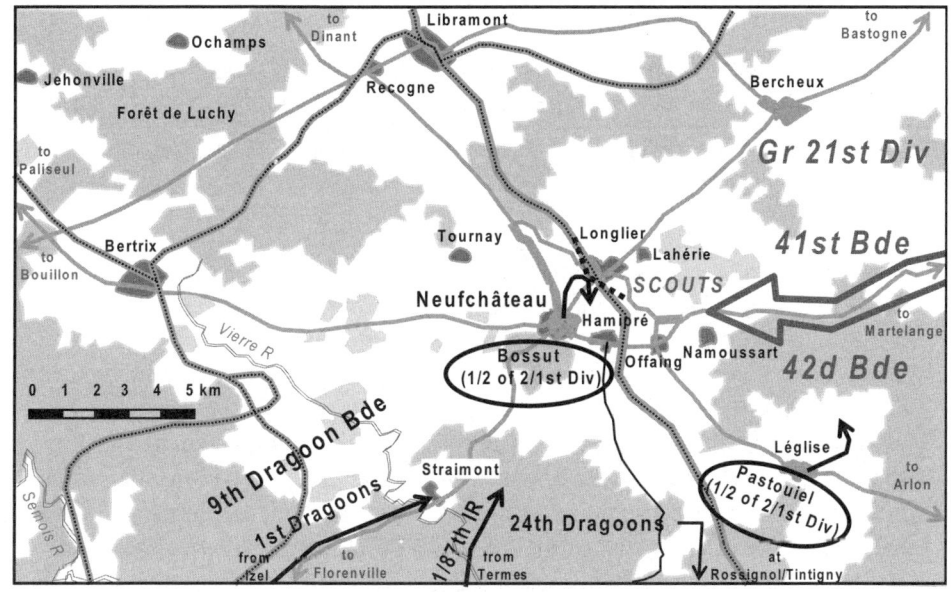

Figure 8. Battle of Hamipré, 0900, 20 August 1914.

Meanwhile, the Germans did not realize how close the French were for several hours, while the bulk of the forces on both sides closed in on Neufchâteau (figure 9). In this interval, L'Espée moved up the 1/87th Infantry Battalion to occupy the town of Hamipré, just east of Neufchâteau, from where it could cover both the road from Martelange and the road from Bastogne. The French commander also brought up the rest of his 9th Dragoon Brigade (commanded by *Général de Brigade* Emmanuel-Philibert-Henri de Sailly), sending one regiment (the 1st Dragoons) to the

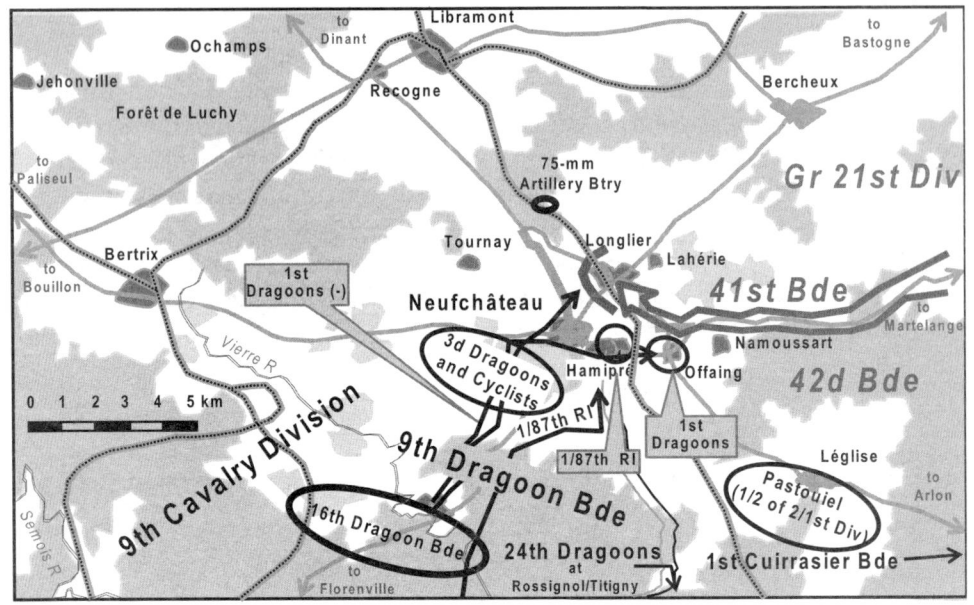
Figure 9. Battle of Hamipré, 1100, 20 August 1914.

right of the infantry battalion at the village of Offaing and reinforcing Bossut in Neufchâteau with the 3d Dragoons and the divisional cyclist company. The other dragoon brigade, the 16th, commanded by *Général de Brigade* Gombau de Séréville, moved forward to Neufchâteau as the division consolidated its light cavalry in one place. L'Espée then sent his heavy cavalry, the 1st Cuirassier Brigade under Colonel Gaspard-Jean-Marie-René de Cugnac, to follow country roads several miles to the south of Neufchâteau easterly to cover the division's flank in that direction. In preparation to support an attack on the Germans blocking the roads his division was assigned to reconnoiter, L'Espée placed several 75-mm artillery batteries on ridgelines north of Neufchâteau, which provided observation over the whole area. While the French were engaged in all this activity, the Germans took a break from their march to eat soup, having been told by their scouts that the way was clear to Longlier.[53]

Shortly after noon, following their break for soup, the soldiers of the German 41st Infantry Brigade resumed their march to Longlier. At this time, the French revealed their presence by opening fire with the artillery battery located to the northwest overlooking Longlier. The artillery fire was the signal for the start of the French attack, spearheaded by the cyclist company in Neufchâteau and supported by Cussac's infantry battalion in

Hamipré (figure 10). Despite the disruption caused by the surprise presence of the French, the Germans quickly deployed out of march formation, with the lead infantry using the masking effect of a nearby hill to move toward the shelter of the buildings in Longlier.[54]

The French cyclist company expected to encounter a small group of scouts in Longlier but ended up facing the bulk of two German infantry regiments. As the Germans deployed, their numbers began to overwhelm the cyclists, who retreated to Neufchâteau before they could be outflanked. To their right, L'Espée gave his infantry battalion commander, Cussac, the mission of moving along a railroad embankment to the north of Hamipré

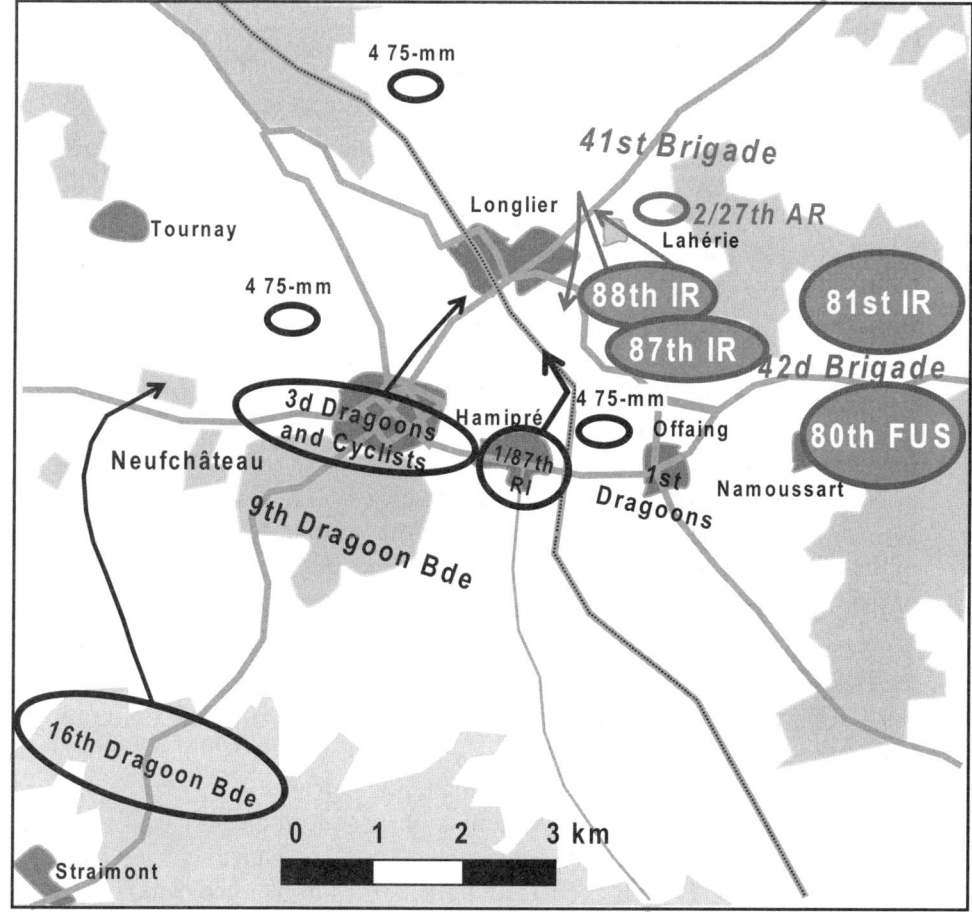

Figure 10. Battle of Hamipré, 1230, 20 August 1914.

and striking at the flank of the German force counterattacking the cyclists. L'Espée still did not know how large a German force he was opposing. At about 1300, now supported by a 75-mm battery, Cussac moved out with three companies, leaving one behind to cover his left at Offaing with the 1st Dragoons. With the French cavalry slightly to the rear in Neufchâteau and Offaing, the Germans concentrated their forces against French infantry. As Von Oven gradually deployed his whole division, Cussac's battalion was soon fighting for its life.[55]

After recovering from the surprise contact with French forces, the 41st Brigade assembled its two regiments in and around Longlier while the 21st Division deployed its artillery to the northeast and began dueling with its French counterparts. While in Longlier, Belgian civilians fired on the Germans, mortally wounding the commander of the German 87th Infantry Regiment, Colonel von Kierstein. In retaliation, the Germans set the building, a hotel, from which the shot came, aflame. Within minutes, the whole town was on fire, with several Belgian civilians and soldiers burned alive.[56]

As Longlier burned, the Germans massed the bulk of eight battalions from two brigades against the single French infantry battalion along the railroad embankment north of Hamipré (figure 11). While Cussac's battalion held off the German infantry, French commander L'Espée finally realized the scope of the German forces near Longlier and began withdrawing his forces, starting with the artillery batteries. The French 1st Cuirassier Brigade, which was posted on the division's right (south), withdrew to the west before the infantry of the German 42d Brigade could deploy and block this move. One cuirassier regiment was detached from the brigade and sent to cover the withdrawal of the artillery posted north of Neufchâteau. The two dragoon brigades also withdrew to the west from Neufchâteau under cover of the cyclist company and artillery posted west of the crossroads. The cyclists then withdrew and dug in in front of the rest of the division 3 miles to the west.[57]

Cussac's battalion of the 87th Infantry did not have such options. Fighting on foot on ground unfavorable to cavalry maneuver, the battalion fell back into a V-shaped defensive line in a ravine just north of Hamipré. While the Germans assaulted Cussac's unit with five battalions in close-order line formations, one infantry battalion advanced westerly north of Longlier to secure the dominating high ground there, on which the Germans soon placed a 77-mm artillery battery. This maneuver forced the withdrawal of the French cyclists and artillery from Neufchâteau. To the south, the German 80th Fusilier Regiment from the 42d Brigade moved to

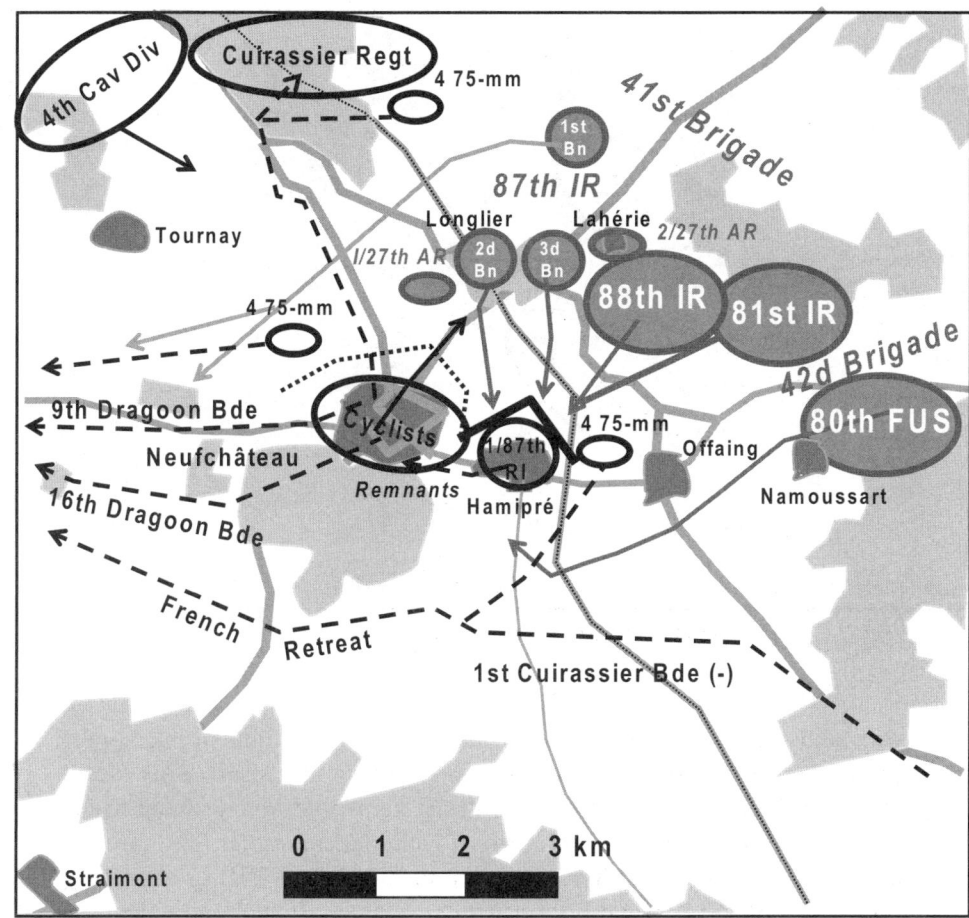

Figure 11. Battle of Hamipré, 1530, 20 August 1914.

surround the French at Hamipré from near the village of Namoussart. After a stalwart defense for several hours, the Germans overran the French 1/87th with less than the equivalent of one company, infiltrating back through Neufchâteau to the French lines. The battalion commander, Cussac, was killed in action along with three of his four company commanders.[58]

With the destruction of the French battalion and dusk approaching, the Germans stopped their advance and bivouacked east of Neufchâteau (figure 12). The 21st Division had already met its march objectives for the day but, after having had to deploy the whole division to fight off the French cavalry, ended the day slightly disorganized. The XVIII Corps remained in the vicinity of Neufchâteau the next day as the German Fourth

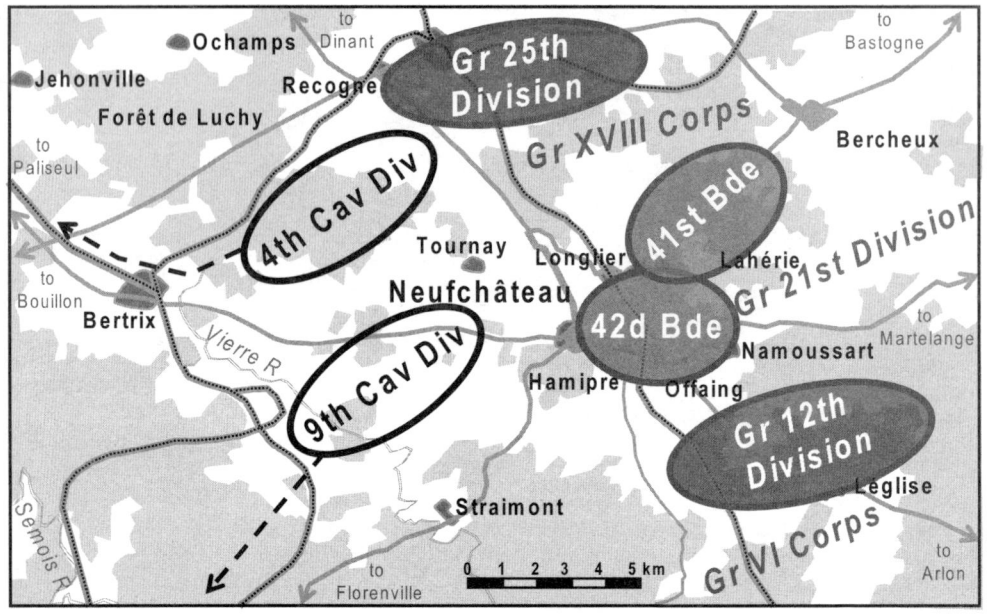

Figure 12. Battle of Hamipré, Dusk, 20 August 1914.

Army adjusted its lines. The XVIII Corps ended up shifting slightly to the right as the XVIII Reserve Corps was brought up on its left. This meant that, when the advance began again, the corps would be marching to the southwest from a starting point north of Neufchâteau rather than through the town. When the advance resumed on the 22d, the XVIII Corps, along with the rest of the German Fourth Army, fought a pitched battle near the town of Bertrix with the main body of De Langle's French Fourth Army, which had advanced that morning, defeating the French and forcing them to retreat.[59]

The French also withdrew from the Neufchâteau area after dusk on the 20th. Abonneau withdrew his corps back to the same assembly areas from which it had marched on that morning. Northeast of Neufchâteau, Abonneau's 4th Cavalry Division was unable to penetrate the cavalry screen in front of the German 25th Division and VIII Corps. For the loss of an infantry battalion, the French cavalry had identified units from several German divisions. However, since contact with these divisions had been lost with the cavalry's withdrawal, on the next day, Abonneau had to send his cavalry forward again to the Neufchâteau area.[60]

Presuming the Germans had marched to the northeast, the focus of this reconnaissance shifted westward about 5 miles. On the 21st, the French effort to find information about German movements and dispositions was not rigorous. In the 9th Cavalry Division, the horses were worn out and were only moved at a walk, with frequent breaks. The Germans, now alerted to the proximity of the French, provided cavalry screens around their troop movements with squadrons provided from divisional cavalry assets. This prevented the French cavalry troops, now, after the destruction of Cussac's battalion, without their own infantry support, from discovering German dispositions and from maintaining contact with German forces they encountered.[61]

The French command did not realize the Germans were still east of Neufchâteau, particularly after secondhand information gleaned from Belgian civilians mistakenly indicated the Germans had marched to the west when, in fact, they had withdrawn to the east. Also unknown was that the Germans were marching southwest not northwest. These erroneous impressions were reinforced when overcast limited the ability of aerial reconnaissance to see into the forest.[62]

Despite the setback at Hamipré, early on 21 August, Joffre ordered De Langle to begin the Fourth Army's offensive into the Ardennes that day, with the advance centered on Neufchâteau. The Fourth Army began its advance with little current and accurate reconnaissance information on German dispositions. In fact, the French infantry soon marched up to the most advanced positions reached by the cavalry. Both Joffre and De Langle believed they were advancing to strike the left flank. When the Germans were encountered on the 22d near Bertrix, however, as on the 20th at Hamipré, the French ran directly and unexpectedly into them while still in march order and were decisively defeated when their own right flank was exposed. Ultimately, such reconnaissance failures forced the Fourth Army to retreat. Similar misconceptions about German dispositions across the northern portion of the front forced the French and their British Allies to retreat until a counterstrike could be made against the overextended Germans on the Marne in early September 1914.[63]

The Battle of Hamipré was a meeting engagement between a French reconnaissance element and a German line-of-battle force whose reconnaissance elements had failed them. In the ensuing battle, the Germans so wore out the French that their reconnaissance effort was hindered for the next several days, blinding the advancing French Fourth Army as it met its German counterpart in battle. The French cavalry division moved forward on 20 August based on faulty assumptions that were not alleviated after the battle. The Germans also moved forward with little knowledge of the enemy situation because operational reconnaissance units had left the area several days earlier and the cavalry units assigned to the German infantry divisions to conduct tactical reconnaissance did so at too close a distance to the following infantry to be effective.[64]

Insights From the Opening Battles

Both sides developed lessons from the cavalry operations of August 1914 on the Western Front. Both sides sought to use the mounted characteristics of its cavalry to maximum effect. However, this mobility required large spaces. Lacking space, as in the Ardennes and between two entrenched lines, cavalry could not effectively operate as a mounted arm. Defensive firepower made frontal attacks most difficult. Massed attacks on horseback became impractical, while firing dismounted became far more important than previously thought, particularly in the close terrain that dominated western European battlefields.[65]

However, old ideas often died hard. At least one German cavalryman rationalized that the enemy had realized Teutonic-mounted superiority and deliberately sought to take advantage of close terrain to negate this advantage.[66]

The German cavalry divisions were saved by the attachment to them of the *Jäger* battalions, originally designed for mountain or forest warfare, but left with no use for their unique skills in German war plans. However, while this was recognized to a point at the time, German cavalry observers still insisted that mounted cavalry could operate alone to conduct operational intelligence.[67]

Aerial reconnaissance complemented ground units. In fact, in August 1914, airplanes, particularly on the French side, rather than ground cavalry units, obtained most of the significant intelligence.[68] However, aviation had several disadvantages. The planes were short ranged and required changes of base when operating with cavalry in a reconnaissance role, as in August 1914. The aviation support elements frequently could not keep up and, in at least one instance, resulted in the planes not being able to conduct an important mission.[69] While generally beyond the scope of this work, after the failures of cavalry in the mobile campaigns of August and September 1914, and the subsequent development of the trench lines, when the weather was good, airplanes in effect provided the only available reconnaissance.[70]

By the end of the war, all sides agreed that cavalry had to be as capable on foot as it was mounted. The revised French regulations spelled this out specifically, declaring that French cavalrymen had to be the equal of infantrymen when not on their horses.[71]

Reconnaissance Operations in World War I After August 1914

August 1914 was the last time on the Western Front that ground reconnaissance units were able to operate with any effectiveness in World War I. The creation of continuous lines of entrenchments and the mass use of artillery relegated most reconnaissance missions to the nascent air forces deployed on both sides. As the war progressed, the Germans converted most of their large prewar cavalry to infantry, while the British and French retained mounted units not for reconnaissance but to pursue the enemy once the long expected breakthrough occurred. Both the French and Germans retained small contingents of cavalry in their infantry division organization. However, these squadrons were almost never used in a reconnaissance role.[72]

When the Germans transformed their offensive tactics in 1917, the attacking forces used a more dispersed, decentralized technique known as infiltration tactics. However, reconnaissance units did not lead the infantry, even before the adoption of infiltration tactics. At Verdun in 1916, most prior reconnaissance was conducted by air. Infantry patrols accomplished what ground reconnaissance there was, usually only to determine damage inflicted by artillery barrages during the preparatory phase before the attack. None of the later successful German offensives in 1917–18 used dedicated reconnaissance units as part of the operation. In most cases, given the nature of the entrenched lines, the locations of enemy positions were obvious, and the elements leading the attack provided their own reconnaissance as a byproduct of the attack. Therefore, when the Germans reorganized their infantry to create elite assault battalions, these units did not include organic reconnaissance elements as they were considered unnecessary.[73]

Large cavalry forces continued to operate where the front was less continuous and the terrain more open—in the east and in Palestine. At the start of the war, the Germans deployed only a single cavalry division in the east. In September 1914, the German High Command transferred a cavalry corps from the west to the Eastern Front where the Russians fielded large cavalry forces of their own, followed shortly by a second corps. Before this transfer, the single German cavalry division screened one Russian army while the German Eighth Army massed against another Russian army, surrounded it, and destroyed it at Tannenberg. While both Russian armies each deployed multiple cavalry divisions, which were given reconnaissance missions, these missions were assigned via nebulous orders, and there was no proper coordination with the infantry forces they supported. Since the Russians also lacked air reconnaissance assets, the two armies maneuvered blindly against the Germans. Although the Germans primarily used their operational-level cavalry for security missions, the Germans were not similarly blinded. The Russians had poor signal discipline, and the Germans intercepted almost every enemy radio message, giving them a detailed understanding of Russian dispositions and projected maneuvers.[74]

After Tannenberg, the vastness of the front, compared to the size of the forces deployed, and its open nature, with few roads initially, allowed for the use of large cavalry forces. At the Battle of Łodz in November 1914, the Germans used two cavalry corps to successfully screen the concentration of their forces. One of these corps also repulsed a Russian cavalry corps trying to conduct reconnaissance while the other German corps conducted its own reconnaissance, discovering the location of two Russian corps separated from the rest of their army. The German cavalry proved to be less capable in dismounted combat.[75]

As the war progressed, the role of cavalry on the Eastern Front declined as it had in the west. The primary reason for this was the proliferation of light machine guns. The Romanian campaign in November 1916 was the last operation in which the Germans used large cavalry organizations. A provisional cavalry corps composed of two divisions was part of the German main effort against the Romanian left (west) flank. This corps' main contribution to the offensive was pursuit operations rather than simple reconnaissance, although the corps did provide zone reconnaissance for the infantry corps assigned to the main effort. The cavalry corps also provided security on the flanks of the German infantry during the Battle of Targu Jiu, and after the Romanians were decisively defeated on 18 November, while the German infantry pursued the retreating enemy closely, the accompanying cavalry attempted to cut the Romanians off from their line of retreat. However, in this mission, the Germans were only partially successful. Throughout the campaign, the cavalry corps provided timely reconnaissance, either as its main mission or as a byproduct of pursuit operations. The rugged terrain of the Transylvanian Mountains emphasized the cross-country mobility of horsemen.[76]

In later operations on the Eastern Front, the Germans did not use cavalry, depending more on a combination of assault infantry using infiltration tactics and the creative employment of massed artillery. By mid-1918, the only cavalry organizations that the Germans maintained were two small cavalry divisions, both being used for occupation duties in the east.[77]

The British campaigns in Palestine in 1917–18, under General Sir Edmund Allenby, are often considered the last great horse cavalry campaigns. In these operations, the British initially used two cavalry divisions and then later a corps, referred to as the Desert Mounted Corps, composed of cavalrymen primarily from Australia and New Zealand. These actions were fought in terrain much more open and rugged than western Europe, and the number of forces used by both sides was not large enough nor was the ability to supply them in the desert adequate enough to maintain an extended continuous front, frequently leaving open flanks or extended areas with no troops in them. With the weapons and organizations used in 1917–18, these conditions were ideal for cavalry operations of the style practiced by the British and the Commonwealth nations as a response to their experiences in the Boer War.

Referring to them as "light horse" or "mounted" troops, the British imperial forces' cavalry was more mounted infantry than traditional cavalry. The troopers' horses were primarily used as transportation, with most combat actions being conducted dismounted, although, in later pursuit operations in 1918, these forces often fought mounted. In Palestine, the cavalry was still capable of shock action under the right conditions where the mobility of the horse, particularly when supported closely by artillery and the dispersion made possible by the openness of the desert allowed the mounted forces to approach defending infantry without being decimated by the firepower of the defenders. The premier example of this use was during the Third Battle of Gaza where the Desert Mounted Corps charged the Turkish 27th Infantry Division at Beersheba on Halloween 1917. After swiftly overrunning the Turkish first line of entrenchments, the Australian horsemen dismounted and then fought and defeated the demoralized Turkish infantrymen on foot, primarily with the bayonet.[78]

Even though it attacked mounted, Allenby's use of the Desert Mounted Corps to play a main role in the Third Battle of Gaza reflected more on his use of the corps as a mobile infantry force on the Turkish open (western) flank than as a traditional cavalry force. Throughout the 1917 and 1918 campaigns, Allenby repeatedly used the mounted force to outflank the Turks and move deep into their rear areas to block their retreat.[79]

The imperial mounted forces scouted and screened on horseback. However, Allenby, particularly in the 1917 campaign, depended more on deception and surprise maneuvers to screen his intentions from the Turks than he depended on his cavalry. And while mounted troopers were used for local (that is, tactical) reconnaissance, the Desert Mounted Corps was not used for operational reconnaissance, this role in the open desert being primarily that of the airplane. While Allenby used large cavalry forces, these units were employed primarily in combat operations similar to those of infantry, only at a faster pace, and not as reconnaissance forces.

While cavalry units continued to exist after August 1914, rarely would they be used in a reconnaissance role for the rest of the war. When able, such units performed other cavalry missions such as security operations and, sometimes in open terrain such as in Palestine, used their mobility to maneuver against enemy forces. However, during the war, reconnaissance operations soon became the primary province of aircraft.[80]

US Army Reconnaissance Units in World War I

Given the state of cavalry and reconnaissance units in the Allied armies by 1917–18, it should come as no surprise that, when the US Army organized infantry divisions to fight in France, these divisions contained no organic reconnaissance elements. However, the story is not as simple as the straight application of an appreciation of combat conditions to the organization of the American Expeditionary Force (AEF). The US Army had a long cavalry tradition. General John Pershing, the AEF commander, was an old cavalryman. The absence of cavalry came about because of circumstances rather than design.

Before US deployment, American planners commissioned two teams to look at Allied force organization and provide recommendations for US Army structure. This mission became known as the General Organization Project, and the consensus of findings from the two teams was called the Baker Board Report (after the chief of one of the teams, Colonel Chauncey Baker). The Baker Board Report did not include any cavalry directly in proposed US Army divisional organizations but postulated the attachment of one squadron to each division from a corps-level cavalry regiment. Each corps would have two such regiments with three squadrons each. Unattached squadrons would be used as training and replacement units.[81]

However, when the first US division arrived in France, cavalry did not accompany it. When the AEF devised transatlantic shipping schedules, cavalry was given a low priority. With a shortage of troop transports, almost no cavalry units went to France, and the few that did came without their mounts. Four regiments did arrive in France dismounted. Most ended up in the rear area providing guard duty or other noncombat functions. The French promised to provide horses, but by early 1918, they had provided only enough to equip one squadron. This one squadron, a provisional unit made up of troops from the 2d Cavalry, fought in the St. Mihiel and Argonne Offensives as a corps asset. The squadron, usually divided into troops, provided tactical reconnaissance for several divisions, moving mounted and fighting dismounted. It was particularly effective in the final phases of the St. Mihiel operation when the Germans began withdrawing to straighten out their lines.[82]

Aside from the single squadron, US forces fought on the Western Front without designated reconnaissance elements. The French and British offered to supply cavalry to the AEF as necessary. In several cases, Allied regiments or squadrons were attached to US divisions for short periods. The French command attached its 5th Cavalry Division to the US I Corps in the Argonne Offensive. This division was to exploit any holes made in the German front, push through the gap, and advance toward Sedan while providing operational-level reconnaissance for the US corps. However, the pace of trench warfare and the ability of the Germans to recover quickly provided no suitable opportunity for using the division. It was returned to French control after a week.[83]

As has been seen in the operations of the other combatants, the airplane dominated reconnaissance in US operations as well. While the AEF lacked ground reconnaissance units, the nascent US Air Service organized for this mission with each infantry corps containing a corps air service headquarters. Under this command were an observation group and a balloon group (figure 13). The observation group typically contained one

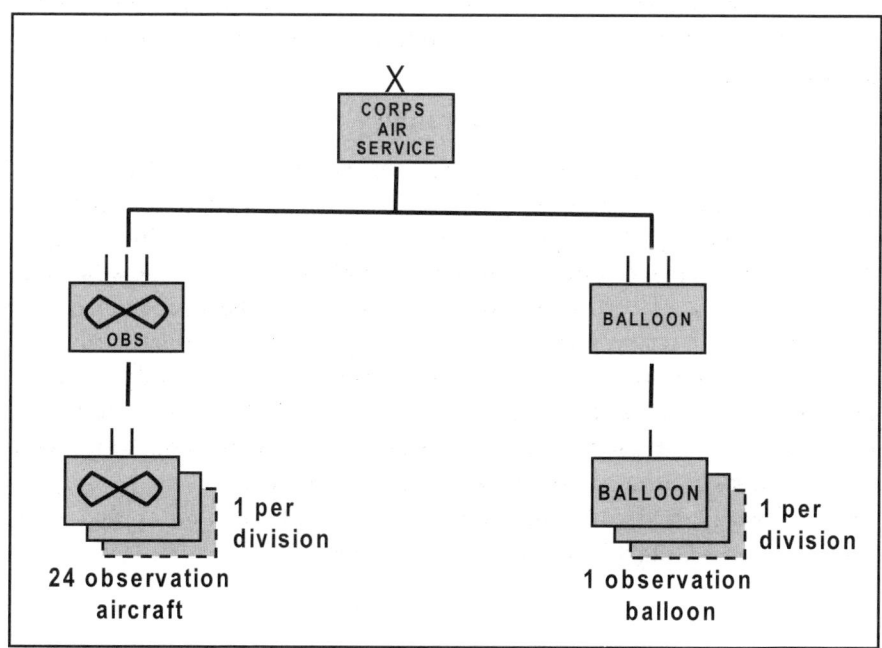

Figure 13. Typical air observation group, AEF, 1918.

41

observation plane or aerosquadron for each division assigned to the corps. Each such aerosquadron had about 24 observation planes and was assigned to support a specific division. The balloon group controlled a number of separate balloon companies that were attached directly to divisions in the front lines. The balloons provided high-altitude observation across the front lines for specially trained observers and teams of support personnel. Each company operated one balloon and followed the advance of the infantry.[84]

By 1918, fixed-wing aerial observation had become sophisticated, and US pilots and observers were expected to conduct four distinct missions: general intelligence gathering, contact, aerial fire, and photographic reconnaissance. Contact was a command and control reconnaissance mission where observers watched and recorded the forward progress of the advance of friendly troops. These observations were then relayed by Morse code transmitters to supporting artillery and higher headquarters. Aerial fire missions were preplanned observation of the effects of artillery fire. Photographic reconnaissance supplemented similar missions conducted by the balloon troops.[85]

As of the date of the armistice, 11 November 1918, the AEF's Air Service was composed of 45 squadrons. Of these squadrons, 18 were devoted to observation support for the Army, while an additional 20 pursuit squadrons provided air cover for the observers. Accordingly, more than 80 percent of the Air Service's missions focused on providing reconnaissance information for the Army.[86]

Summary

By the end of the war, most reconnaissance conducted to support ground troops was done by air.[87] The World War I period was one in which the combatants equated organized ground reconnaissance units with the cavalry as had been traditional since the development of gunpowder. The immobility of the entrenched opposing forces and the firepower of the defense made cavalry ineffective in the reconnaissance role. And even in those places where cavalry could operate more effectively, such as in Palestine, horse soldiers were used more often than not as mounted infantry rather than as reconnaissance troops. The reconnaissance mission had completely passed to the air component. The return of ground reconnaissance units required a departure from the notion that only organizations equipped with horses could conduct reconnaissance.

Notes

1. A good discussion of this issue can be found in Kay Brinkmann, "German Observations of the U.S. Civil War: A Study in Lessons Not Learned," MMAS thesis, US Army Command and General Staff College, 2000. The cavalry on both sides (French and German) before World War I seemed to be more concerned with developments on the other side rather than those from outside of Europe. See US War Department, Office of the Chief of Staff, *Reorganization of the French Cavalry: Extract From the Report of the Military Committee of the Chamber of Deputies, Session of 1912* (Washington, DC: Government Printing Office, 1913), 8, 9, 12, 13. Aside from lances and edged weapons, the French cavalry was also equipped with 1892 Lebel 8-mm carbines as secondary weapons. Cuirassiers carried them in saddle buckets while the rest of the French cavalry slung them on their backs. See Anthony Clayton, *Paths of Glory: The French Army, 1914–18* (London: Cassell, 2003), 207; General Staff, War Office [UK], *Handbook of the French Army, 1914* (Nashville: Battery Press, 1998), 236. The German cavalry also was equipped with a carbine, the 7.9-mm Karabiner 98, usually carried in a bucket on the saddle. See General Staff, War Office [UK], *Handbook of the German Army in War, April 1918* (Nashville, TN: Battery Press, 1996), 64.

2. Dennis E. Showalter, *Tannenberg: Clash of Empires, 1914* (Washington, DC: Brassey's, 2004), 151; *Handbook of the German Army in War*, 63–64; Hermann Cron, *Imperial German Army, 1914–18: Organisation, Structure, Orders of Battle*, trans. C.F. Coltron (London: Helion & Company, 2002), 1.

3. Erskine Childers, *German Influence on British Cavalry* (London: Edward Arnold, 1911), 2–3; M. von Poseck, *The German Cavalry: 1914 in Belgium and France*, ed. Jerome Howe, trans. Alexander Strecker, Oscar Koch, Gordon Gordon-Smith, and Anton Hesse (Berlin: E.S. Mittler & Sohn, 1923), 232.

4. Poseck, 47, 222, 232. The British Army, unlike the French and German Armies, with its recent experience in the Boer War, considered dismounted fighting to be the norm for cavalry. This realistic view did not, however, prevent the British cavalry from conducting at least one disastrous charge onto German artillery on 24 August 1914 at Mons and from the British cavalry divisional headquarters losing control of its subordinate brigades during the retreat to the Marne. See Nikolas Gardner, "Command and Control in the 'Great Retreat' of 1914: The Disintegration of the British Cavalry Division," *The Journal of Military History* 63 (January 1999): 29–54.

5. *Reorganization of the French Cavalry*, 10–11. The French considered cavalry corps to be temporary organizations.

6. *Handbook of the French Army*, 233, 236. A heavy division had a cuirassier brigade and two dragoon brigades. A light division had only light cavalry and dragoon brigades. A mixed division had a cuirassier brigade, a dragoon brigade, and a light cavalry brigade.

7. Ibid., 109, 208, 234–235.

8. *Handbook of the German Army in War*, 54, 56, 58, 62.

9. When mobilized, however, this corps received only a single infantry regiment. See Colonel [nfn] Boucherie, *Historique du Corps de Cavalerie Sordet*, 2d ed. (Paris: Charles-Lavauelle, 1924), 13, 28.

10. Poseck, 41; Boucherie, 8; Clayton, 27.

11. Cron, 116.

12. In 1911, when a French general proposed a complete integration of reservists into the French active force structure, he was replaced. See Robert A. Doughty, "French Strategy in 1914: Joffre's Own," *Journal of Military History* 67 (April 2003): 437–438.

13. *Reorganization of the French Cavalry*, 12, 14.

14. Ibid., 10, 12.

15. Cron, 127–129; *Handbook of the German Army in War*, 63.

16. Cron, 94.

17. Poseck, 3–5.

18. Doughty, 429, 442; Poseck, 4–7.

19. *Handbook of the French Army*, 239; *Reorganization of the French Cavalry*, 11–13. At least one observer partially blames early French defeats in 1914 on the poor quality of divisional cavalry composed of reservists. See Clayton, 28.

20. *Handbook of the German Army in War*, 63.

21. Poseck, 134.

22. Boucherie, 29, 39, 45.

23. Before Plan XVII, the French referred to their temporary large cavalry commands as "groups of cavalry divisions" (*groupments des divisions de cavalerie*). Although Plan XVII adopted the term "cavalry corps" (*corps de cavalerie*) and included one such command, this force was still considered a temporary expedient. Sordet's headquarters was originally authorized a chief of staff, three officers, a liaison section consisting of four automobiles, and a small signal detachment. In the period between the adoption of the plan and mobilization, Sordet successfully lobbied for a more robust headquarters, receiving the projected attachment of a military police detachment, a larger signal element, an infantry brigade, and trucks. See Boucherie, 7–8, 115–117.

24. Poseck, 4–5.

25. Ibid., 3–6, 10.

26. Doughty, 441.

27. French Army *Grand Quartier Général (G.Q.G.)* General Order No. 1, 8 August 1914; Doughty, 447.

28. Poseck, 14, 21–27.

29. The commander of the I Cavalry Corps was the uncle and namesake of the famous aviator who at that time was a lieutenant with the 1st *Uhlan* Regiment in the IV Cavalry Corps in northern Lorraine.

30. Poseck, 42.

31. Ibid., 137.

32. Ibid., 222–223.

33. Ibid., 48.

34. Boucherie, 23.
35. Ibid., 27–28.
36. Ibid., 27–28, 30–33. On the day of Sordet's movement, two of the three German cavalry divisions at Liege were actually crossing the Meuse north of Sordet. The French commander would have encountered only the German 9th Cavalry Division with his three divisions if he had completed his movement.
37. Boucherie, 23, 29, 37–41, 45; Poseck, 43.
38. Doughty, 449.
39. Service Historique de l'Armée de Terre, "Niveau G.Q.G.," 25 June 1984, document in the author's files; French Fourth Army Order Number 426, dated 2000 hours, 17 August 1914; Le 9e Division Cavalerie, *Historique des Faits les 5-25 août 1914*, Service Historique de l'Armée deTerre, Republique Française, Paris, a war diary extract in the author's files.
40. Ibid.; Major William T. Haldeman, "Operations of the Provisional Cavalry Corps Abonneau (4th and 9th Cavalry Divisions) in Belgium, the 18th, 19th, and 20th August 1914—Review of Cavalry, 1927," Group Research Project, Second Year Class, US Army Command and General Staff School, Fort Leavenworth, KS, 1932, copy in archives, Combined Arms Research Library (CARL), Fort Leavenworth, KS.
41. Clayton, 26–27; *Feldwebel* C., 1st Sergeant, 88th Infantry Regiment, 21st Division, 18th Army Corps [German Army], *The Diary of a German Soldier* (New York: Alfred A. Knopf, 1919), 42–43. Joffre believed the Germans did not have enough troops to be strong both in central Belgium (as they appeared to be) and in the Ardennes. See Doughty, 441.
42. Poseck, 14.
43. Major R.E. Moses, "A Study of the Action of the German IV Army Preparatory to the Battle of the Ardennes, August 1914," Second Year Class, US Army Command and General Staff School, Fort Leavenworth, KS, 1931, copy in archives, CARL, Fort Leavenworth, KS.
44. *Diary of a German Soldier*, 43.
45. Service Historique de l'Armée de Terre, Republique Française, "Niveau 4e Armee," 25 June 1984, document in author's files; Major R.C. Allen, "A Study of the Initial Operations of the French Fourth Army in the Battle of the Ardennes," Second Year Class, US Army Command and General Staff School, Fort Leavenworth, KS, 29 May 1931, copy in archives, CARL, Fort Leavenworth, KS.
46. Le 9e Division Cavalerie, *Historique des Faits les 5-25 août 1914*; Major Paul V. Kane, "A Study of the Preliminary Steps of the Development of the Third and Fourth French Armies in the Battle of the Ardennes," Second Year Class, US Army Command and General Staff School, Fort Leavenworth, KS, 1931, copy in archives, CARL, Fort Leavenworth, KS.
47. Moses. The French 1/87th Infantry's parent regiment was assigned to the 6th Brigade, 3d Infantry Division, II Corps. The 4th Cavalry Division similarly had an infantry battalion (from the 9th Infantry Regiment) attached to it. See F. Gazin, *La Cavalerie Française dans la Guerre Mondiale, 1914–1918* (Paris:

Payot, 1930), 75; Le 87e Régiment Infanterie, *Historique des Faits, les 5, 14-22 août 1914*, Service Historique de l'Armée de Terre, Republique Française, Paris, a war diary in author's files. Haldeman.

48. Le 9e Division Cavalerie, *Historique des Faits les 5-25 août 1914*; Allen. The first names of Bossut and Pastouiel are not found in available records.

49. Allen; Poseck, 137. The French were aware of the presence of this German cavalry division but did not realize it was deployed only in the extreme south of the Neufchâteau region and that its area of operations did not extend north to Neufchâteau and Bastogne. See Haldeman.

50. *Diary of a German Soldier*, 43; Le 9e Division Cavalerie, *Historique des Faits les 5-25 août 1914*.

51. Times used in the account of the Battle of Hamipré are French ones. German time was 1 hour earlier and has been modified in this work accordingly.

52. Le 9e Division Cavalerie, *Historique des Faits les 5-25 août 1914*.

53. Ibid.; *Diary of a German Soldier*, 44.

54. *Diary of a German Soldier*, 44.

55. Le 9e Division Cavalerie, *Historique des Faits les 5-25 août 1914*; Historical inscription at the Battlefield of Hamipré, Belgium, copy of the inscription in author's files (from a site visit) and at "1914–18, Nos Héros & Leur Guerre>1-Bataille des Ardennes les Combats d'Hamipré–Longlier," *La Guerre de nos Héros 1914–1918*, http://www.google.com/search?q=cache:3HbsAo-dmKgJ: www.1914-18mibb.com/index.php%3Ffile%3DGallery%26op%3Dcategorie%2 6cat%3D116%26orderby%3Dnews%26p%3D3+Cussac+commandant+87&hl=e n&ct=clnk&cd=6&gl=us (accessed 27 August 2007).

56. *Diary of a German Soldier*, 45–48. Kierstein's full name is not attested in available sources. Until they encountered the French infantry, the Germans still thought they were fighting small Belgian rear guard forces that had disputed their advance. In particular, the French cyclists were thought to be Belgian. See *Diary of a German Soldier*, 49.

57. Le 9e Division Cavalerie, *Historique des Faits les 5-25 août 1914*.

58. Ibid.; Historical inscription at the Battlefield of Hamipré, Belgium.

59. *Diary of a German Soldier*, 48–49; Captain John Dahlquist, "A Study of the Operations of the Fourth German Army in the Battle of the Ardennes, August 22d–23d, 1914, Based on the Account Contained in Volume I, *Der Weltkrieg* (Official History of the World War)," Second Year Class, US Army Command and General Staff School, Fort Leavenworth, KS, 1931, copy in archives, CARL, Fort Leavenworth, KS. For detailed accounts of the Battle at Bertrix, see Kane and Dahlquist, as well as Bruce I. Gudmundsson, "Unexpected Encounter at Bertrix," *Military History Quarterly* 13 (Autumn 2000): 20–27; Bruce Gudmundsson, "Encounter at Bertrix," *Tactical Notebook* (October 1993): 1–11; *Infantry in Battle*, 2d ed. (Washington, DC: Infantry Journal, 1939), 122–126, 415–416.

60. Le 9e Division Cavalerie, *Historique des Faits les 5-25 août 1914*; Kane; Major J.W. Cunningham, "The French 9th Cavalry Division: Ardennes," Group Research Monograph, Second Year Class, US Army Command and General Staff School, Fort Leavenworth, KS, 1933, copy in archives, CARL, Fort Leavenworth, KS.

61. Ibid.
62. Ibid.
63. Kane; Cunningham. For more on Bertrix, see the references cited in note 59.
64. French reconnaissance failures were not limited to the Ardennes in August 1914. Simultaneous with the Battles of Hamipré and Bertrix, the French Fifth Army along the Sambre River to the north was badly beaten by German forces that crossed the river and advanced on the French before the French realized they were there in force. For one division's experience in this battle, see Leonard V. Smith, *Between Mutiny and Obedience: The Case of the French Fifth Infantry Division During World War I* (Princeton, NJ: Princeton University Press, 1994), 42–45. A combination of their own misconceptions, the speed of the German advance, and the lack of good reconnaissance placed the French at a marked disadvantage in almost every initial engagement with the main body of German forces in August 1914.
65. Poseck 221–224.
66. Ibid., 221–224, 232.
67. Ibid., 221–224.
68. For examples of this, see Boucherie, 38. On 15 August 1914, the French theater commander, Joseph Joffre, ordered the Fourth Army to use its airplanes to reconnoiter the area around Neufchâteau. See Allen.
69. Boucherie, 31.
70. Poseck, 231.
71. Ibid., 234.
72. Cron, 105–106; James Sawicki, *Cavalry Regiments of the US Army* (Dumfries, VA: Wyvern, 1985), 96. The French continued to assign two cavalry squadrons (roughly 300 troopers) to each infantry division for the bulk of the war, while the British retained a cavalry brigade in each corps. The Germans retained one or two cavalry squadrons in their divisions throughout the war.
73. Bruce I. Gudmundsson, *Stormtroop Tactics: Innovation in the German Army, 1914–1918* (Westport, CT: Praeger, 1989), 60–61, 141–142, 159.
74. Cron, 94; Colonel Frederick E. Jackson, "Tannenberg: The First Use of Signals Intelligence in Modern Warfare," Strategy Research Project (Carlisle Barracks, PA: US Army War College, 2002), 10, 14–15, 17.
75. Gudmundsson, *Stormtroop Tactics*, 107–109; Major Ernest Harmon, "A Critical Analysis of the German Cavalry Operations in the Łodz Campaign to Include the Breakthrough at Brzeziny, With Particular Reference to the I Cavalry Corps," Individual Research Paper, Second Year Class, US Army Command and General Staff School, Fort Leavenworth, KS, 1933, 20–24, copy in archives, CARL, Fort Leavenworth, KS. As at Tannenberg, at Łodz, the Russian cavalry failed completely in its reconnaissance function even though more than enough assets were available.
76. Major A.T. Lacey, "The Effect of the German Cavalry on the Rumanian Campaign in November 1916," Individual Research Paper, US Army Command and General Staff School, Fort Leavenworth, KS, 1930, 1–8, copy in archives,

CARL, Fort Leavenworth, KS; Captain Jonathan House, *Toward Combined Arms Warfare: A Survey of 20th Century Tactics, Doctrine, and Organization*, Research Survey No. 2 (Fort Leavenworth, KS: Combat Studies Institute, US Army Command and General Staff College, 1984), 32–34.

77. Gudmundsson, *Stormtroop Tactics*, 100; Cron, 105.

78. Jean Bou, "Cavalry, Firepower, and Swords: The Australian Light Horse and the Tactical Lessons of Cavalry Operations in Palestine, 1916–1918," *Journal of Military History* 71 (January 2007): 110–114, 116.

79. Ibid., 120; Major O. Welsch, "Cavalry in the Palestine Campaign," *Cavalry Journal* 17 (April 1927): 296.

80. Edgar Raines Jr. *Eyes of the Artillery: The Origins of Modern US Army Aviation* (Washington, DC: US Army Center of Military History, 2000), 10.

81. John Wilson, *Maneuver and Firepower: The Evolution of Divisions and Separate Brigades* (Washington, DC: US Army Center of Military History, 1998), 52, 54; Sawicki, 96, 98. Since the French retained two troop-sized squadrons in their divisions, the squadron, equivalent to a French regiment, which US planners envisioned for AEF divisions, was slightly larger than the French allocation.

82. Sawicki, 100; Captain Ernest Harmon, "The Second Cavalry in the St. Mihiel Offensive," *Cavalry Journal* (April 1927): 282, 287–289.

83. Sawicki, 100.

84. Raines, 11; 385; Mauer Mauer, ed., *The US Air Service in World War I: Volume I, The Final Report and a Tactical History* (Washington, DC: Office of Air Force History, 1978), 385.

85. Raines, 13.

86. Robert F. Futrell, *Ideas, Concepts, Doctrine: Basic Thinking in the United States Air Force, 1907–1960*, vol. 1 (Maxwell Air Force Base, AL: Air University Press, 1989), 23.

87. Ibid., 18.

Chapter 2

Reconnaissance Theory and Organization in the Interwar Period

Introduction

World War I ended with the armies of the major combatants depending on observation aircraft to provide most tactical and operational reconnaissance. This role fell to the air force because of the lack of any other effective alternatives. However, dependence on aviation alone for a major function necessary to ground operations began to look more perilous during the interwar period as most air forces moved away from supporting the army to strategic bombing and air superiority roles.

While all major armies retained horse cavalry units, these forces focused primarily on combat, security, and pursuit missions in what was termed "open warfare" or "war of movement"—in other words, nontrench warfare. Such operations postulated the availability of an open flank for cavalry to maneuver around. Even Germany, the one power that had gone the furthest to abandon cavalry during the war, in its interwar field service regulation considered that "[c]ombat is the cavalry's principal mission. Attack against the flank and rear of the enemy is the most effective form of maneuver."[1]

Interwar development of reconnaissance units, therefore, followed several organizational and theoretical strains. These included the development of alternative ground reconnaissance units to supplement air reconnaissance; the divorce of horse cavalry from the reconnaissance role; and the development of nonhorse, motorized, and mechanized reconnaissance forces. In addition, once new reconnaissance organizations were established, developmental concepts required decisions on how to equip such units. The choices on equipment often depended on how the army involved intended to use such units: either to gain information through stealth and speed or to gain it from combat action. Developments in the interwar period foreshadowed a proliferation of reconnaissance units at the tactical level in World War II and a waning of such units at the operational level.[2]

The American Experience

The Air Force as the Army's Reconnaissance Element

In its postwar organizational structure, the United States continued the wartime trend of dependence on aviation to conduct reconnaissance. The 1920 version of the infantry division, which was retained for most of the interwar period, had an aero observation squadron with 13 airplanes as the division's organic reconnaissance element. If necessary, nondivisional cavalry units could provide ground reconnaissance to the infantry division. The observation squadron remained part of the divisional organization.[3]

Dependence on airplanes as the sole reconnaissance agent for ground troops soon faced challenges from air power theorists and advocates, led by Brigadier General William Mitchell. Mitchell believed that aviation forces should be centralized under a separate air commander and that the premier role for air power should be an independent, strategic bombing one. Mitchell's views, while extreme in 1920, soon became a common theme among Air Service officers. During World War I, the Air Service organization comprised a structure that was 80-percent observation support and 20-percent bomber. Originally, Major General Mason Patrick, the American Expeditionary Force (AEF) Air Chief, agreed that this was the proper ratio. But by 1926, even Patrick believed the Air Service's main role should be that of strategic bombardment.[4]

While emphasizing strategic bombing and giving observation support a much lower priority, American postwar air power proponents opposed the way aerial observation was handled in the war and retained in the postwar organization even while grudgingly accepting the need for such support. These Air Service officers thought that observation units needed to be centralized at higher levels of command rather than be divided among combat divisions. Nevertheless, in the immediate postwar reorganization, the War Department retained observation units as components of divisions while retaining pursuit and attack aircraft at the field army echelon.

Even as the Air Service gained increased autonomy, beginning with its redesignation as the Army Air Corps in 1926, observation squadrons remained in Army infantry division organizational structures. This design lasted until July 1941 when the War Department centralized observation squadrons under five air support commands under the Army Air Force (AAF) (as the Air Corps had been redesignated a month earlier). As part of this reorganization, the War Department and Army leadership recognized that the observation squadrons had become the orphans of the Air Force and that "observation equipment and tactics had not progressed since 1918."[5]

In 1941 when the Army Air Force deployed a total of 11 observation squadrons in its Active Component, this represented only 10 percent of the overall AAF Active structure. Even including the pursuit planes that provided air cover for the observers as one of their missions, this total represented only 40 percent of the AAF's organizational structure, with the bulk of the

AAF devoted to bombing. By 1941, however, ground reconnaissance, in the form of mechanized cavalry units and in reconnaissance companies and platoons in combat regiments and battalions, had returned to the US Army's force structure.[6]

The Development of Mechanized Cavalry

Although no ground reconnaissance elements were in the infantry division, the US Army retained 17 cavalry regiments after the war. Four of these regiments were organized into a division, with the remainder assigned various functions such as border security or as backup support for coast artillery units. Peacetime force developers did not specify the actual role expected of the US Army's cavalry division, although its 1920 organizational structure emphasized mobility and firepower. Machine-gun squadrons at the brigade level primarily represented this increase in firepower. It was clear that Army cavalry proponents believed the main role of the horse cavalry units was to conduct traditional cavalry combat missions (offense, defense, flank protection, shock action, pursuit) rather than reconnaissance and counterreconnaissance. In addition to combat missions, the Army's Cavalry branch anticipated a reconnaissance role for the Army's single cavalry division—conducting large-scale tactical reconnaissance in front of friendly forces. The branch refused to discount the all-weather, all-terrain mobility of mounted units in a war of movement. In fact, drawing primarily on examples from Allenby's campaigns, cavalry proponents believed that, despite the technological advances in World War I, the role of horse cavalry, except in the operational reconnaissance area, had not changed at all. It could remain an all-purpose mobile combat force. At the tactical level, although the airplane had supplanted the horse as the divisional reconnaissance element, postwar cavalry analysts still believed that divisions should have a regiment or squadron of cavalry attached as necessary but they should not be organic components.[7]

Despite this conservative mindset, US Army cavalry officers discussed the possible adoption of motorized and mechanized elements, nascent in World War I, into the cavalry division as early as 1919 when an AEF-appointed cavalry board recommended that 12 armored cars and an unspecified number of motorcycles be included in the postwar divisional organization. When the Army Chief of Staff approved the first postwar cavalry division organization in 1920, it included 14 armored cars, 28 trucks, and 65 motorcycles.[8]

Although there were technological advances in motorized and mechanized vehicles throughout the 1920s, tight budgets ensured that most American experimentation with such vehicles was primarily theoretical. Toward the end of the decade, changes began to take place. The beginning of limited motorization began in 1927 when an infantry regiment experimented with using trucks to move itself operationally. The Army expanded this experiment with a plan to permanently motorize eight infantry regiments using trucks left over from World War I stocks. In 1931, Congress provided funds for the Army to buy new trucks to motorize the supply trains of three Active infantry divisions. Field artillery units in both the Regular force and the National Guard were then completely motorized in the 1930s.[9]

Motorization initially had a limited impact on the cavalry with its dependence on the horse for transportation. However, mechanization, the development of armored tracked and wheeled vehicles for combat use, also began in the US Army in 1927 with the creation of a brigade-sized organization known as the Experimental Mechanized Force (EMF). The impetus for the creation of the EMF was American notice of the British Army's mechanized maneuvers of 1927. The reconnaissance element of this force was an armored car troop consisting of 14 light and medium armored cars. The EMF conducted field tests using experimental equipment for several months in the latter half of 1928. The force was then temporarily disbanded, although there were plans to reestablish it in 1930 when funds became available to procure new mechanized equipment.[10]

The EMF used, as its name implied, experimental equipment, a series of armored cars equipped with machine guns, and generally based on civilian vehicles. In general, these vehicles were lightly armored, weighed between 1 and 4 tons, could maintain high speeds of up to 70 miles per hour (mph), and had a range of 150 miles. The appendix provides performance data for these and all platforms described in this special study.

After the demise of the EMF, the Cavalry branch retained the armored car troop and assigned it to the 1st Cavalry Division in 1929 as the initial component of a projected divisional armored car squadron. The troop participated in the 1929 cavalry maneuvers with a mix of light and medium armored cars whose primary mission was reconnaissance. During these maneuvers, for the first time, the issue of whether reconnaissance vehicles should be light or heavy (in the form of medium armored cars) arose without resolution. Cavalry observers thought that the armored car's lack of cross-country mobility limited reconnaissance activities to long-range missions aimed at discovering the location of large enemy concentrations. The observers also thought that even the heavier medium armored cars were too light to do anything but reconnaissance, depending on speed and stealth in the operations. Despite a good overall performance in the maneuvers, mechanized cavalry, in the form of armored cars, remained an auxiliary force at best to horse cavalry. The cavalry retained the troop and organized a second troop in 1930.[11]

In 1931, General Douglas MacArthur became the new Army Chief of Staff. As such, MacArthur saw the value of the mechanization experiments, now being organized by a successor organization to the EMF, the Mechanized Force. However, he believed that the decentralization of such testing on a branch basis was a better way of maximizing results. Therefore, the Mechanized Force was disbanded shortly after it was established. However, MacArthur thought that both horses and mechanized vehicles had a place in the cavalry, a vision he shared with the Chief of Cavalry, Major General Guy Henry. After the demise of the Mechanized Force, MacArthur directed Henry to mechanize one regiment of cavalry.[12]

Figure 14. M1 (T4) medium armored car.

On the termination of the Mechanized Force, the War Department transformed its headquarters into the 7th Cavalry Brigade (Mechanized), a force to control Henry's projected mechanized cavalry regiment. The 1st Cavalry Regiment (Mechanized) joined the brigade in 1933 and remained the nucleus of the brigade until a mechanized cavalry regiment, the 13th, and a motorized field artillery battalion in 1936 were added. A motorized infantry regiment was also frequently attached to the brigade.[13]

The mechanized cavalry regiment had 2 squadrons of combat cars (a euphemism for tanks) and a troop of 15 armored cars. As in its experimental predecessor organizations, the armored car troop was the cavalry regiment's reconnaissance element. The troop's vehicles were only lightly armored. It was not designed to fight but to obtain information through a combination of stealth and speed. Operationally, the troop was usually divided into five vehicle platoons or two vehicle sections.[14]

Through a series of maneuvers, reorganizations, and equipment upgrades, the 7th Cavalry Brigade developed into a combined arms mechanized force whose primary missions included the former cavalry ones of providing shock action and of being an all-purpose mobile combat force. In addition, it was also to be a main battle force similar to the infantry. Therefore, although nurtured in the Cavalry branch, by 1940, the brigade became the core of a new combat arm, the Army's Armored Force, the brigade itself becoming that force's 1st Armored Division. This resulted in the de facto transfer of the cavalry's former combat missions to the new Armored Force.[15]

Although the mechanized cavalry brigade eventually evolved into a separate combat arm, its armored car troop provided the antecedent for all the separate mechanized cavalry reconnaissance units developed in the US Army in World War II and for the armored reconnaissance battalions found in its World War II armored divisions. The latter will be discussed in the next chapter. Mechanized cavalry units developed in a parallel manner in the bulk of the cavalry with that in the 7th Brigade. When the Army fielded the M3 scout car, a light armored car, in 1939, the first 64 vehicles were sent to the 7th Cavalry Brigade.[16]

While the armored car troop in the 7th Cavalry Brigade (Mechanized) came from the second armored car troop raised as part of the 1930 mechanized force, the Cavalry branch had retained the original armored car troop from the 1928 EMF and attached it to the 1st Cavalry Division. By 1938, the use of armored cars in that division and in nondivisional horse regiments was extended when a troop was added to each cavalry regiment in the Army. The new unit, similar to the revised version in the mechanized cavalry regiment, had 17 armored cars divided into 4 platoons and a section of 5 motorcycles. Through technological advances and testing both by the 7th Brigade and the horse cavalry, the Cavalry branch now considered the armored car to be superior to the horse in the reconnaissance role.[17]

In addition to the armored car units, the cavalry embraced mechanization in the late 1930s with a hybrid organization, the horse-mechanized (H-M) cavalry regiment. Created as a response to German success using mechanized forces in Poland in September 1939, this unit contained two cavalry squadrons, one horse mounted and the other with armored cars and motorcycles. The concept for the H-M regiment was that it would be used at the corps level to provide operational reconnaissance and counterreconnaissance and that the horse squadron would be moved operationally by specially designed horse-carrying trucks and offloaded and used tactically in places more accessible to horse and rider than to armored cars. The truck-horse combination was referred to as "portee" cavalry. The armored car squadrons in the H-M regiment were the US Army's first squadron-sized mechanized reconnaissance units.[18]

Initially, three Regular Army regiments were converted to the H-M structure. When the National Guard's cavalry was mobilized in late 1940 and early 1941, the Army converted seven of these regiments to the H-M regiments. The hybrid organization lasted until after the United States entered World War II, but in 1943, the 10 regiments were converted to mechanized or armored units as the horse was completely eliminated from the US Army's combat force structure.[19]

With the approach of war in 1941, ground reconnaissance had become the exclusive realm of the Cavalry branch and its nondivisional cavalry regiments with their mix of horses and light armored vehicles. When the US Army ultimately went to war in 1941–45, its cavalry deployed 91,948 troops. Except for the dismounted troopers fighting as infantry in the 1st Cavalry Division in the Pacific, these forces were found in 73 mechanized cavalry units whose primary function was to conduct reconnaissance.[20]

Divisional Reconnaissance Elements

Since the end of World War I, the US Army infantry division contained no ground reconnaissance unit. Even before the AAF's observation squadron was withdrawn from the division in July 1941, ground reconnaissance assets had returned to the divisional structure. As early as 1936, the Army began experimenting with the conversion of its four-regiment square division organization to a sleeker three-regiment triangular division. In the earliest proposals, the division also contained a small reconnaissance squadron. This squadron was to be equipped with unspecified lightly armored or unarmored vehicles capable of traveling off roads. An Army division tested the structure in 1937. As a result of these tests, organizational revisions removed the reconnaissance squadron from the division. At least theoretically, the squadron was moved to corps level.[21]

The Regular Army infantry divisions changed to the triangular structure in 1939. Shortly after the Polish campaign, Army force developers decided that the triangular division needed a troop-sized reconnaissance element. When the Cavalry branch organized these troops, it developed them as mechanized rather than horse units. This divisional reconnaissance troop, along with armored division reconnaissance battalions, is discussed in more detail in the next chapter.[22]

The German Experience
Doctrine and Theory

At the beginning of World War I, the Germans had deployed the largest and most thoroughly trained cavalry force. By the end of the war, almost all the German cavalry had been dismounted and the notion of dedicated reconnaissance troops abandoned at the operational level and minimized to a single cavalry squadron per infantry division at the tactical level. In the *Reichswehr*, the 100,000-man army that the provisions of the Treaty of Versailles allowed the Germans, horse cavalry forces formed a large part of the force: 18 regiments organized into 3 cavalry divisions. Despite their World War I experience, German cavalry leaders still clung to pre-1914 concepts and ideas. The lance was not officially eliminated from the *Reichswehr* until 1927. And as late as 1931, German cavalry generals, similar to their counterparts in the United States, intended to reorganize their cavalry into a heavy main battle force. In contrast to what happened in the US Army in the same period, the German cavalry leadership's devotion to the cavalry in the main battle led to the cavalry's ready surrender of the operational-level reconnaissance mission to the motorized troops branch, the predecessor of the armored forces. Despite later attempts to shift this role back to the cavalry, the motorized troops retained the mission. The Germans became the first major army to effectively divorce operational reconnaissance from horse cavalry, at least in theory.[23]

However, at the tactical level, the Germans still respected the role of the horse, particularly in support of infantry. Even such armored proponents as Heinz Guderian retained this view. The result was that the German Army entered World War II with its infantry divisions containing horse cavalry elements in which to conduct tactical reconnaissance alongside its panzer and motorized divisions.[24]

Within the *Reichswehr*'s infantry divisions, as originally formed, there was no reconnaissance element. To fulfill this role, when mobilized, a single troop-sized squadron would be attached from one of the cavalry divisions. Although the Treaty of Versailles restricted *Reichswehr* organizational changes, its chief, *Generaloberst* Hans von Seeckt, presented postulated future changes in the force's field service regulation (Army Regulation 487, *Leadership and Battle With Combined Arms*) in 1921 and 1923. Von Seeckt's theoretical changes were based on his and the *Reichswehr* staff's perceived lessons of the war. In the reorganized infantry division, Von Seeckt expanded the reconnaissance element from the single cavalry squadron, creating a new organization known as a reconnaissance battalion. This battalion contained two cavalry squadrons as well as a bicycle company and an armored car detachment (figure 15). With treaty restrictions, the design was only notional as the elements of the reconnaissance battalion remained components of cavalry regiments until the era of rearmament began in the late 1930s. But Von Seeckt's concept became the basis for the original reconnaissance battalion found in the German infantry division in the first campaigns of World War II.[25]

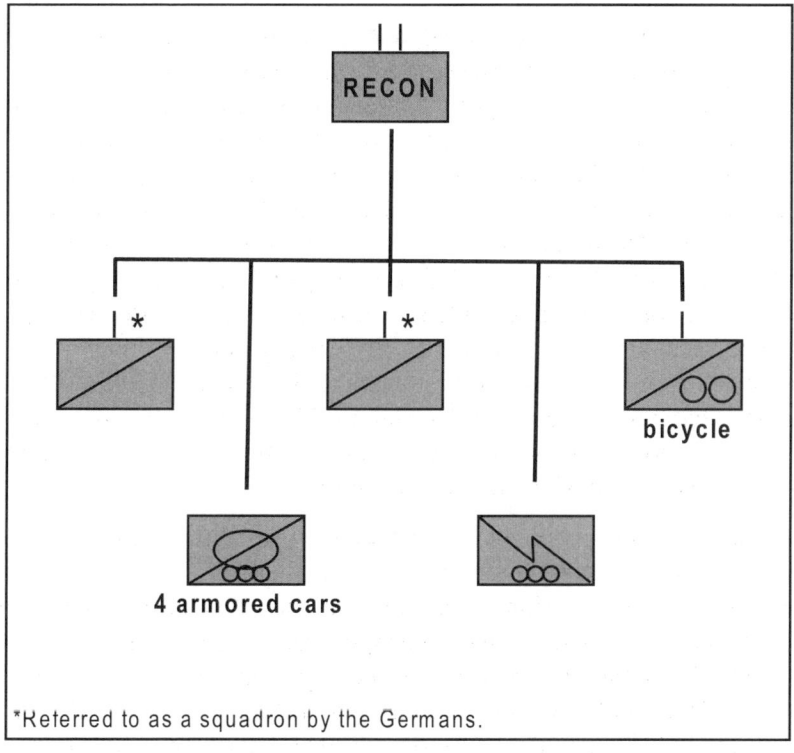

Figure 15. Proposed German infantry division reconnaissance battalion, 1923.

The subsequent German field service regulations of 1933, which (as previously noted) reflected on cavalry as primarily a main battle force, devoted a separate chapter to reconnaissance. In that chapter, reconnaissance was divided into operational and tactical levels. A subset of the latter was combat reconnaissance—that is, reconnaissance conducted once contact with the enemy was made. The 1933 regulations, while reflecting the German doctrinal dichotomy existing between motorized (the then German term for what Americans called mechanized) and horse units, did not assign particular roles at the operational and tactical levels to each type of reconnaissance unit. Instead, the document delineated each type by its perceived capabilities. The advantages of motorized units were speed on roads and long range. Horse cavalry was able to operate with greater stealth in all kinds of terrain, day and night, while requiring less supply than motorized units. Unlike the US Army's H-M regiments, the Germans believed that motorized and horse units should not be in the same organization, as such a force would then include the disadvantages of both.[26]

With rearmament beginning almost immediately after the Nazi accession to power in 1933, the panzer forces grew. As in the US Army, the German cavalry branch sought simultaneously a place in mechanization/ motorization while retaining its traditional role. However, unlike in the United States, development of armored forces in the German Army did not originate in experimental cavalry units but in the ranks of the motorized supply troops. However, the cavalry played a role as well. In 1934, with the formation of a Motorized Combat Troops Directorate (*Inspektion der Kraftfahrtruppen*), an independent arm responsible for the development of what became the panzer forces, the cavalry provided personnel and equipment from four cavalry regiments and the headquarters of the 3d Cavalry Division to the new organization. These units were used to form panzer and motorized infantry regiments, leading to the creation of the first three panzer divisions the following year.[27]

The remaining 14 *Reichswehr* regiments of cavalry were organized into 2 cavalry divisions under a corps headquarters. In 1938, when two additional panzer divisions were formed, the cavalry was completely reorganized. The most dramatic change was the conversion of the two divisional headquarters and some of the regimental troops into three and later four large motorized units, referred to as "light divisions." The exact role of the light divisions was murky. While Guderian believed they were organized to conduct reconnaissance operations at the highest level, and several other sources cite specific screening and reconnaissance missions, the actual employment of the divisions in the 1939 Polish campaigns imply that the cavalry branch saw the divisions as replacements for its cavalry divisions in the former main battle role similar to the employment of the panzer divisions but with less firepower and armor.[28]

Organizationally, the division contained both a strong reconnaissance (armored car) and motorized infantry contingent (figure 16). The motorized infantry, officially known as cavalry rifle (*Kavallerie-Schützen*), units were formed into two regiments of two battalions each. The division also

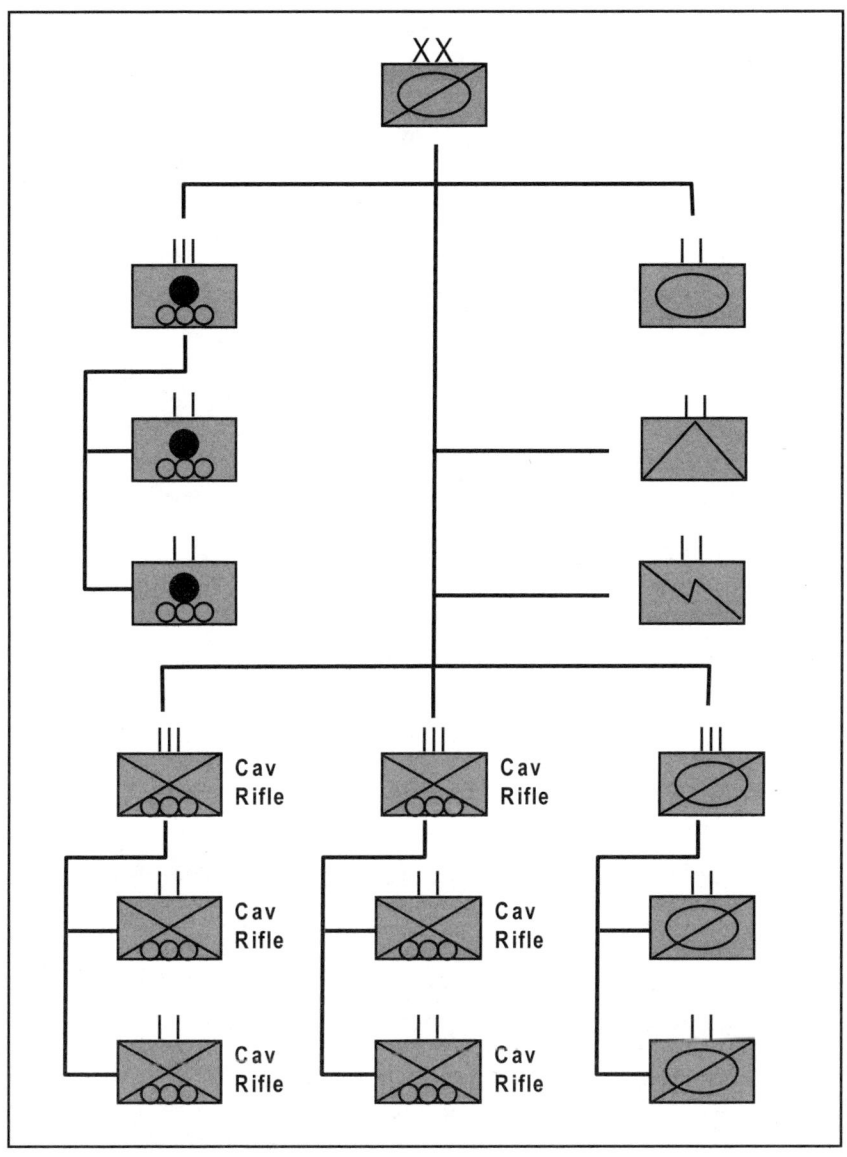

Figure 16. German light division, 1939.

included an expanded reconnaissance regiment consisting of two armored car regiments and a tank battalion equipped with 90 Panzer I or Panzer II light tanks.[29]

When formed, the light divisions were placed under their own corps command (the XV). At the same time, the Inspectorate of Cavalry, the cavalry branch headquarters, was abolished, and all cavalry forces were placed under a new command headed by Guderian, the Chief of Mobile Troops (*Chef der Schnellen Truppen*). This command encompassed both the cavalry and the motorized troops.[30]

At the same time the light divisions were formed, the remaining horse cavalry regiments were also reorganized. Except for two regiments formed into a cavalry brigade, the remaining regiments restructured into two subordinate battalions each, one composed of horse cavalry squadrons (equal to US Army troops in size) and one with motorcycle squadrons. A regiment was assigned to each corps to provide the divisional reconnaissance assets for the portion of the 35 peacetime infantry divisions of the Wehrmacht (as the Nazi-era successor to the *Reichswehr* was now called) assigned to the corps. On mobilization in late August 1939, the regimental headquarters were dissolved and the subordinate squadrons parceled out according to a prearranged scheme among the infantry divisions.[31]

The organizational scheme for the German infantry division's reconnaissance component in 1939 somewhat resembled Von Seeckt's 1923 proposal, with a unit of mixed assets. The battalion had a horse cavalry squadron, a motorcycle squadron, and a heavy motorized squadron (figure 17). The latter unit contained three armored cars, a motorized antitank platoon with three 37-mm towed antitank guns, and a platoon with three 75-mm guns.[32]

This organizational structure applied only to the 35 peacetime infantry divisions. Additional horse cavalry squadrons were only available for the 16 divisions of the second wave of the division formation. Subsequent divisions typically received additional motorcycle squadrons in lieu of the horse units.[33]

Reconnaissance and the Development of Panzer and Motorized Forces

The armored or panzer forces of the interwar German Army developed from the motorized support units of the 100,000-man interwar *Reichswehr*. The terms of the Treaty of Versailles prescribed the *Reichswehr*'s organizational structure. The treaty prohibited the Germans from developing tanks. The only motorized or mechanized equipment allowed by Versailles was that found in the divisional truck battalions. These units were not combat forces but, rather, supply troops equipped with cargo trucks. But out of necessity, the motor transport troops (*Kraftfahrtruppe*) began

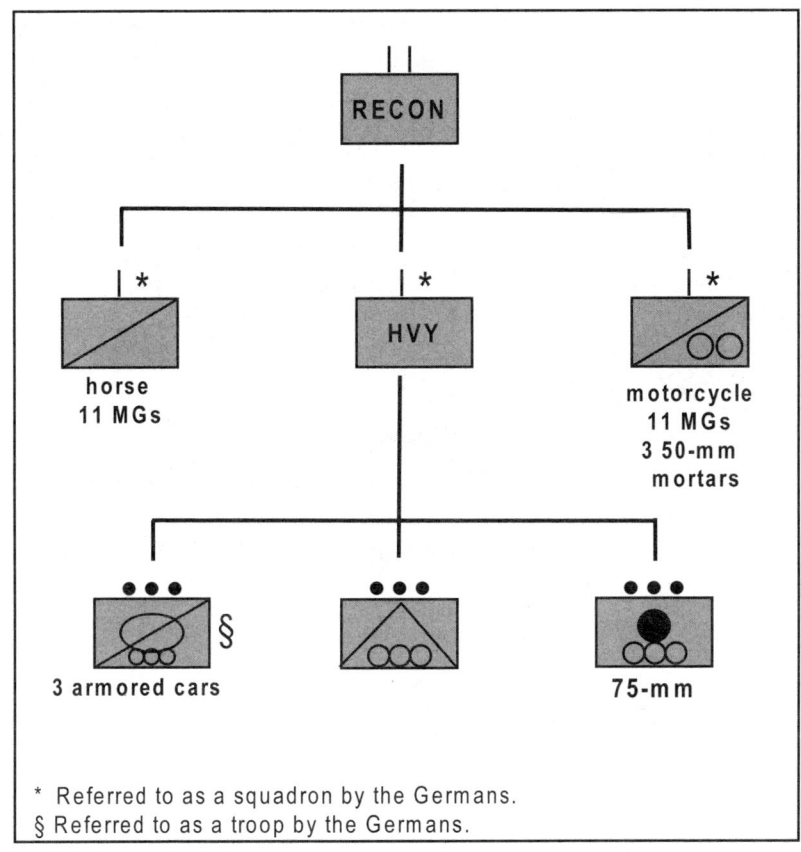

Figure 17. German infantry division reconnaissance battalion, 1939.

evolving into combat troops (*Kraftfahrkampftruppe*) in the late 1920s, partially through a secret program where motor transport officers trained on tanks in the Soviet Union. In 1931, Guderian was given command of the 3d *Reichswehr* Division's transport battalion. With support from the chief of the motor transport troops, he converted this battalion into a motorized infantry unit. On forming his motorized infantry battalion, Guderian created two additional subordinate units: an armored reconnaissance company with armored cars and a motorcycle company. The armored car platform used in these early units was the *Kfz 13*, a light (2.1-ton) four-wheeled vehicle capable of speeds up to 45 miles per hour and ranging out to a little less than 200 miles. Starting in 1934, an improved armored car, the *SdKfz 221*, replaced the *Kfz 13* in panzer division reconnaissance battalions. The slightly heavier (4-ton) *SdKfz 221* became the standard scout vehicle in the German Army in World War II. It had a range similar

Figure 18. The *SdKfz 221* light armored car.

to the *Kfz 13* and a faster highway speed (55 mph). Initially armed with an MG 36 light machine gun, later versions had a 28-mm cannon mounted in a turret.[34]

From this humble beginning, the German panzer arm and its armored reconnaissance forces evolved. In June 1932, the head of the *Reichswehr*, *Generaloberst* Wilhelm Adam, decided to form the first motorized reconnaissance battalions. The motor transport branch successfully pried this mission away from the cavalry branch, which was more concerned with maintaining its horse cavalry units intact. In the subsequent fall maneuvers, both sides used provisional motorized reconnaissance battalions consisting of various combinations of armored cars, motorcycles, bicycles, and horses. As the motorized forces evolved into the panzer troops (*Panzertruppen*), the German tank specialists developed reconnaissance battalions as part of their evolving force structure. By 1935, the new Wehrmacht formed its first panzer divisions, each with an armored reconnaissance battalion. In the next 5 years, up to the initiation of hostilities in Poland, the Wehrmacht deployed 11 such battalions. In addition to battalions found in the five panzer divisions, the 1st Light Division, 1st Cavalry Brigade, and four motorized infantry divisions also had organic armored reconnaissance battalions.[35]

Unlike the reconnaissance battalion of the infantry division, which was only formed in wartime, the armored reconnaissance battalions were permanent peacetime organizations. The main vehicles of the 1939 armored reconnaissance battalions were armored cars and motorcycles. The battalion fielded four troop-sized squadrons (figure 19). Two of these units were equipped with 18 armored cars. The motorcycle squadron deployed 31 motorcycles, most with sidecars equipped with either machine guns or mortars.

As in the nonarmored reconnaissance battalion, the armored variant contained a heavy weapons squadron equipped with a platoon-sized troop each of engineers, towed antitank guns, and cannons. Armored reconnaissance squadrons in motorized infantry divisions initially fielded only a single armored car troop and a motorcycle troop.[36]

Guderian outlined the concept for the employment of armored reconnaissance battalions in *Achtung-Panzer*, his 1937 tome on armored

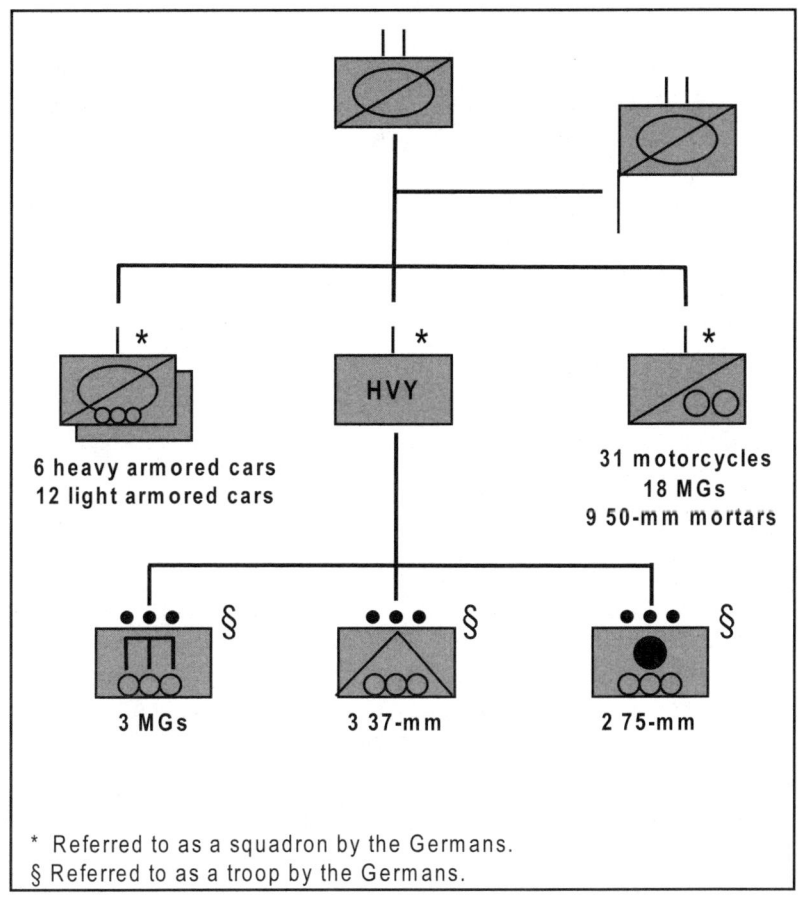

Figure 19. German armored reconnaissance battalion, 1939.[37]

warfare. Unlike the reconnaissance battalions in the infantry divisions, Guderian believed that, in addition to providing tactical reconnaissance for its assigned division, armored reconnaissance units should also be used as the army's prime ground agency for operational reconnaissance, augmenting the efforts of the air force. Armored cars provided speed and range, particularly on roads, and were the main reconnaissance element in the battalion. The motorcyclist and heavy weapons elements of the battalion provided support to the armored cars, particularly when negotiating the main enemy defensive zone.[38]

Guderian recognized the vulnerability of armored cars and motorcycles. However, he believed that armored cars offered speed and agility. Their armament and firepower were, by design, intended to be only strong enough to defeat enemy reconnaissance elements. These elements were to fight only if necessary to complete their reconnaissance mission, depending on the initiative provided by offensive action. Guderian also believed that the reconnaissance units had the capabilities to execute other traditional cavalry missions such as pursuit, covering unit movements, and flank security. Once the war started, Guderian served as an operational panzer commander at the corps and army levels rather than as the chief of all German mobile troops. Nevertheless, the wartime employment of panzer and motorized forces reflected his views. In particular, doctrinal and training manuals and the operational use of reconnaissance battalions in the field followed the guidelines found in Guderian's writings.[39]

Reconnaissance Troops in Other Armies in the Interwar Period

Apart from the Americans, the Germans ultimately faced British, French, and Soviet enemy reconnaissance elements in World War II. During the interwar period, those nations also mechanized or motorized their reconnaissance assets to various extents.

The British

By 1939, the British had developed their tank and reconnaissance forces into a single entity called the Royal Armoured Corps (RAC). Apart from two armored divisions being formed, the RAC controlled tanks used for infantry support as well as various battalion-sized reconnaissance units equipped with armored cars, motorcycles, light tanks, and fully tracked armored scout carriers. The British differed from the Germans primarily in their use of light tanks and fully tracked personnel carriers for reconnaissance in addition to armored cars and motorcycles. In terms of horses, the British were most radical. By 1939, there were none in the British reconnaissance forces that would face the Germans.

The British had ended World War I with the largest tank (20 battalions) and armored car (12 battalions) force of any of the combatants. But austerity in the early 1920s reduced this to four battalions. However, in 1926, the British Army created its own experimental mechanized force, which included a reconnaissance unit consisting of two armored car companies and one of miniature tanks called tankettes. After 2 years of testing, this force was disbanded.[40]

Nevertheless, the British mechanized their first two cavalry regiments in 1928 using armored cars from war stocks. These two battalion-sized regiments retained their armored cars up to the start of the war. In 1939, the regiments were considered corps- or army-level assets. One regiment accompanied the British Expeditionary Force (BEF) to France, and the other was in Egypt with the Middle East Command. By early 1940, each regiment had been attached to the armored division in France and in Egypt to provide divisional reconnaissance support.

Tanks developed along three tracks in the interwar British Army: heavy (called infantry tanks), medium (called light cruiser tanks), and light. Reconnaissance units contained the latter two categories. The heavy tanks were organized into tank brigades consisting only of subordinate tank battalions starting in the early 1930s. Such brigades provided tank support to the infantry. As such, they were equipped with slow-moving but heavily armored tanks equipped with machine guns. One tank brigade deployed to France in 1939 and 1940 as part of the BEF.[41]

Although the British had fielded large cavalry forces in Allenby's 1918 campaign, in 1936, after Hitler began rearming Germany, they completely abandoned horse cavalry, mechanizing 18 of 20 line horse regiments by 1939, with the remaining 2 regiments following by 1941. This mechanization took the form of two organizational structures: a divisional reconnaissance regiment and a nondivisional regiment that could be consolidated with similar units into brigades. Both types stressed the use of light tanks and light cruiser tanks as the primary method of conducting reconnaissance. The nondivisional units had the mission of operational-level reconnaissance.[42]

The nondivisional mechanized cavalry regiment was a battalion-sized organization of two company-sized light tank squadrons and a company-sized squadron of light cruiser tanks. These tanks differed primarily in that the cruisers had thicker armor. Both were armed with machine guns, although the cruiser tanks also had small guns.[43]

These types of mechanized cavalry regiments were a major component of the first large mechanized unit the British formed. In 1938, six mechanized cavalry regiments were combined with three heavy tank battalions, two artillery battalion equivalents, and two motorized infantry battalions to form the Mobile Division. The Mobile Division theoretically conducted operational-level reconnaissance. However, by 1940, when the division, renamed the 1st Armoured Division, began to deploy to France, it had been reorganized with the lessons of Poland in mind. The reorganized division had six battalion-sized tank units instead of nine. All these units, whether of cavalry or tank origin, were standardized in their structure. The division's mission was no longer considered reconnaissance by the inclusion of a platoon-sized armored car or troop carrier reconnaissance troop in each tank regiment and an armored car regiment at division level. Two other mechanized cavalry regiments formed a brigade-sized component in a second armored division being formed in Egypt as the war started. Of the mechanized cavalry units, one had been completely motorized, and a single armored division was deployed.[44]

As in the German Army, British divisional reconnaissance was not an organic component of the division but was considered a general headquarters (GHQ) asset. While the British Army fielded a specific unit type designated to provide tactical reconnaissance for an infantry division, there were not enough of these fielded for each division. When the BEF deployed to France in 1939 with 10 infantry divisions, only 5 had the battalion-sized reconnaissance regiments. One of the remaining five divisions, the 50th, was organized with a unique motorized infantry table of organization. Its reconnaissance unit was an infantry battalion mounted on motorcycles.

The divisional mechanized cavalry regiment contained a combination of motorcycles, light tanks, and small armored personnel carriers organized under a headquarters squadron and three mechanized cavalry squadrons. Each cavalry squadron consisted of 2 troops of light tanks (a total of 6 tanks per squadron) and 4 scout troops equipped with Bren carriers (a total of 12 carriers per squadron). The headquarters squadron had the motorcycle troop and its 41 vehicles (figure 20). Compared to a German divisional reconnaissance unit, the British regiment was fully mechanized. The main vehicles for reconnaissance were a combination of light tanks and scouts in mechanized vehicles as opposed to the German reliance on armored cars.

By the start of hostilities in 1939, the British tank and mechanized cavalry forces had been amalgamated under the banner of the Royal Armoured Corps. When the BEF deployed to France in 1939, it had 3

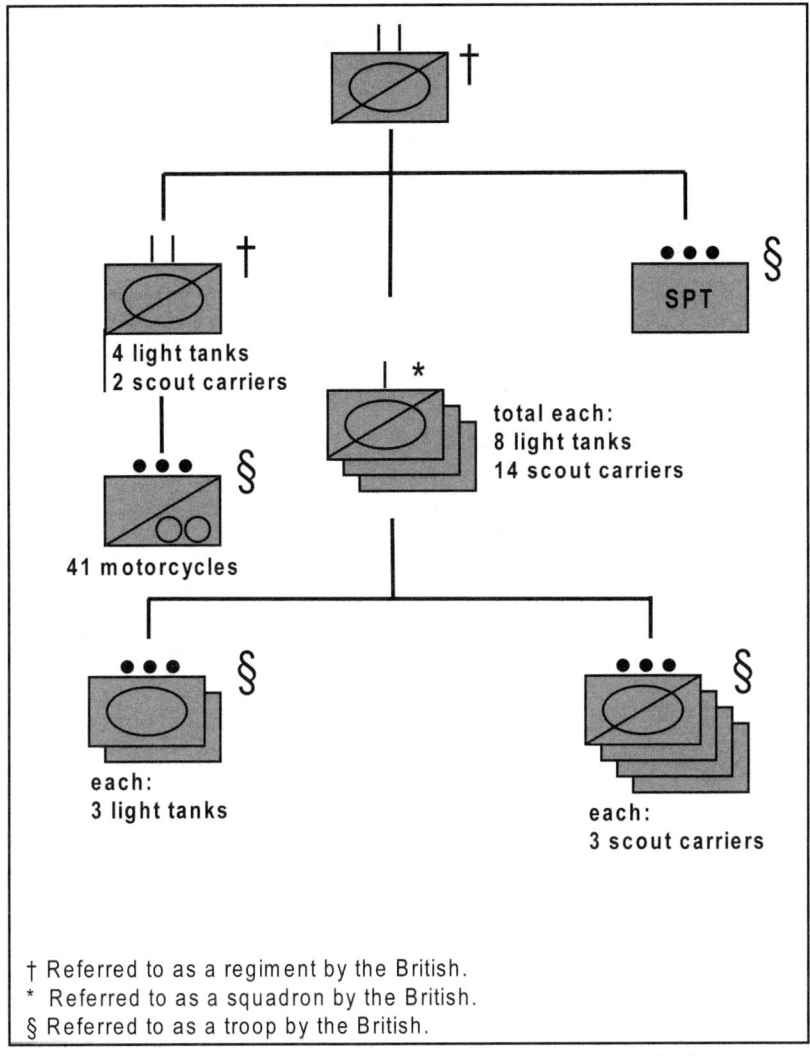

Figure 20. British divisional mechanized cavalry regiment, 1939.[45]

corps and 10 infantry divisions. Four battalion-sized divisional mechanized cavalry regiments and one motorcycle infantry reconnaissance battalion went as well.

The French

In 1940, the French deployed three armored divisions (*Division Cuirassée de Réserve* (*DCR*)), three light armored divisions (*Division Légère Mécanique* (*DLM*)), and five light cavalry divisions (*Division Légère de Cavalerie* (*DLC*)). Each of these contained motorized or mechanized

67

elements designed specifically to conduct reconnaissance operations. Two *DLM*s were joined operationally under a corps headquarters.

As early as 1922, the French were experimenting with combining cavalry with armored cars and bicycles to provide operational-level reconnaissance. Five such "light" divisions (*Division Légère* (*DL*)) were created and maintained until 1932. In that year, the five *DL*s were converted into a new organizational structure, the 1932 cavalry division (*Division de Cavalerie* (*DC*)). The *DC*s consisted of two cavalry brigades (*Brigades de Cavalerie* (*BC*s)), each with two battalion-sized horse regiments; an armored car battalion (*Groupe d'Autos-Mitrailleuses* (*GAM*)); a half-track-mounted mechanized infantry battalion (*Bataillion de Dragons Portés* (*BDP*)); and a motorized artillery regiment. Both the *GAM* and *BDP* also had a company-sized motorcycle squadron.[46]

As with the US H-M regiment, the French hybrid *DC* proved to be unsatisfactory. A combination of supply difficulties and the different movement speeds of the horse and mechanized elements slowed division operations to the pace of the most sluggish horse soldier. Therefore, the French General Staff decided that at least some of the *DC*s should become fully mechanized. In 1935 and 1936, two *DC*s were converted to a fully mechanized *DLM* organization. By 1940, three *DC*s had been converted to the *DLM* structure. Between September 1939 and May 1940, the two *DC*s were converted into five new-style "light" divisions (*DLC*s). The *DLC*s consisted of a brigade of cavalry, a battalion of armored cars, and a regiment of mechanized infantry. Their mission was to conduct operational and tactical reconnaissance as a backup to the *DLM*s.[47]

The *DLM*s resembled the German light divisions in structure. They were designed to fulfill the role that Sordet's cavalry corps had in 1914, including operational reconnaissance. By 1940, the French Army fielded three *DLM*s, with two divisions formed under a cavalry corps headquarters. This corps was then used as the advance guard for the Allied advance into Belgium. The *DLM* organization in 1940 consisted of a brigade each of light tanks and light motorized infantry. The motorized infantry brigade had its own company of light tanks and motorcycles and a battalion-sized reconnaissance regiment equipped with armored cars and motorcycles. The tank brigade contained two subordinate battalion-sized regiments each with 40 tanks.[48]

For action in 1940, the French also employed a brigade-sized tank force with each infantry corps. These brigades provided tank support to the infantry divisions. In response to the German development of the heavier panzer division and its effectiveness in Poland, the French created a similar organization from some of their infantry support tank forces, creating the *DCR*, consisting of two half-brigades with two battalions of heavy tanks each, supported by a single battalion of motorized infantry.[49] Three *DCR*s were fielded before the 1940 campaign but were still forming when the campaign began. Unlike the contemporary German panzer divisions, which were intended to strike a mailed fist at the enemy and to make deep penetrations, the French viewed the *DCR*s as massed tank support for attacking infantry.[50]

Apart from large units, in 1940, the French Army also deployed 105 reconnaissance battalions (*Groupe de Reconnaissance* (*GR*)) for tactical reconnaissance purposes. The *GR*s were divided between those designed to support corps (*Groupe de Reconnaissance de Corps d'Armée* (*GRCA*)) and those designated to support infantry divisions (*Groupe de Reconnaissance de Division d'Infanterie* (*GRDI*)). The *GRCA* organization consisted of two half-battalions, one horse and the other motorized. The horse unit contained two company-sized cavalry squadrons and two horse-drawn 25-mm antitank guns. The mechanized half-battalion comprised a company-sized motorcycle squadron and a heavy weapons squadron armed with machine guns and two towed 24-mm antitank guns.[51]

At the divisional level, the French Army deployed a reconnaissance battalion similar to that of the Germans, combining horse cavalry with motorized vehicles. The *GRDI* had three company-sized squadrons: a horse cavalry squadron equipped with eight light machine guns, four heavy machine guns, two 25-mm antitank guns, and a 60-mm mortar; a motorcycle squadron with about 60 cycles, 16 light machine guns, and a 60-mm mortar; and a squadron similar to a German heavy squadron that had eight medium machine guns and four 25-mm antitank guns.[52]

The Soviets

Throughout the interwar period, the Soviets maintained a large force of horse cavalry but also raised motorized and mechanized forces. Mobile operations were always at the forefront of Soviet military thought. The Red Army produced its share of armored warfare theorists, headed by Marshal Mikhail Tukhachevsky. While Tukhachevsky believed in mobile warfare as much as Guderian did, the Soviet marshal was also in an official position to implement his ideas. Starting in the early 1930s, under his direction, the Red Army developed a doctrine called deep battle that envisioned the use of large tank and mechanized forces in attacking waves to a battlefield depth of 60 to 120 miles. While raising mechanized forces to support this doctrine, the Soviets retained their horse cavalry as well, using an interpretation of the results of field exercises to prove the horse's continued relevance.[53]

In 1930, the Soviets formed an experimental mechanized brigade. After adjustments, the brigade's combat element consisted of two tank battalions and a motorized infantry battalion. Its regimental-sized reconnaissance group included a battalion each of tankettes, armored cars, armored cars with machine guns, and artillery. In 1932, the first mechanized corps was formed. By 1937, the Soviets had raised four mechanized corps and numerous separate mechanized and tank units. Each corps contained a battalion of light tanks for reconnaissance purposes. Separate mechanized brigades included a reconnaissance armored car company. While cavalry was retained, each cavalry division now also had a mechanized reconnaissance regiment consisting of an armored car battalion, two tank companies, and one tankette company.[54]

In 1937 and the following years, the Soviet mechanized forces received a series of setbacks beginning with Tukhachevsky's execution, followed by operational setbacks in Spain, Poland, and Finland. Mechanized forces were redesignated "tank" forces, and the 1937 tank corps included a mechanized reconnaissance battalion in each of its two component tank brigades and an additional battalion at the corps level. By 1939, the Soviet High Command had decided to eliminate the tank corps and distribute its massed tanks in infantry support roles, while forming a series of motorized rifle divisions, each with its own reconnaissance battalion, primarily equipped with armored cars. This transformation was well underway when the fall of France in mid-1940 made the Soviet leadership rethink the value of large armored forces. Between mid-1940 and the German invasion in June 1941, the Red Army reformed mechanized corps and tank divisions.[55]

In 1941, just before the German invasion, Red Army rifle and motorized divisions contained a reconnaissance battalion consisting of an armored car company with 10 vehicles, a light tank company with 10 tanks, and a motorized rifle company. Tank divisions contained an armored car reconnaissance battalion with about 90 vehicles, and mechanized corps had an organic motorcycle reconnaissance regiment.[56]

Summary

The Germans entered World War II with their largest reconnaissance organization being the battalion. Armored reconnaissance battalions assigned to mobile divisions conducted operational-level reconnaissance as well as tactical-level reconnaissance for their supported divisions.

Reconnaissance elements were relatively light and mobile and were not expected to fight unless absolutely necessary. The main vehicle was the wheeled armored car. Reconnaissance units in infantry divisions still consisted partially of horse cavalry. Infantry divisional reconnaissance units were organized to conduct only tactical-level reconnaissance in support of the division.

The United States entered World War II several years later with a mixture of reconnaissance assets. By 1941, armored cars had replaced horses in the reconnaissance role in US Army divisions. However, at the operational level, in contrast to the Germans, the Army fielded a nondivisional unit with that specific mission. Again, in contrast to the Germans who retained horses at the tactical level but removed them from the operational level, the United States fielded a mixed unit of horse cavalry and armored cars at the higher echelon. Each of these horse-mechanized regiments provided reconnaissance support to a corps. However, in both armies, the overriding organizational theory was that the reconnaissance units would gain information by stealth, speed, and mobility rather than through combat. World War II would test these organizations and concepts.

While developments in France paralleled German developments with hybrid horse-motorized reconnaissance units at division level, both the British and French placed light tanks in their reconnaissance units, depending less on armored cars. The British completely mechanized their deployable reconnaissance forces and issued the first armored personnel carrier to the scouts in their units. The Soviets initially developed large mechanized reconnaissance forces but, on the eve of war, were in the midst of reorganizing these forces. All nations studied retained operational mechanized reconnaissance forces at levels above division except the Germans, who saw this mission as one of the functions of the armored reconnaissance battalion found in the panzer, light, and motorized infantry divisions. As with the Americans and Germans, the British, French, and Soviet reconnaissance organizations, doctrine, and theoretical concepts would all be tested in World War II.

Notes

1. Bruce Condell and David Zabecki, trans. and ed., *On the German Art of War: Truppenführung* (Boulder, CO: Lynee Rienner Publications, 2001), 184.
2. An American postwar cavalry study believed that the airplane had totally supplanted the cavalry in the operational reconnaissance role. See Matthew D. Morton, "Men on 'Iron Ponies': The Death and Rebirth of the Modern US Cavalry," PhD diss., Florida State University, 2004, 5.
3. John B. Wilson, *Maneuver and Firepower: The Evolution of Divisions and Separate Brigades* (Washington, DC: US Army Center of Military History, 1998), 93–94; John B. Wilson, "Mobility Versus Firepower: The Post-World War I Infantry Division," *Parameters* 13 (September 1983): 51.
4. Robert F. Futrell, *Ideas, Concepts, Doctrine: Basic Thinking in the United States Air Force, 1907–1960*, vol. 1 (Maxwell Air Force Base, AL: Air University Press, 1989), 24, 36, 41, 43; Edgar Raines Jr., *Eyes of the Artillery: The Origins of Modern US Army Aviation* (Washington, DC: US Army Center of Military History, 2000) 14.
5. Raines, 105.
6. Ibid., 43, 50, 102, 104–105.
7. Morton, 19–20, 23, 30. As late as 1930, the Army Chief of Staff believed that US cavalry could have played a decisive role in France in 1918 and that a peacetime cavalry corps needed to be formed. See General Charles P. Summerall, "Cavalry in Modern Combat," *Cavalry Journal* 39 (October 1930): 491–493.
8. Morton, 21; Wilson, *Maneuver and Firepower*, 95.
9. Wilson, *Maneuver and Firepower*, 121.
10. Captain Harold Holt, "The 1st Armored Car Troop," *Cavalry Journal* 37 (October 1928): 599; Wilson, *Maneuver and Firepower*, 122–123.
11. Wilson, *Maneuver and Firepower*, 115; Major Edward C. McGuire, "Armored Cars in the Cavalry Maneuvers," *Cavalry Journal* 39 (July 1930): 386–399; Morton, 45.
12. Wilson, *Maneuver and Firepower*, 123; Morton, 50–51, 53–55.
13. John J. McGrath, *The Brigade: A History—Its Organization and Employment in the US Army* (Fort Leavenworth, KS: Combat Studies Institute Press, 2004), 45–46.
14. Major Louis A. DiMarco, "The U.S. Army's Mechanized Cavalry Doctrine in World War II" (MMAS thesis, US Army Command and General Staff College, 1995), 10–11.
15. Ibid., 2, 16–17; Morton, 77. The Infantry branch had also organized a tank brigade of three regiments that was reassigned to the Armored Force and used to form the 2d Armored Division. See Wilson, *Maneuver and Firepower*, 125, and Mary Lee Stubbs and Stanley R. Connor, *Armor-Cavalry Part I: Regular Army and Army Reserve* (Washington, DC: US Army Center of Military History, 1984), 58. The Cavalry branch was actually offered the opportunity to form what became the Armored Force under its own auspices, but its chief, Major General John Herr, a believer in the future of the horse, declined the mission, and the cavalry lost most of its mechanized elements.

16. *The American Arsenal: The World War II Official Standard Ordnance Catalog of Artillery, Small Arms, Tanks, Armored Cars, Artillery, Antiaircraft Guns, Ammunition, Grenades, Mines, Et Cetera* (Mechanicsburg, PA: Stackpole: 1996), 75.

17. Morton, 74–75; DiMarco, 12–14.

18. Morton, 157, 185; DiMarco 17–18.

19. DiMarco, 17–18; Shelby Stanton, *Order of Battle: US Army, World War II* (Novato, CA: Presidio, 1984), 311–318. After the conversion of the H-M regiments, only the cavalry regiments in 1st and 2d Cavalry Divisions retained their horses. The 1st Cavalry Division was dismounted in 1943 and fought in the Pacific as an infantry organization. The 2d Cavalry Division was partially converted to an armored division in 1942 and briefly reactivated in 1943. In early 1944, the division was broken up in North Africa.

20. Morton, 10.

21. Wilson, *Maneuver and Firepower*, 127–128, 131.

22. Morton, 184; Wilson, *Maneuver and Firepower*, 133, 144.

23. James S. Corum, *The Roots of Blitzkrieg: Hans von Seeckt and German Military Reform* (Lawrence: University Press of Kansas, 1992), 71–72; Heinz Guderian, *Panzer Leader*, trans. Constantine Fitzgibbon (Washington, DC: Zenger, 1952), 24–26. The *Reichwehr*'s motorized troops were originally its transportation and supply forces, which were gradually converted to more combat-oriented missions.

24. Major General Heinz Guderian, *Achtung-Panzer: The Development of Armoured Forces, Their Tactics and Operational Potential*, trans. Christopher Duffy (London: Arms and Armour Press, 1995), 163.

25. Corum, 39, 43–46; Morton, 32.

26. Condell and Zabecki, 39, 42, 45.

27. Albert Seaton, *The German Army: 1933–1945* (New York: St. Martin's Press, 1982), 60–61; Mary R. Habeck, *Storm of Steel: The Development of Armor Doctrine in Germany and the Soviet Union, 1919–1939* (Ithaca, NY: Cornell University Press, 2003), 208–209.

28. Guderian, *Panzer Leader*, 36–37; Seaton, 90–91; Robert Citino, *Armored Forces: History and Source Book* (Westport, CT: Greenwood Press, 1994), 57; Walter Goerlitz, *History of the German General Staff, 1657–1945*, trans. Brian Battershaw (New York: Praeger, 1957), 300. The 4th Light Division was created from the Austrian Army's motorized division after Germany annexed that country in 1938.

29. Citino, 57; Georg Tessin, *Verbände und Truppen der deutschen Wehrmacht und der Waffen-SS im Zweiten Weltkrieg 1939–1945, Band 2: Die Landstreitkräfte. Nrn. 1-5* (Osnabrück, GE: Biblio Verlag, 1973), 175. As an exception to light division organization, the 1st Light Division only had a single armored reconnaissance battalion. See Helmut Ritgen, *The 6th Panzer Division, 1937–45* (London: Osprey, 1982), 7.

30. Seaton, 90; Guderian, *Panzer Leader*, 62–63. Guderian had planned to reorganize the cavalry by upgrading the light divisions and by reorganizing the

mishmash that divisional reconnaissance had become. However, he was unable to do so before the war started, less than a year after he took his new appointment.

31. Morton, 153; Seaton, 60–61; Frido von Senger und Etterlin, *Neither Fear Nor Hope*, trans. George Malcolm (Novato, CA: Presidio, 1989), 15.

32. Wilhelm Necker, *The German Army of To-Day* (London: Lindsay Drummond, 1943), 56–59; George Nafziger, *The German Order of Battle: Infantry in World War II* (Mechanicsburg, PA: Stackpole, 2000), 31. Nafziger erroneously translated the term "cyclists" in the reconnaissance battalions to mean bicycle riders when, in fact, it is motorcycles to which he refers. This is clearly indicated in numerous other sources (such as Guderian, *Panzer Leader*, 63) and in the German designation for the unit *Kradschützenschwadron*.

33. Nafziger, 28, 196–204; Guderian, *Panzer Leader*, 63.

34. Seaton, 60–62; Guderian, *Achtung-Panzer*, 133–134.; Guderian, *Panzer Leader*, 24; Peter Chamberlain and Hilary Doyle, *Encyclopedia of German Tanks of World War Two: A Complete Illustrated Directory of German Battle Tanks, Armoured Cars, Self-Propelled Guns, and Semi-Tracked Vehicles, 1933–1945* (London: Arms and Armour Press, 1993), 190–191.

35. Morton, 59–60; Citino, 54–55; Robert Citino, *The Path to Blitzkrieg: Doctrine and Training in the German Army, 1920–1939* (Boulder, CO: Lynee Rienner, 1999), 204–206, 212–214; Guderian, *Panzer Leader*, 24, 28. The reconnaissance battalions did not receive the armored designation until after the Polish campaign. See Bryan Perett, *German Armoured Cars and Reconnaissance Half-Tracks, 1939–45* (London: Osprey, 1982), 20.

36. Perett, 19–20, 21.

37. These battalions were officially called reconnaissance battalions (motorized) (*Auklärungs Abteilung (mot.)*) until 1943. See Martin Windrow and Richard Hook, *The Panzer Divisions*, rev. ed. (London: Osprey, 1982), 6–8.

38. Guderian, *Achtung-Panzer*, 163, 165.

39. Ibid., 164–165; Perret, 19–20; Military Intelligence Service, US War Department, "Information Bulletin Number 1, German Armored Car Reconnaissance," 20 December 1941, http://www.lonesentry.com/manuals/armored-car/index.html (accessed 10 September 2007).

40. Richard Ogorkiewicz, *Armor: A History of Mechanized Forces* (New York: Praeger, 1960), 150; Citino, *Armored Force*, 43.

41. George Forty, *British Army Handbook, 1939–1945* (Stroud, Gloucestershire: Sutton, 2002), 66; Ogorkiewicz, 156.

42. Forty, 3; Chris Ellis and Peter Chamberlain, ed., *Handbook on the British Army, 1943* (New York: Hippocrene Books, 1976), 41, 228; Ogorkiewicz, 57–60.

43. Ellis and Chamberlain, 166; Leo Niehorster, "British Army Authorized Organization Light Armoured Brigade 3 September 1939," *World War II Armed Forces—Orders of Battle and Organizations*, 2006, http://niehorster.orbat.com/017_britain/39_org/brig_armd_lt.html#brig_armd_lt (accessed 24 September 2007).

44. Ogorkiewicz, 58–60.

45. Leo Niehorster, "British Army Authorized Organization Infantry Division Divisional Cavalry Regiment (RAC) 3 September 1939," *World War II*

Armed Forces—Orders of Battle and Organizations, 2006, http://niehorster.orbat.com/017_britain/39_org/div_inf_rac.html (accessed 24 September 2007).

46. N. Leulliot, "The Divisions Légères de Cavalerie (DLC–Light Cavalry Divisions) Part 1: Organisations," *France 1940*, http://france1940.free.fr/oob/oob.html (accessed 24 September 2007).

47. Ibid.

48. Citino, *Armored Force*, 59; Ogorkiewicz, 65; David Lehman, "The French Cavalry Corps in 1940," 2005, http://www.militaryphotos.net/forums/archive/index.php/t-43179.html (accessed 21 September 2007).

49. Ogorkiewicz, 58–60.

50. N. Leulliot, "French Army Order of Battle, 10 May 1940," *France 1940*, http://france1940.free.fr/armee/dlc/html (accessed 24 September 2007); Citino, *Armored Forces*, 59.

51. Leulliot, "The Divisions Légères de Cavalerie (DLC–Light Cavalry Divisions) Part 1: Organisations"; Stephane Commans, "GRCA and GRDI," *French Orders of Battle*, http://france1940.free.fr/armee/gr.html (accessed 24 September 2007).

52. Stephane Commans, "Order of Battle Division Infanterie (1940) (Infantry Division)," *French Orders of Battle*, http://enpointe.chez-alice.fr/di.html (accessed 24 September 2007).

53. Habeck, 126–127, 171–172; Kurt S. Schultz, "The Revolution Rearmed: Development of Soviet Mobile Warfare Doctrine, 1920–1941," *Historical Analysis of the Use of Mobile Forces by Russia and the USSR*, ed. Jacob W. Kipp et al., Occasional Paper No. 10 (College Park, TX: Center for Strategic Technology, The Texas Engineering Experiment Station, Texas A&M University System, 1985), 124.

54. Colonel David Glantz, *The Motor-Mechanization Program of the Red Army During the Interwar Years* (Fort Leavenworth, KS: Soviet Army Studies Office, 1990), http://stinet.dtic.mil/cgi-bin/GetTRDoc?AD=ADA232707&Location=U2&doc=GetTRDoc.pdf (accessed 24 September 2007), 22, 30–32; Habeck, 261, 264–267.

55. Glantz, 34, 40–41, 43–44; Habeck, 261, 264–267; Leo Niehorster, "Soviet Armed Forces Organization Soviet Mechanized Division 22 June 1941," *World War II Armed Forces—Orders of Battle and Organizations*, 2006, http://niehorster.orbat.com/012_ussr/41_organ/40_mech-div.html (accessed 24 September 2007).

56. Glantz, 46; Phillippe Carmoy and Evgeniy Drig, "Soviet Armed Forces: Organization Rifle Division, 22 June 1941," *World War II Armed Forces—Orders of Battle and Organizations*, 2006, http://niehordster.orbat.com/012_ussr/41_organ/41_rifle_div_00.html (accessed 25 September 2007); Leo Niehorster, "Soviet Armed Forces Organization Soviet Tank Division, 22 June 1941," *World War II Armed Forces—Orders of Battle and Organizations*, 2006, http://niehorster.orbat.com/012_ussr/41_organ/40_tank-div.html (accessed 25 September 2007); Leo Niehorster, "Soviet Armed Forces Organization Soviet Mechanized Corps, 22 June 1941," *World War II Armed Forces—Orders of Battle and Organizations*, 2006, http://niehorster.orbat.com/012_ussr/41_organ/40_mech-corps.html (accessed 25 September 2007).

Chapter 3

Reconnaissance Units in World War II

Introduction

The interwar period introduced the concept of cavalry reconnaissance units without horses. By 1939, there was a general acceptance of the superiority of mechanized or motorized vehicles in the reconnaissance role. Some armies had almost completely abandoned horses (Britain and the United States), while those that did retain them always combined them with mechanized or motorized forces (Germany, France, and the Soviet Union). On the eve of World War II, almost all armies assumed that mechanized or motorized reconnaissance units needed to be light to move fast and gain information primarily through stealth. Most nations used armored cars and motorcycles in this role. Some nations also used light tanks. By the start of the war, the British had consolidated their tank and reconnaissance forces into one branch of the army and used a combination of light tanks and scouts in armored personnel carriers to conduct reconnaissance at the tactical level.

After the war started and the combatants gained experience, much prewar theory, particularly that related to the sharp division between reconnaissance missions and combat actions, evaporated in the face of battlefield reality. Most telling, light reconnaissance forces often could not survive to effectively use their speed and nimbleness. As the war progressed, organizations adjusted, and most armies became heavier, either in design, by fielding heavier equipment, or through habitual augmentation.

The German Experience in World War II

General German Theory, Doctrine, and Organization

As discussed in the previous chapter, the Germans were the first to organize and mass mechanized forces on a large scale and treat these forces as an independent combat arm. Throughout the Wehrmacht period, German armored reconnaissance units depended on wheeled armored cars (*Panzerspähwagen*) as their primary vehicles. Such units were found only in panzer and panzergrenadier divisions. The armament of the armored cars progressively increased. Early versions (*SdKfz 231*) mounted a 20-mm cannon and a machine gun. The last developed vehicle (*SdKfz 234/4*) was equipped with a turret-mounted 75-mm antitank gun. Early in the war, the Germans also extensively used motorcycle battalions for reconnaissance, but they were phased out by 1943 because of their battlefield fragility. Despite the weak armor and poor cross-country mobility of armored cars, the Wehrmacht continued to favor them because they were quiet and fast when used on roads.[1]

The initial German armored reconnaissance theory called for such units to gather information but not fight if possible. As the war progressed and armored car armament increased, reconnaissance units often fought both for information and simply as part of the operations of their parent units where, often in the later years of the war, no gun could be left unused in defensive battles.[2]

Nonpanzer German reconnaissance elements atrophied during the war. By 1944, more than half the infantry divisions fighting in Normandy had no reconnaissance element at all, while the remaining units replaced it with a general-purpose infantry battalion mounted on trucks or bicycles. In the latter stages of the war, German infantry commanders needed mobile reserves more than they needed specific tactical intelligence.[3]

The Polish and French Campaigns—Ardennes Redux

The Germans began the war with five light (mechanized cavalry) divisions. Theoretically, the light divisions, with their large organic reconnaissance regiments, were available to conduct operational reconnaissance missions. However, in actual practice, the armored reconnaissance battalions of the panzer and motorized divisions, as Guderian had planned, assumed this role. In fact, in the Polish campaign, all four light divisions were initially held in reserve and then used as regular combat units rather than as specialized operational reconnaissance forces. For example, the 1st Light Division was used similar to that of the panzer divisions. Supported by air strikes, the unit led the advance of the XIV Corps, breaking through the Polish defenses and pursuing their retreat to the Vistula River. After this, the division blocked the Polish retreat in a different sector.[4] While the German General Staff thought the light divisions had performed well in Poland, Guderian's criticism that the divisions were too light to fight the French and British was accepted, and the light divisions were converted to the panzer division organizational structure immediately after the end of the Polish campaign. From this point on in the war, the Germans did not even theoretically field a reconnaissance force larger than a battalion or provide any echelons above division with their own dedicated reconnaissance assets. For the rest of the war, a combination of Luftwaffe air and panzer division ground reconnaissance provided operational-level reconnaissance to German field commanders.[5]

Figure 21 shows a comparison of the German and French concepts of ground reconnaissance before the 1940 campaign. While the French maintained cavalry forces at the army, corps, and division levels, the

Level	French		German	
Operational				
Army	XX ⌀ *DLM* 3 *DLM*s were organized into a corps	XX ⌀ *DLC*	None (Panzer divisional armored reconnaissance battalions fill this role)	
Primary Equipment	Light tank brigade and motorized infantry brigade with light tanks, armored cars, and motorcycles	Horse cavalry brigade and mech infantry regiment with armored car battalion	NA	
Corps	⌀ *GRCA*		None (Panzer divisional armored reconnaissance battalions fill this role)	
Primary Equipment	1 horse cavalry half-battalion 1 motorcycle half-battalion 4 25-mm antitank guns		NA	
Tactical				
Division	⌀ *GRDI*		⌀ panzer and motorized divisions	RECON infantry divisions
Primary Equipment	1 horse cavalry squadron 1 motorcycle squadron 4 25-mm antitank guns		18 armored cars, 31 motorcycles, 5 towed guns	1 horse cavalry squadron, 1 motorcycle squadron, 3 armored cars, towed guns
Below Division	None ⌀		•••	
Primary Equipment	NA		Motorcycle scout platoons at panzer and motorized infantry regimental and battalion levels	

Figure 21. The echeloning of German and French reconnaissance units, 1940.[6]

Germans had no dedicated reconnaissance assets apart from those in their infantry and panzer divisions.[7] In preparation for the projected German offensive, the French planned to counter with a plan to advance their best

79

forces into central Belgium where they expected to face the main German attack along a flat expanse known as the Gembloux Gap. Spearheading this movement was a cavalry corps of two *Division Légère Mécanique*s (*DLM*s). Despite this massing of the French Army's best mechanized assets, the corps' mission was reconnaissance. The French command expected the main battle to be an infantry one, so the *DLM*s had to find and delay the main German advance for 5 days 20 miles forward of the main infantry positions along the Dyle River. If all went according to plan, the infantry would use the time to dig in and reinforce defensive positions.[8]

When the German attack started on 10 May 1940, the Gembloux Gap was not the main effort, but an elaborate diversion. Nevertheless, the French cavalry corps moved forward and engaged two panzer divisions of the German XVI Corps on the third day of the offensive and fought the Germans to a standstill. The French force, designed for reconnaissance more than for a major tank battle, included numerous light tanks and armored cars, but it also had four battalions of heavier tanks. The French forces were quantitatively superior to those of the Germans but assumed defensive positions. The Germans, by using superior combined arms tactics and being supported by concentrated close air support, massed against one of the French *DLM*s and broke through. Since the French defended in a linear fashion, the breakthrough compelled the cavalry corps to retreat to the main French position. Weak communications hindered command and control, permitting the *DLM*s only the ability to move en masse behind the infantry defensive line rather than to conduct a delay operation. The French First Army then dispersed the corps assets among the infantry. The cavalry corps did accomplish its assigned delay mission. However, this tactical victory soon proved to be an operational defeat as it fed the French belief that they were opposing the German main effort along the Dyle River. Meanwhile, the panzer divisions of the actual German main effort were crossing the Meuse River in force to the south.[9]

At Gembloux, the German panzer divisions used their reconnaissance forces, primarily armored cars, to probe and infiltrate around the French strongpoints, supported by infantry. When the Germans massed against one French *DLM*, reconnaissance troops supported by antitank guns screened the 6-mile front of the other division. German reconnaissance in this action was ineffectual at the operational level—the French successfully dispersed and camouflaged their forces. But at the tactical level, once in contact, it was very effective. On the other side, the French had detached a *Groupe de Reconnaissance de Division d'Infanterie* (*GRDI*) from an uncommitted motorized infantry division and used it to cover the retreat of the cavalry corps. The *GRDI*'s motorcyclists and armored cars held positions between the two *DLM*s as they withdrew to the west. The cavalry corps had effectively delayed the Germans until the main force could occupy the Dyle River positions. However, this German advance was not the main effort.[10]

The decisive sector was to the south. While the French and British considered this area to be of secondary importance, it was, in fact, the area of the German primary attack. Belgium had maintained a strict neutrality, so French forces could not deploy into that country until the Germans attacked. When this happened, the French planned to deploy their hybrid light cavalry divisions (*Division Légère de Cavalerie (DLC)*) forward into delaying positions to determine the dispositions of the attacking Germans and then slow their advance while maintaining strong infantry forces in predetermined defensive lines along the Franco-Belgian border.[11]

When the Germans attacked on 10 May 1940, the French Army sent its *DLC*s forward into Belgium, according to plan, to detect the German dispositions and delay the enemy advance. The French cavalry ultimately failed at both tasks. In the Ardennes sector, the Germans cleared the forested region 12 hours before their own timetables. And even after meeting large German armored forces and retreating behind the Semois River, the French did not realize that the Ardennes was the German main effort. Of course, the French reconnaissance soldiers encountered only German spearheads moving along narrow routes and did not realize the mass of armor behind the ones they fought. Nevertheless, as late as 14 May, 5 days after the beginning of the German offensive, the French still believed the Ardennes sector was a diversion. The French *DLC*s uniformly retreated across the Meuse River by the third day of the German offensive and assumed defensive positions between the French infantry divisions.[12]

Figure 22 shows the actions outlined in this section. The Germans made their main effort in southern Belgium, massing most of their panzer divisions into a concentrated strike force advancing through the same Ardennes terrain described in chapter 2. For this particular thrust, the German command assembled seven panzer divisions and three motorized infantry divisions organized under four corps headquarters. The immediate German goal was to pass through the Ardennes as fast as possible and force a crossing of the Meuse River near Sedan before the French realized what was happening. As in 1914, the restrictive terrain and road net of the Ardennes was a key hindering factor in the German advance. *Panzergruppe* Kleist, the command controlling three of the four corps, designated four routes of advance through the Ardennes. Because of the restrictive terrain,

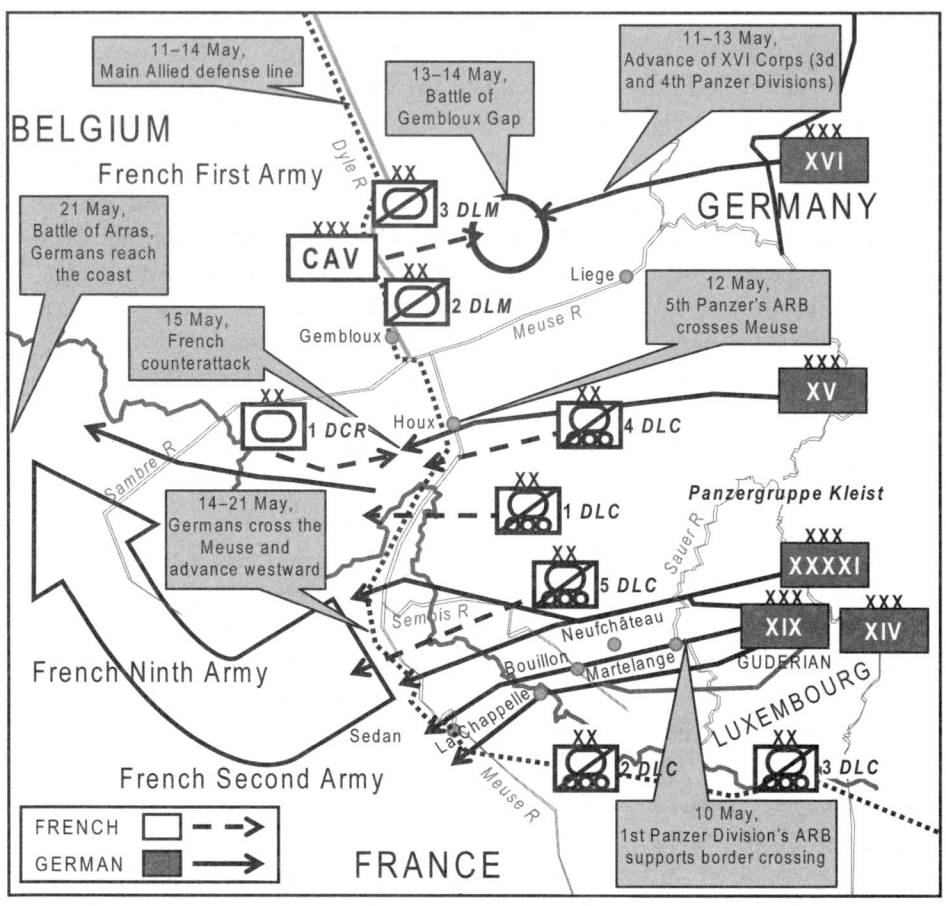

Figure 22. Operations in southern Belgium, 1940.

the corps advanced initially in echelon, with Guderian's XIX Corps leading along all four axes. Following Guderian was the XXXXI Corps, which was supposed to attack across the Meuse on a line with and to the north of Guderian's forces.[13]

Unlike the French, the Germans maintained no separate reconnaissance forces above division level. However, throughout the campaign, each corps usually had an air reconnaissance squadron (*Staffel*) from the Luftwaffe at its disposal. On the ground, lead elements of the panzer divisions were the reconnaissance units at both the operational and tactical levels. In the May 1940 campaign, however, the panzer divisions generally task organized themselves into an advance guard force, a main body element, and a rear guard. The advance guard force usually consisted of tanks and the divisional motorcycle troop assets. In the narrow passages of the Ardennes, reconnaissance units generally did not lead or were part of larger tank forces in the advance guard. When they did lead, such elements usually ended up in combat with defending Belgian or French forces. Sometimes, the advance guard included armored car assets from the divisional reconnaissance battalion, but usually, the bulk of that battalion was restricted to either covering the division's flanks or rear or maintaining links with adjacent units.[14]

When a force larger than a battalion was required for such missions and lacked a dedicated operational-level reconnaissance force, the Germans used whole divisions in this role. For example, in the initial advance in the Ardennes, panzer group commander Ewald von Kleist specifically assigned the 10th Panzer Division to cover the southern flank of Guderian's corps advance. Later in the campaign, the independent *Grossdeutschland* motorized infantry regiment, reinforced with the 1st Panzer Division's armored reconnaissance battalion, augmented the 10th Panzer Division in this role.[15]

The Germans depended on motorcycle troops more than any other element to lead advances and conduct concurrent reconnaissance. While in the panzer division, the reconnaissance battalion contained one company of cyclists, the infantry brigade also had an infantry motorcycle battalion, and each tank and infantry battalion and regiment had a small scout platoon equipped with motorcycles. The cyclists were often task organized into a composite battalion, including elements from all the division's cycle assets.[16]

There were three notable uses of divisional reconnaissance forces in the German advance into France. On 10 May, the 1st Panzer Division of Guderian's corps forced its way across northern Luxembourg to the Sauer River border crossing, leading with motorcycle and armored car elements from the divisional reconnaissance battalion in its advance guard's forward detachment. At Martelange on the Belgium border, the defenders quickly stopped the German advance. Under the direction of the division's infantry regimental commander, the German cyclists dismounted and crossed the shallow Sauer River, which demarcated the border, and assaulted the Belgian position. The surprised defenders withdrew. Based on audacity, the first action of an armored reconnaissance battalion in the Western campaign had been a success. However, using reconnaissance troops for a combat action rather than as stealthy information gatherers portended such an extensive combat use throughout the war.[17]

In the second example, reconnaissance troops again had to fight rather than gain stealthy intelligence. On 12 May, the third day of the offensive, the 10th Panzer Division easily crossed the Semois River and advanced toward the Meuse River, the French main defensive line. The division's reconnaissance battalion led this movement. When reaching the French frontier defenses at La Chappelle, the battalion assaulted them so as not to slow the advance. The German scouts overcame the French defenders who were withdrawing to the Meuse. When leading the advance, reconnaissance forces found that they had to fight combat actions because of their position at the front of the march column.[18]

In the last example, reconnaissance troops were the first to cross the Meuse River, the major river obstacle facing the German advance. On 12 May, elements of the motorcycle squadron of the 5th Panzer Division's armored reconnaissance battalion discovered a crossing site over the Meuse at Houx and immediately crossed. After securing a small bridgehead, the rest of the battalion was ferried across, followed by the division's infantry regiment.[19]

Within the assembled panzer force, Guderian's XIX Corps provided the German main effort, and of Guderian's forces, the 1st Panzer Division was the corps' main effort. Opposing Guderian was the French 5th *DLC*. Initially, things went according to plan for this unit. The division, as did four other *DLC*s, crossed into Belgium on news of the German invasion of that country and, by mid-morning on 10 May, had assumed its designated screening positions around Neufchâteau. In 1940, the 5th *DLC* had a horse brigade and a light mechanized brigade. For the Ardennes operation, the two brigades mixed their forces together into task forces, each consisting of a battalion-sized horse cavalry regiment and armored cars and light tanks, supported by infantry mounted in trucks and half-tracked armored personnel carriers.

After the border crossing at Martelange, the Germans chose to lead their advance either with the motorcycle infantry battalion that was part of the panzer division's infantry brigade or with one of its panzer regiments rather than with the reconnaissance battalion. With speed as the essence, the German command wanted the advance guard to be strong enough to swiftly overcome any opposition while still in the Ardennes. The advance was, however, delayed for several hours by a Belgian fortified position only a few miles beyond the frontier. This setback and Belgian obstacles, which slowed the tight German march, allowed the French 5th *DLC* to take up its screening positions around Neufchâteau ahead of the German advance.[20]

When two of Guderian's panzer divisions finally reached the French positions near Neufchâteau on the morning of 11 May, their column movement formation forced the commitment of the lead panzer units without support from the reconnaissance battalion or the divisional motorized infantry. The lead panzer regiment found itself unable to eject the defending French mechanized reconnaissance troops from Neufchâteau. However, the following panzer regiment bypassed both the French position and its predecessor regiment. This maneuver, coupled with the arrival of the German motorized infantry and Stuka dive bomber support, forced the French to evacuate Neufchâteau and retreat to the west behind the Semois River where the rest of the French cavalry division had already retreated.[21]

The 1st Panzer Division closely pursued the French reconnaissance and cavalry forces with its advance guard tank units reinforced with the divisional armored reconnaissance battalion, encountering elements of the French 5th *DLM* for the first time, which was reinforcing the delaying force. The Germans brushed off this new threat but could not initially force the Semois line. However, elements of the reconnaissance battalion quickly found a ford along the Semois just north of Bouillon. The lead tank company from the accompanying panzer regiment immediately crossed the river.[22]

The bulk of the 1st Panzer Division stalled at the chokepoint of Bouillon on the Semois, preparing to assault the town on the 12th. However, the situation elsewhere in Guderian's corps sector and beyond compelled the French to retreat from the riverside city without a fight. To the south, the 10th Panzer Division easily crossed the river on the morning of 12 May and advanced to the west and the Meuse. While Guderian's northernmost division, the 2d Panzer, had been seriously delayed in the Ardennes, the French cavalry forces farther to the north, opposite the advancing German XV Corps (5th and 7th Panzer Divisions), retreated precipitously to the Meuse early on the 12th, forcing the French commander opposite Guderian to order his own retreat westward to the Meuse River.[23]

Both German corps followed the retreating French closely and reached the Meuse before the end of the 12th. The 1st Panzer Division advanced across Semois to the Meuse with two battle groups mixed between tanks, infantry, motorcycle infantry, and artillery and reached Sedan on the Meuse within hours. The massed German armor had, therefore, made its way through the tight confines of the Ardennes in less than 3 days.[24]

Upon reaching the Meuse in strength, elements from seven panzer divisions immediately assaulted across the river. For this operation, assault infantry led the way. Reconnaissance troops generally held flanks or supported the infantry assaults by fire. The 10th Panzer Division held its reconnaissance battalion in reserve during the Meuse crossing, organized into two mobile task forces.

Once across, the Germans immediately advanced westward, breaking through the French main line. The French responded with uncoordinated counterattacks. Guderian's XIX Corps alone faced off against 5½ French divisions on 14 May. Along the Meuse front, *DLC*s fought beside infantry, making local counterthrusts using armored cars. The French command committed the 1st *Division Cuirassée de Réserve (DCR)*, with its large tank force, against the German XV Corps. While the French fought hard, superior German command and control, facilitated by a proliferation of radios, won the day. With the counterattacks repulsed, the German panzer forces continued their advance, which by the 16th had turned into a pursuit. Guderian's forces reached the coast near the mouth of the Somme River on 21 May, effectively cutting off the best units in the French Army and almost the entire British contingent in northern France and Belgium.[25]

Figure 23. Guderian (center) and the staff of the 4th Armored Reconnaissance Battalion (Lieutenants Voss and Munck in black panzer uniforms standing behind Guderian and battalion commander Major Alexander von Scheele to his left) at Bouillon, Belgium, 12 May 1940.

During the advance to the coast, German reconnaissance battalions often covered the open flank of the advancing divisions. The reconnaissance battalion of the 7th Panzer Division, XV Corps, commanded by *Generalmajor* Erwin Rommel, was in this role on the same day Guderian reached the coast when the British organized a counterattack near Arras against the division's other flank. While the counterattack was a failure, it is significant because both sides fought without reconnaissance. The British task organized into two attack columns, each led by a tank battalion from an army tank brigade and supported by a battalion each of infantry, field artillery, and antitank guns. Each column had a small motorcycle scout unit that covered the rear rather than the front or side of the advance. The French supported the attack on the right (west) with the 3d *DLM*. This division also did not assist by providing reconnaissance, one of its primary functions, but, rather, only provided flank protection. The Germans were advancing from east to west perpendicular to the British attack axis when the British struck. The German advance guard, the division's single panzer regiment, had just passed to the west when the British attacked blindly, with their attack drifting off its projected axis.[26]

The Germans were equally blind. The divisional reconnaissance battalion was far to the rear in the column behind the two infantry regiments on the southern flank of the march column. The Germans, personally led by Rommel, soon recovered from their surprise and beat back the British attack. The French mechanized division covered the British retreat. After Arras, the Allies never truly threatened the Germans with an effective counterattack.[27]

German infantry divisions contained mixed horse-mechanized reconnaissance battalions. Aside from a horse squadron, the battalion contained a motorcycle squadron and three armored cars and towed guns. Being the mobile part of divisions paced to the foot march of its infantry, these units were used more often in the division vanguard, particularly in areas where the panzers had not preceded the infantry. The reconnaissance troops often set out to secure bridges over unfordable rivers in advance of the division to secure the far bank. As with the armored reconnaissance battalions, such units often found themselves unavoidably in combat situations.[28]

After the Germans reached the coast, the British evacuated most of their units and some of the French forces trapped north of the breakthrough via the port of Dunkirk. In a second phase to the campaign, in June 1940, the Germans, primarily by using panzer forces, overran most of the rest of France, forcing that nation's surrender. During this phase of operations, reconnaissance battalions from both mobile and infantry divisions often ranged far in front of and to the flanks of divisional main columns.[29]

Several trends for reconnaissance forces developed in the 1940 campaign from the German perspective. The campaign unfolded in a way that the Germans wanted to combine reconnaissance and immediate combat action to maintain the tempo of their advance. Since antitank defenses were not strong at this stage of the war, leading with tanks, especially in open terrain, gave the advantage of being able to find the enemy, defeat him in one stroke, and continue the advance. In rough terrain, motorcycle infantry forces were favored for the same reasons. The cyclist infantry could immediately attack or cross a river. Designed for stealth, armored car forces often did not have the firepower or off-road mobility to fight their way through, although in many cases, that was the mission they were given.

Later German Organizational Developments

At the start of the war, German panzer and motorized infantry regiments contained small organic reconnaissance platoons consisting of motorcyclists. By early 1942, however, new organizational schemes replaced the motorcycles with a platoon of five light tanks in the panzer regiment and a platoon of half-track mounted scouts in the motorized infantry (late panzergrenadier) regiment. The light tanks were later replaced with the standard medium tanks that the Germans used in their line panzer companies.

The replacement of the motorcycle with armored vehicles was the major development in the German armored reconnaissance battalion after 1940.[30] Before 1942, the Germans maintained a motorcycle infantry battalion and a motorcycle reconnaissance squadron in each panzer division. Surprisingly, considering their role in the 1940 campaign, the Germans greatly reduced the use of motorcycles as the war continued. The cycles had proved to be vulnerable in the Russian campaign, and the divisional motorcycle battalion was dissolved. Its assets were briefly merged into the reconnaissance battalion. At this point, battalion designations were changed to match panzer division numbers, and the cavalry designation "squadron" was replaced with the noncavalry "company." During this period, panzer division armored reconnaissance battalions contained an armored car company and three motorcycle companies. In 1942 and 1943, the motorcycles were progressively replaced by half-tracked armored personnel carriers. Whereas the primary role of the old motorcycle squadron was to provide machine-gun support to the armored car element, the primary mission of the new half-track company was reconnaissance.[31]

By 1944, the armored reconnaissance battalion was primarily a half-track-mounted organization (figure 24). The battalion contained four reconnaissance companies equipped with 77 scout half-tracked armored personnel carriers. Almost all the battalion's support assets were now mounted in half-tracks as well, including the assault engineer troop and the mortar and howitzer troops. The replacement of motorcycles and trucks enhanced both the survivability and firepower of the battalion.[32]

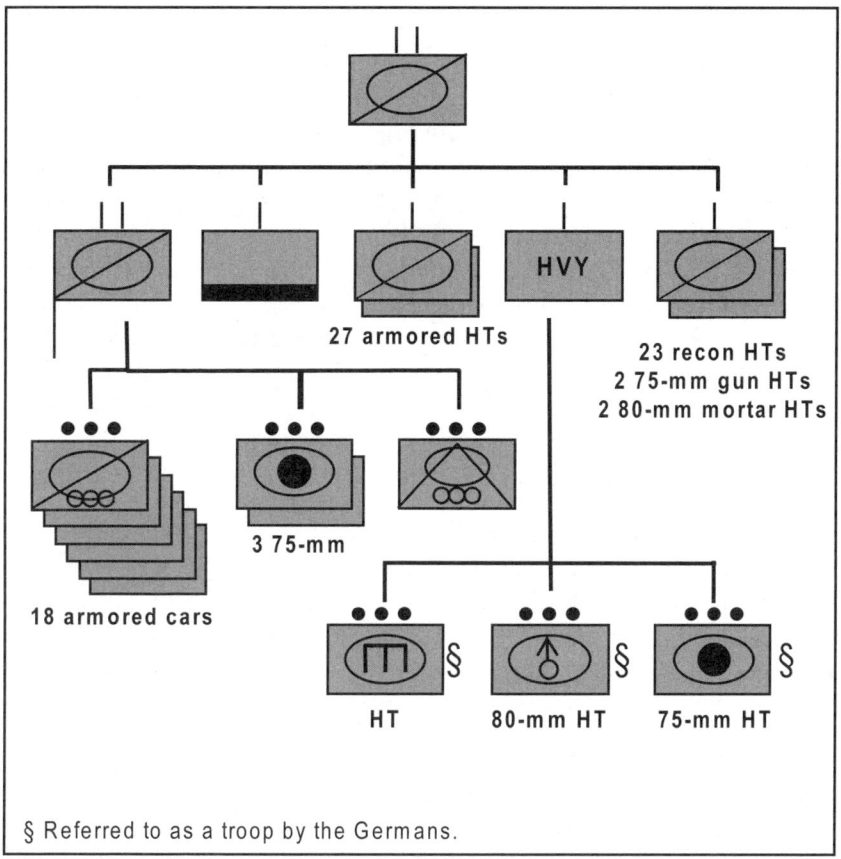

Figure 24. The German armored reconnaissance battalion, 1944.

The main German half-track was the *SdKfz 250/251*, which came in many variations and began to be fielded in 1941. It was designed to carry an infantry squad (*Halbgruppe*) or half of a scout section. The vehicle had a slower maximum road speed to German armored cars used later in the war (35 mph versus 50 mph) and a shorter range (130 miles between a minimum of 180 miles) but was more useful in combat situations and off roads.[33]

Despite the proliferation of half-tracks, because of their speed and range, armored cars still played a prominent role in the organizational structure of the 1944 German armored reconnaissance battalion. The revised organization contained 18 armored cars, organized into 6 troops in its headquarters company, along with an additional 3 75-mm howitzers

89

mounted on armored cars and 3 armored cars with 50-mm antitank guns.[34]

Technology continued to improve armored cars throughout the war, with, as mentioned previously, formerly towed antitank and assault guns being mounted directly on the armored cars. In addition, the Germans developed a series of heavy armored cars specially designed for unusual operating conditions such as in the desert or the cold. The last of these, the *SdKfz 234 Schwere Panzerspähwagen*, was so well designed that, despite having heavier armored plating, it still had a longer range and only a slightly lower maximum road speed than the armored cars it replaced. Armored cars used later in the war all mounted turrets with cannons no smaller than 20-mm. The Germans also made maximum use of captured enemy armored cars, including almost 200 Panhards, formerly the primary vehicle in French reconnaissance groups.[35]

After the French campaign, the Germans progressively increased their number of panzer divisions, primarily by reducing by half the overall number of tanks in the division from four battalions to two battalions, and upgraded their motorized infantry divisions to armored infantry (panzergrenadier) status. These units all contained armored reconnaissance battalions built around armored cars and, ultimately, half-tracks.[36]

The distinction between panzer and panzergrenadier divisions gradually blurred, at least on paper, in the latter years of the war. The major distinction was that, while 1944 panzer divisions contained two tank battalions, panzergrenadier divisions contained only one tank or an assault gun battalion. The divisional armored reconnaissance battalion in the panzergrenadier division contained only nine armored cars, and often, its reconnaissance companies were equipped with Volkswagen *Kubelwagen* sedans instead of half-tracks.[37]

Later in the war, the *Waffen SS* developed into a major armored component of the German Armed Forces. *Waffen SS* divisions, including their reconnaissance battalions, were similarly organized to comparable German Army units.

North Africa and Russia

Arduous campaigns in Russian and North Africa in 1941 and 1942 produced long advances and retreats across open terrain similar to the second phase of the 1940 French campaign. In these circumstances, German reconnaissance units were often far ranging in advance or on the flanks of their parent units.

Starting in February 1941, the Germans deployed armored and infantry forces to North Africa under the command of the then *Generalleutnant* Rommel, who had commanded the 7th Panzer Division in France. The Germans deployed to support the Italian Army in Libya. British armored forces had just defeated an Italian invasion of Egypt and occupied the eastern half of the Italian colony of Libya. The heart of the German forces was the Afrika Korps (*Deutsches Afrika Korps* or *DAK*), which consisted of the 15th and 21st Panzer Divisions. Each division had an armored reconnaissance battalion of the 1940 pattern. Although Rommel sought a special organization heavy in armored cars, when these battalions were upgraded in early 1942, the motorcycles were replaced with half-tracks as elsewhere in the German Army. However, each division formed within its reconnaissance battalions a battery from captured British 25-pdr guns.[38]

While the *DAK* remained a separate command, Rommel soon led a panzer group, which was later upgraded to a panzer army. Under this command, in addition to the *DAK* and aside from various Italian units, there were several specially organized *Afrika* infantry divisions. The first of these, the 90th Light Africa (later Infantry) Division, initially contained only a company-sized reconnaissance unit. In April 1942, this company was expanded and organized similar to the *DAK* panzer divisions' armored reconnaissance battalions. When the German command formed an additional light division, the 164th, from a former infantry division garrisoning Crete, in September 1942, it too contained the standard African version of the armored reconnaissance battalion.[39]

From the beginning, Rommel and his subordinate commanders used their reconnaissance units to lead sweeping advances, conduct long-range reconnaissance, and screen the advance of armored forces. When the army was on the defensive, scouts provided early warning of enemy movements via strings of outposts and covered the southern flank facing the empty wastes of the Western Desert. Usually when assigned such missions, the reconnaissance battalions reported directly to Rommel.[40]

This centralization was by design. Without any operational-level reconnaissance units under their direct control, Rommel and other German commanders in North Africa often detached reconnaissance battalions from their parent divisions and used them independently or to reinforce the light divisions or Italian divisions. Rommel had a particular affection for the 3d Armored Reconnaissance Battalion of the 21st Panzer Division. It was considered his pet unit as the battalion had been the first German unit to arrive in Libya and had begun conducting operations against the British in less than 2 days. Sometimes, the battalions were combined into a larger force in defensive operations and used in a counterattack role. For example, during the Battle of El Alamein on 31 October 1942, DAK commander *General der Panzertruppen* Wilhelm Ritter von Thoma personally led such a counterattack.[41]

While the reconnaissance battalions took heavy casualties in the Battle of El Alamein, in the subsequent 1,200-mile retreat across Libya to Tunisia, the scouts frequently provided the rearguard for the German forces and, on several occasions, forestalled British attempts to outflank and cut off part of Rommel's forces. During the retreat, these units usually worked directly under Rommel's control. At one point, the Desert Fox combined two reconnaissance battalions into a battle group with the specific mission of preventing the British from turning the German flank through the desert.[42]

Once the German forces were consolidated in the Tunisian bridgehead in February 1943, they counterattacked against the US forces at Kasserine. The 21st Panzer Division's reconnaissance battalion tried to seize the Kasserine Pass in a surprise night attack on 18–19 February. The attack failed, although follow-on forces took the pass the next day. The early success of the German counterattack only slightly delayed the inevitable surrender of the bridgehead to superior British, US, and French forces in early May 1943. As the German and Italian forces retreated closer and closer to Tunis, the reconnaissance battalions covered exposed flanks and provided rearguards. The Axis surrender ended the African phase of the war.[43]

The 1941 Russian campaign was much larger. Early in the campaign, the Germans advanced on a broad front with panzer and motorized divisions consolidated into panzer corps and groups. Long advances often resulted in the creation of large pockets of surrounded Soviet units. By the early winter of 1941, the German offensive had reached its zenith. Soviet counterattacks pushed the Germans back in many places. Throughout these operations, reconnaissance forces played a prominent role.

One German commander described the use of reconnaissance troops in the 1941 Russian campaign as leading divisional advances along various axes out to a distance of 12 to 24 miles to find enemy locations ahead of the division. In this role, the battalions were performing the operational-level reconnaissance mission often done by higher echelon scout units in other armies. Larger units, such as corps, depended on the divisional reconnaissance battalions to provide intelligence on the enemy situation. While in this role, scouts often proved invaluable in obtaining terrain information, seizing bridges or other key terrain, capturing enemy documents, and immediately discovering Soviet withdrawals.[44]

Most frequently, accounts cite the divisional battalions as covering flanks during advances rather than leading them. Sometimes, the motorcycle infantry battalion assisted in this mission. Slower advance rates of adjacent infantry divisions often exposed panzer division flanks. As in France, the motorcycle battalion frequently led the advance, particularly in rough terrain, and often combined with a tank battalion. When the 3d Panzer Division crossed the Soviet border on 22 June 1941, as happened at Martelange in 1940, reconnaissance and motorcycle troops led the way. However, once the fixed border obstacles were crossed, the division reorganized into several combined arms task forces, each containing part of the reconnaissance battalion, but led by motorcycle infantry elements.[45]

The long German advances of the early portion of the Russian campaign often proved to create flanks too broad for divisional reconnaissance battalions to cover, or the momentum of the advance caused gaps in the coverage. Sometimes, Soviet units managed to infiltrate between advancing German units after reconnaissance units protecting the flanks had passed them. The Germans were frequently surprised by the sudden appearance of Soviet units attacking from unexpected directions. Often, headquarters staffs were forced to defend themselves from such attacks.[46]

In the large encircling battles of the summer of 1941, sometimes, commanders gave divisional reconnaissance battalions defensive sectors to keep the trapped Soviet troops from escaping from the pockets. Generally, in defensive operations, the motorcycle units and heavy squadron of the reconnaissance battalion were retained as frontline fighters while the armored cars remained in division reserve. As in North Africa, the scouts were often used as a counterattack force. In the retreats of late 1941, the reconnaissance troopers covered division withdrawals and screened rear and left and right flanks while the armored cars kept the division commander posted on the status of the pursuing enemy.[47]

The lack of German operational-level reconnaissance forces led, as in France, to the use of whole divisions to cover large flanks at levels above division. The most notable example of this was the posting of the 16th Motorized Division at Elista on the Kalmyk Steppe in late summer of 1942. This posting placed the division between Army Group B fighting in Stalingrad and Army Group A fighting in the Caucasus. This gap extended almost 200 miles. The division covered it for more than 5 months from its central base at Elista through a series of strongpoints and through extensive motorized patrolling by its reconnaissance battalion along the major rail line connecting the Caucasus region with the rest of Russia.[48]

After the Battle of Kursk in mid-1943, the Germans remained on the defensive in Russia for the rest of the war as the front gradually advanced to the west. Reconnaissance units increasingly were used more for their mobility and less for their original function. The Soviets frequently massed forces for their offensives, and even in the panzer divisions, the reconnaissance unit became more valuable as a mobile reserve. Nowhere was this more apparent than in the much less mobile infantry divisions that made up the bulk of the German ground forces.

Fusilier Battalions and the Last Years of the War

Germany began World War II with its first-line infantry divisions containing a hybrid horse-motorized reconnaissance battalion that had a squadron each of horses and motorcycles and a heavy support squadron containing an armored car platoon. From the start, a shortage of horse units meant that units formed later did not contain the cavalry squadron. Third- and fourth-wave divisions formed in August 1939 contained an extra motorcycle squadron instead of the cavalry one. Higher numbered waves formed in 1939 sometimes had only a single company-sized motorcycle squadron as the reconnaissance unit. By 1941, almost all divisions had replaced horses with motorcycles or with infantry on bicycles.[49]

As the war continued, the need for a dedicated reconnaissance unit for the infantry became less compelling than the need for a mobile reserve force. With the pressing needs of the war, some newer divisions did not even field a reconnaissance unit. Given the overall defensive posture and equipment and personnel shortages, coupled with the perceived vulnerability of motorcycle troops, in late 1943, the German Army began replacing the reconnaissance battalions in its infantry divisions with a new type of unit, the fusilier battalion (*Füsilier-Battaillon*) (figure 25). The fusilier battalion was organized like a typical 1944 German infantry battalion. At least on paper, the new unit, unlike its specialized predecessor, provided the division commander with a small semimobile general-purpose reserve unit under his direct control. By design, the battalion contained one company mounted on bicycles and enough trucks to move the remaining companies, although in practice, this was usually not the case.[50]

Even after the adoption of the fusilier battalion, the Germans did not have enough equipment and troops to maintain the new organization across the board. Many divisions, particularly those considered static units or those converted from static divisions, did not contain a fusilier battalion. During the 1944 Normandy campaign, of the 28 nonmechanized German divisions that participated in the campaign, 13 contained fusilier battalions, while an additional 3 divisions created fusilier battalions from

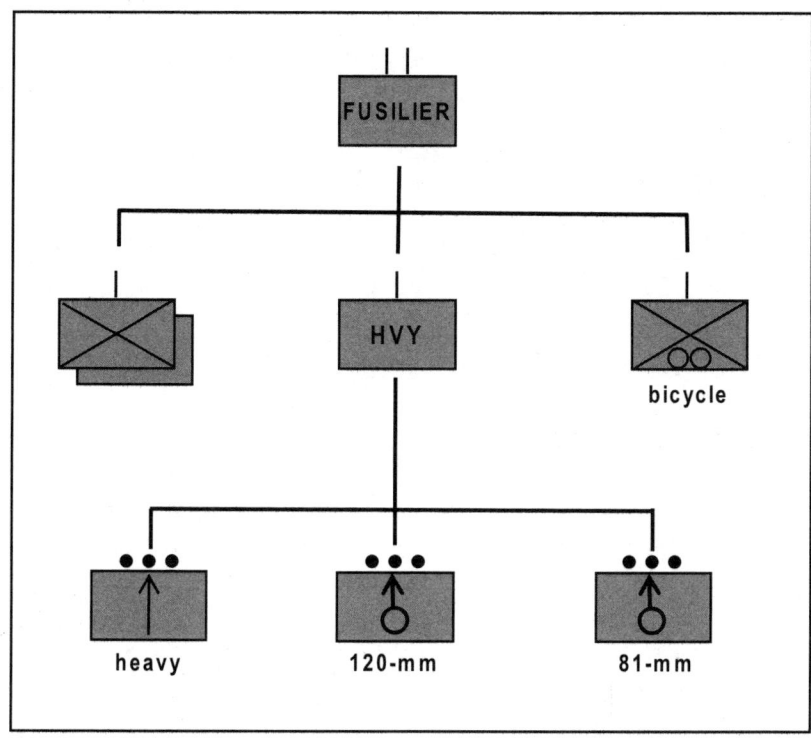

Figure 25. German infantry division fusilier battalion, 1944.[51]

regular infantry battalions. When new tables of organization were drawn up for lower grade infantry units called *Volksgrenadier* (*VGD*) divisions created in late 1944, they included only a single fusilier company mounted on bicycles, although most *Volksgrenadier* divisions already organized retained fusilier battalions with four companies.[52]

As the Allies pressed the German Armed Forces from all sides, armored reconnaissance battalions were used in defensive operations as mobile reserves and flank protection. When the Germans launched their last great offensive in the same Ardennes terrain fought over in 1914 and 1940, in December 1944, panzer divisions spearheaded the attacks. As in 1940, the tight confines of the hilly and forested Ardennes forced the attackers to advance in narrow columns. In general, the German attackers reinforced their reconnaissance battalions with infantry, antitank, and armored assets and made them a separate column.[53]

How the Sixth Panzer Army employed its armored reconnaissance battalions in the offensive illustrates the state of German reconnaissance near the end of the war. The 1st SS Panzer Division used its armored reconnaissance battalion to scout between its main columns on back roads to find intact bridges across streams and rivers. The battalion cleared the route of march for one of the following divisional task forces and then joined the lead task force containing the division's armored spearhead whose advance was stunted when various US units loosely surrounded it. The reconnaissance unit fought unsuccessfully to reopen the supply corridor to the spearhead against US forces at Stavelot. The 12th SS Panzer Division's scout unit followed the advance of the division's secondary column, ready to reinforce it as necessary. The division's attack was stopped cold by the US 99th and 2d Infantry Divisions.[54]

The 2d SS Panzer Division reinforced its reconnaissance battalion with an artillery battalion, an engineer company, and an antitank company. Fuel shortages delayed the movement of this task force, but once in action, it played a key role in the early days of the offensive. In the lead of its division, the task force moved around the town of St. Vith and forced the American evacuation of that strongpoint. The battalion's commander, *SS-Sturmbannführer* Ernst-August Krag, was awarded the Oak Leaves to the Knights Cross after the operation. At Salmchâteau, Krag's reconnaissance troops fought a US task force of tank destroyers, field artillery, and mechanized cavalry elements. When surrounded, the Americans managed to retreat to the west through a loose German cordon. Several days later, Krag's force led the final major German attack in the Ardennes at Sadzot against elements of the US 75th Infantry Division. After a seesaw battle, the US counterattackers repulsed Krag's scouts who had been reinforced with three battalions of divisional panzergrenadiers.[55]

Summary

The Germans fought World War II initially with light, mostly motorized reconnaissance battalions. Although no reconnaissance units were above the division echelon, when necessary, commanders of larger units detached the reconnaissance battalions and placed them directly under their own control. As the war progressed, the Germans gradually decreased the motorized component in their scout units, replacing motorcycles with half-tracked armored personnel carriers, upgrading armored cars and using obsolete light tanks, then standard medium tanks in armored regimental and battalion reconnaissance platoons.

The American Experience in World War II
General

For combat in World War II, the US Army deployed units designed specifically to conduct reconnaissance operations at all levels from battalion to corps. Figure 26 compares the American echeloning with that of the

Level	American		German	
Operational				
Army and Corps	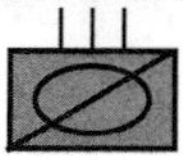 Group headquarters with two subordinate squadrons		None (Panzer division armored reconnaissance battalions fill this role)	
Primary Equipment	Armored cars, jeeps, 75-mm assault guns		NA	
Tactical				
Division	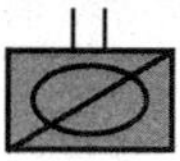 panzer and panzergrenadier divisions	 infantry divisions	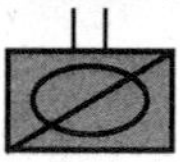	None
Primary Equipment	Armored cars, jeeps, 75-mm assault guns	Jeeps, scout cars, mortars	Armored cars, half-tracks	Fusilier (motorized/bicycle infantry) battalion replaced former recon battalion
Below Division	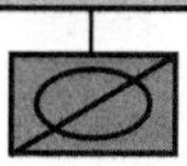 separate battalions	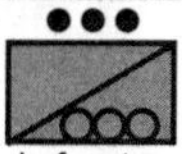 infantry regiment		
Primary Equipment	Separate battalions	Jeeps	Light tank or mech infantry (HT) reconnaissance platoons at panzer and panzergrenadier regiment and battalion levels	

Figure 26. The echeloning of German and American reconnaissance units, 1944.

Germans. As recounted in the previous chapter, in 1940, the Americans organized the Armored Force to field armored divisions, each with its own reconnaissance battalion. There were also small reconnaissance elements at the battalion level in the armored division's major combat elements.

In the infantry division, as fielded for the war, were two echelons of reconnaissance units. At division was a reconnaissance troop, while at the regimental level was an intelligence and reconnaissance platoon. The Cavalry branch retained control over separate units of nondivisional cavalry units of regimental and squadron size. The World War II US Army also contained a large number of separate combat battalions (tank, tank destroyer, engineer). Organizationally, as most of these units were considered self-contained, they usually had a reconnaissance element of up to company size. Each of these points will be discussed in greater detail.[56]

The Mechanized Cavalry Group

The largest reconnaissance organization fielded in the US Army was the mechanized cavalry group. This group was a direct descendent of the two-squadron hybrid horse-mechanized cavalry regiments of the immediate prewar period. Against the wishes of the Chief of Cavalry, Army Chief of Staff General George Marshall decided to completely mechanize the hybrid regiments. This mechanization was finished in the summer of 1942.[57]

In 1943, before any of the regiments were used in combat, they were administratively broken up. The regimental headquarters became a mechanized cavalry group headquarters, while the two subordinate squadrons became separate mechanized cavalry squadrons. This change was part of an Armywide transformation to a flexible group/separate battalion system begun in December 1942. The system applied to nondivisional units in the field artillery, antiaircraft artillery, combat engineers, and mechanized cavalry. The groups were designed to be a flexible tactical headquarters able to freely attach and detach separately organized battalions. However, in the mechanized cavalry, the change was not so drastic. Each newly formed group headquarters was the former regimental headquarters of the two now separate squadrons attached to the group. In practice, the group retained control of these two battalions, except for short periods of temporary detachment, usually to direct field army control or to the control of infantry divisions, throughout wartime service.[58]

The cavalry group became the highest echelon of reconnaissance unit in the US Army in World War II. As such, groups were normally assigned to field armies, which then almost always attached them to a corps subordinate to that army. All 13 groups that went overseas were deployed to the European Theater of Operations (ETO), and all but one served under a corps. While the groups were frequently moved around between tactical commands, overall groups served under corps 48 percent of the time and under infantry divisions 38 percent of the time.[59]

The group headquarters was austere, consisting only of a small headquarters troop and a light truck company. The two cavalry squadrons were organized identically (figure 27). Each contained a tank company with 17 light tanks, an assault gun troop with 6 75-mm assault guns, and 3 reconnaissance troops. Each reconnaissance troop had three platoons. The platoons were each organized into an armored car and a jeep section. Thus, the mechanized cavalry squadrons combined tanks, artillery, scouts on jeeps, and scouts in armored cars in the same organization.[60]

According to the US Army's 1941 field service regulation, mechanized cavalry units were organized specifically to perform reconnaissance missions, not combat missions. The squadrons were only to participate in

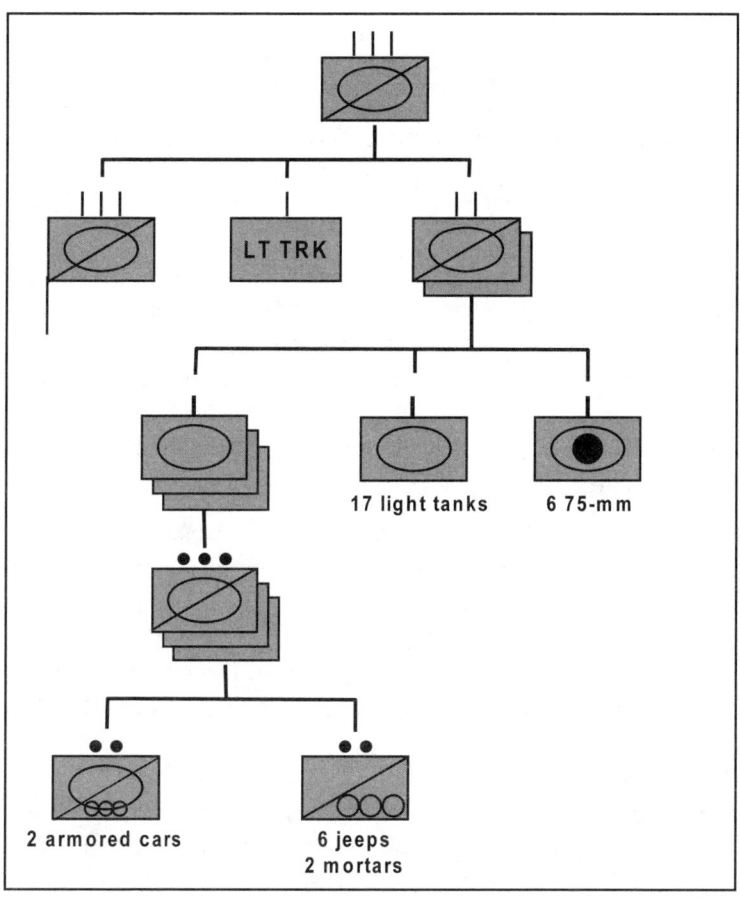

Figure 27. US Army mechanized cavalry group in World War II.[61]

combat actions to obtain information and were to minimize fighting whenever possible.[62]

In actual field employment, mechanized cavalry groups rarely performed reconnaissance missions. A postwar analysis of group operations indicated that such missions consumed only 3 percent of the time spent in combat. Much more common were defensive missions (33 percent), special operations (29 percent), security missions (25 percent), and offensive actions (10 percent). To execute nonreconnaissance missions, cavalry groups always required reinforcement, typically, as a minimum, the attachment of a battalion each of field artillery and tank destroyers and a company of engineers. Even security missions, which included the traditional counterreconnaissance missions of screening flanks and maintaining contact with adjacent units, required reinforcement.[63]

The postwar ETO General Board, which compiled these statistics, stated that corps-level cavalry groups performed combat missions much more frequently than the reconnaissance missions for which they were designed, but the board did not specifically indicate why. However, it is obvious that field commanders indicated a much stronger need for additional combat assets rather than reconnaissance ones. It is significant that the main adversary in the war, the Germans, did not even field reconnaissance forces above division level. The only place that the Germans detached divisional units to create de facto corps- and army-level reconnaissance units was in the North Africa theater where, ironically, the US Army deployed no cavalry groups (then still called regiments). In the cases where the Germans needed a force to cover flanks or maintain contact between two army groups, the Germans generally used whole divisions in this role, as in the case of the 10th Panzer Division in France in 1940 and the 16th Motorized Infantry Division at Elista in 1942.[64]

The US Army created and deployed only 89 combat divisions in World War II, compared to original estimates of a requirement for between 350 and 400 divisions. In contrast, the Germans fielded 165 divisions for the 1940 campaign alone and averaged 222 divisions for the bulk of the war, with a population of only 60 percent of that of the United States in 1940. While the Germans had difficulty keeping their divisions up to strength later in the war and US divisions were usually close to full strength, nevertheless, the number of operational units available to US commanders was fewer than those available to German commanders. Consequently, US commanders frequently used their mechanized cavalry groups as additional combat operational units, reinforcing them with nondivisional combat assets available to the corps or army echelons.[65]

The experience of the 14th Cavalry Group during the December 1944 German Ardennes offensive is a good example of the operational employment of a cavalry group. This unit was assigned to the First Army and attached to the VIII Corps. In mid-December 1944, the VIII Corps was defending in the Ardennes sector generally along the German-Belgian and German-Luxembourg borders with three infantry divisions. To the south of the corps was the Third Army. To the north was the V Corps. On the left of the corps sector was a small pass in the Schnee Eifel mountain range called the Losheim Gap. Before the German offensive, the 14th Cavalry Group had held the gap with a reinforced squadron for almost 2 months. The group had been recently attached to the newly arrived 106th Infantry Division. The 106th was responsible for the 21-mile northern sector of the VIII Corps front. The cavalry group, whose second squadron was in reserve refitting, held a 5-mile sector on the corps left (northern) flank. However, the 14th's sector was open ended on both flanks. On its left (north), a 2-mile space was jointly patrolled with a regimental reconnaissance platoon from the V Corps' 99th Infantry Division. On the right (south) was a 1.5-mile space between the cavalry's positions and those of the neighboring infantry regiment of the 106th Division. The infantry had responsibility for patrolling this space.[66]

The 14th Group's 18th Cavalry Squadron, reinforced with a company from the 820th Tank Destroyer Battalion (equipped with towed 3-inch antitank guns), covered the group sector with platoon-sized strongpoints in a positional defense (figure 28). The length of the group's sector precluded a linear defense with its available assets. While the 106th's predecessor, the 2d Infantry Division, had planned to cover the cavalry's weakness with a reserve infantry battalion, the new division, which took over the sector only a couple of days before the start of the German offensive, had not yet produced revised defensive plans.[67]

The cavalry group suffered from being astride the main advance routes of two German thrusts—one by the Sixth Panzer Army in the north, the other from the Fifth Panzer Army in the south. Each advance consisted of a lead infantry division, followed by one or more panzer divisions. The 3d Parachute (*Fallshirmjäger*) Division led the I SS Panzer Corps' thrust in the north, followed by the 1st and 12th SS Panzer Divisions. This column was to advance against US positions in the northern portion of the 14th's sector, then continue to the northwest into the rear of the V Corps' sector. The southern thrust was under the Fifth Panzer Army's LXVI Corps. Spearheading it was the 18th *Volksgrenadier* Division, followed by the *Führer* Escort (*Begleit-FB*) Panzer Brigade and other unspecified panzer elements.[68]

101

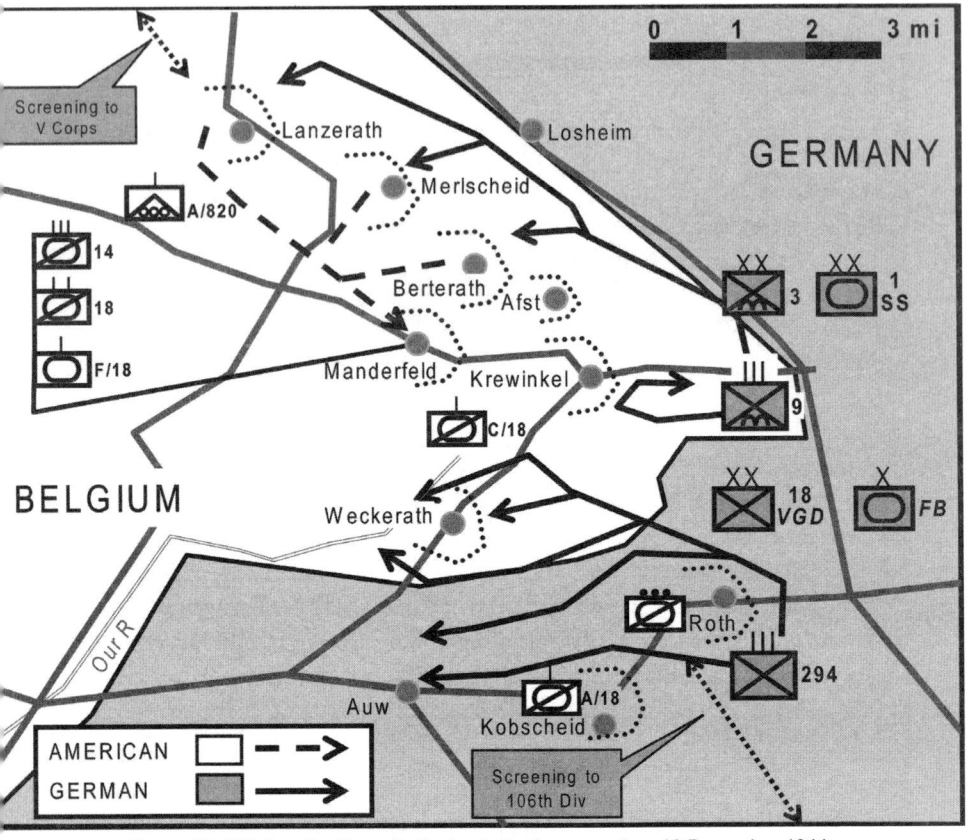

Figure 28. 14th Cavalry Group in the Losheim Gap, morning, 16 December 1944.

The German attack began before dawn on 16 December 1944. In the south, the infantry of the 18th *Volksgrenadier* Division quickly infiltrated around the American village positions and cut off the advance elements of A Troop, 18th Cavalry Squadron. Slightly to the north, light tanks supported the defense, and Troop C, 18th Cavalry Squadron, at the villages of Weckerath and Krewinkel, held off the lead German infantry and paratroopers from both thrusts. However, in the extreme northern portion of the group sector, the tank destroyers of the 820th Battalion were forced to retreat to the group headquarters at Manderfeld. The group commander, Colonel Mark Devine, summoned the reserve squadron and decided to pull back to the ridgeline centered on Manderfeld, 1.5 miles west of the previous forward positions.[69]

By 1100, the cavalry group's reserve unit, the 32d Cavalry Squadron, had begun arriving near Manderfeld. However, when the forward units were ordered to retreat, many were unable to successfully disengage from the Germans. The garrisons of A Troop, 18th Cavalry Squadron, at Roth and Kobscheid in the south were forced to remain in position and either surrender or wait until dark to exfiltrate to the west. In the center, C Troop garrisons at Afst, Krewinkel, and Weckerath successfully withdrew to the main position. At Weckerath, a reconnaissance platoon withdrew just before a massive German artillery barrage signaled a deliberate attack on the village.[70]

While Devine's forces regrouped on the Manderfeld Ridge, it was already clear the new position was untenable. To the south, elements of the 18th *Volksgrenadier* Division were streaming to the southwest, causing a temporary loss of contact with the 106th Division. Contact with the 99th Infantry Division was similarly lost to the north near the village of Lanzerath as the troops of the German 3d Parachute Division moved to the northwest. To reestablish contact with the 99th Division on the left, where the Germans seemed weakest, Devine organized a counterattack force consisting of a reconnaissance troop and an assault gun troop. The force ended up in a firefight with German infantry supported by assault guns south of Lanzerath. By this time, the German advance in the south threatened to cut off the Manderfeld position. At about 1600, the group requested and received permission to retreat westward to the next north-south ridgeline about 2 miles away. Within an hour, all the forces at Manderfeld were in motion, and the withdrawal was successfully executed (figure 29).[71]

Devine's withdrawal had reestablished a tenuous contact with the 106th Division, but contact with the 99th Division to his north was lost. Devine planned to plug this hole on the 17th, but during the night, his subordinate commanders adjusted their positions, mostly on their own initiative, based on their fears of being infiltrated. As a result, the group was even more overextended. The lead elements of the 1st SS Panzer Division, traveling in several different columns, were, in fact, already beginning to pass the 14th Cavalry Group's new position both to the north and the south. In the south on the morning of the 17th, German tanks pushed back the rightmost troop, while on the other flank, German troops were spotted already far to the west. Devine ordered two new withdrawals during the day on 17 December. On the evening of the 17th, Devine's command group was ambushed while traveling to the 106th headquarters at St. Vith. The cavalry units were disrupted by their retreats and German movements. These forces ended up being consolidated into the defense force for St. Vith under the command of the 7th Armored Division.[72]

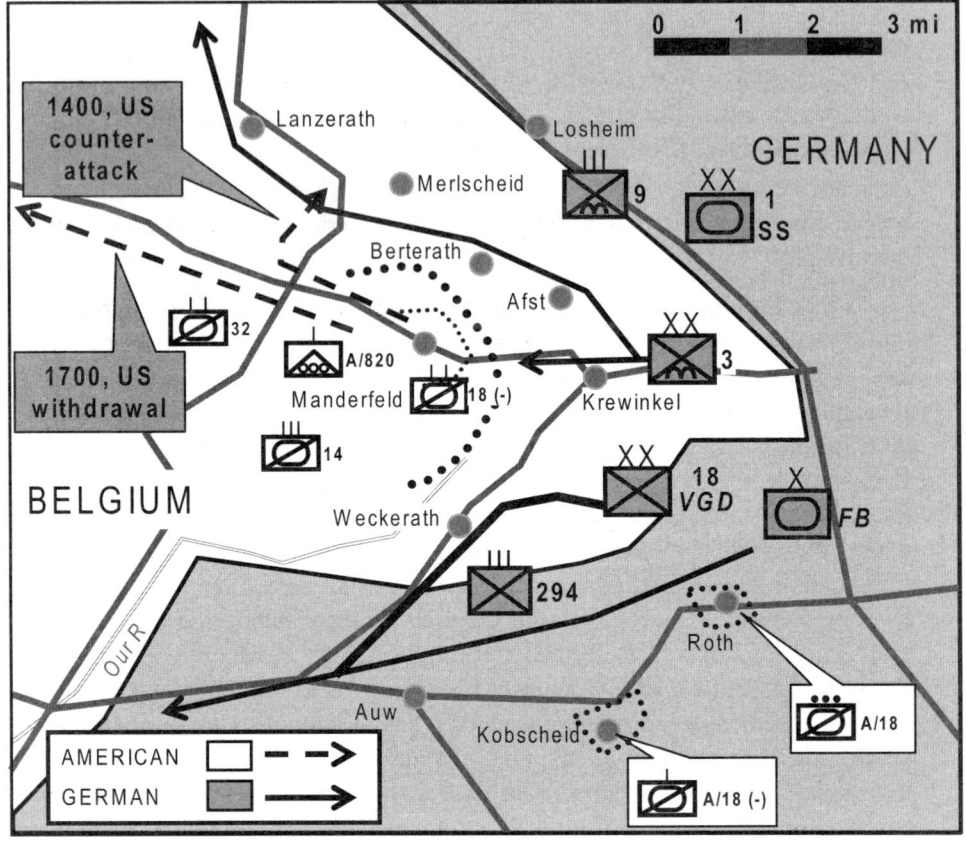

Figure 29. 14th Cavalry Group situation, afternoon, 16 December 1944.

The operations of the 14th Cavalry Group give an extreme example of a cavalry group being used as a combat force. The General Board study of mechanized cavalry completed after the war by the US Forces, European Theater (USFET), provides many additional examples of various types of cavalry group operations.[73]

The Armored Division

The divisional reconnaissance unit of the World War II US Army armored division was the direct descendent of the original armored car troops formed in the interwar years. The Army deployed two basic armored division organizations in World War II, a heavy version used by two divisions and a light version used by the remaining 14 divisions. The structure of the battalion-sized divisional reconnaissance element was similar in both divisions. For simplicity's sake, this work looks only at the light organizational structure's mechanized cavalry reconnaissance squadron.⁷⁴ Figure 30 shows the organization of this unit.

The squadron was equipped with a mix of light tanks, armored cars, assault guns, and jeeps. It had four subordinate reconnaissance troops, a 75-mm assault gun troop, and a tank company. Each reconnaissance troop had three platoons that included a jeep section and an armored car section.⁷⁵

With four reconnaissance troops, division commanders could attach troops to the three subordinate combat commands and still retain troops under direct control of the squadron. Operational employment of the divisional cavalry squadron varied from division to division. Of the 13 light-style armored divisions in the ETO, in their typical employment, all divisions retained the squadron headquarters under their control, but only

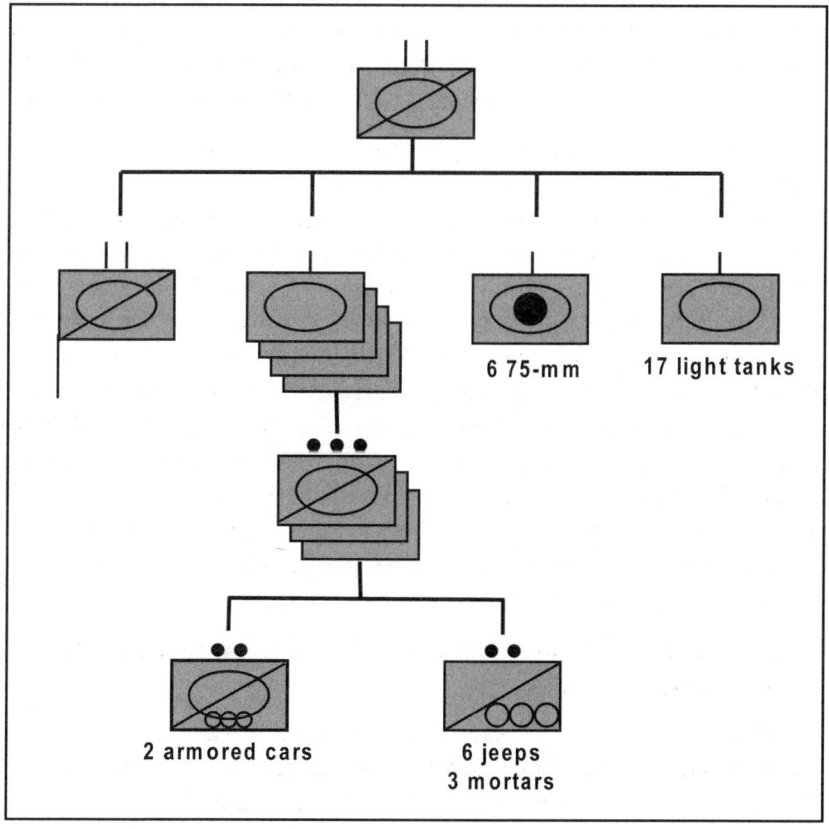

Figure 30. US Army armored division mechanized cavalry reconnaissance squadron, 1944.

3 of these divisions retained the squadron intact. Most gave one troop to each of the two combat commands (A and B) in the divisional command structure. Some divisions organized the small Combat Command Reserve (CCR) headquarters into a third subordinate command and also provided it with a troop. In most cases, the combat command retained the cavalry troop under its control, but in several cases, the troop was parceled out among the subordinate combined arms battalion task forces that formed the combat punch of the division.[76]

In contrast to the Germans, use of the reconnaissance element in the US armored division did not need to be centralized. The presence of higher reconnaissance organizations allowed American commanders the flexibility to decentralize their assets. Operational-level reconnaissance was not an additional mission of US divisional squadrons.

During the war, the Army revised its doctrine for the armored division's reconnaissance squadron. The 1944 update increased the emphasis on reconnaissance as the squadron's primary mission and downplayed the role of security and counterreconnaissance. Since counterreconnaissance implied combat action to deny the enemy information, therefore, doctrinally the squadron was not expected to fight to complete its basic mission.[77]

However, to some extent, postwar critiques of the actual use of armored division reconnaissance assets paralleled the findings for cavalry groups. While the divisional squadrons spent 13 percent of the time on reconnaissance missions, compared to 3 percent for groups, and an additional 24 percent on security missions (25 percent for cavalry groups), the bulk of the time (63 percent) was devoted to combat missions, particularly rear area security and mobile reserve (48 percent). However, the ETO General Board did not recommend drastic changes in the squadron structure. The board recommended the deletion of one cavalry troop but the addition of a dragoon troop. The dragoon troop was essentially an infantry company mounted in half-tracks. The cavalry troops were still primarily equipped with armored cars and jeeps. The light tank company was retained, while the assault gun troop was to be converted into a howitzer troop with eight 105-mm self-propelled field artillery pieces.[78]

The Infantry Division, Regimental, and Separate Battalion Reconnaissance Units

While the cavalry and the Armored Force were developing mechanized reconnaissance units, the de facto divorce of the horse from the reconnaissance function resulted in the creation of reconnaissance elements in nonmechanized forces as well. The War Department accepted the concept of an organic infantry division reconnaissance troop after the 1940 field maneuvers. The utility of this troop was validated in the 1941 maneuvers. As originally devised, the troop contained three platoons, each with four scout cars and two motorcycles. By 1942, the organization had evolved into three troops of three platoons, with each platoon containing three reconnaissance sections, each with an armored car and four jeeps (figure 31).

Postwar statistics indicated that divisional reconnaissance troops only conducted reconnaissance operations 6 percent of the time. Security or counterreconnaissance operations were most common (50 percent), followed by rear area security or mobile reserve activities (39 percent). The size of the troop usually precluded it from being used in offensive or defensive operations (5 percent). Unlike most other types of reconnaissance units, divisional troops were usually not reinforced for operations, nor were they split up and used in separate platoon-sized detachments. The ETO

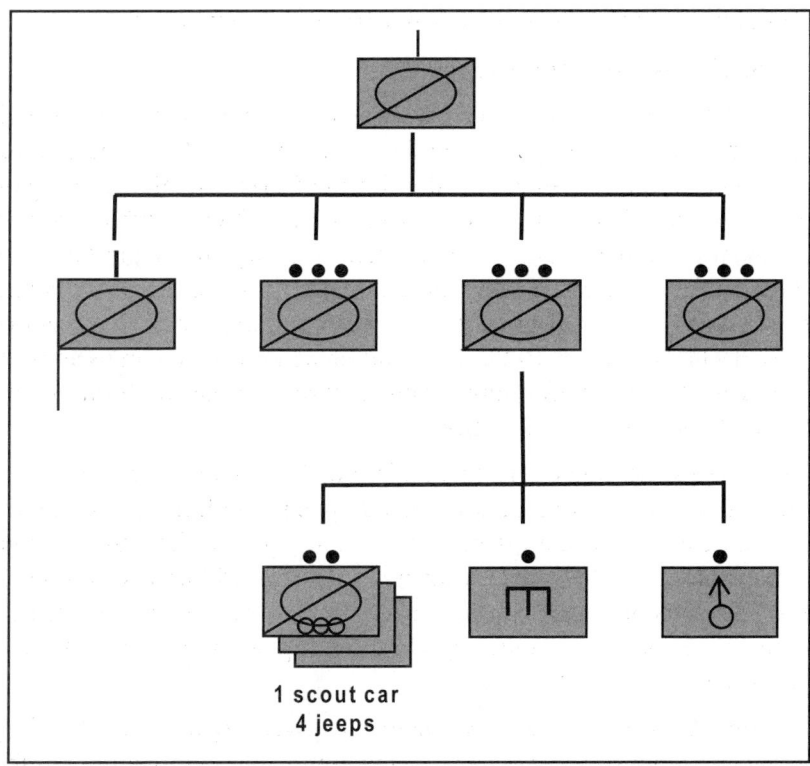

Figure 31. US Army infantry division mechanized cavalry reconnaissance troop, 1942.

General Board recommended that the troop be expanded to a squadron in the postwar Army.[79]

At the regimental level and below, the infantry had organized its own scout units. The prewar infantry regiment contained an intelligence platoon, while each battalion had a small scout section under the control of the battalion intelligence officer (S2). In 1941, the Infantry branch upgraded the regimental intelligence platoon by equipping it with eight jeeps and redesignating it the intelligence and reconnaissance platoon.[80]

As part of the separate battalion concept used in the US Army during World War II, such combat battalions were organized as self-contained organizations. This meant that elements, such as reconnaissance units, previously found at regimental level were now found in battalions. Tank destroyer battalions, the antitank branch of the World War II Army, each contained a reconnaissance company organized similar to the reconnaissance troop of the armored division squadron. Tank battalions included a light tank company that functioned as the reconnaissance element. Armored infantry battalions contained a jeep-mounted reconnaissance platoon, while combat engineer battalions had a 10-man reconnaissance section.[81]

Marine Corps Reconnaissance Units

The US Marine Corps greatly expanded during World War II, fielding three corps headquarters and six divisions by 1945. The first real reconnaissance unit organized in the Marine Corps was the Amphibious Reconnaissance Company, Fleet Marine Force, Pacific, which became operational in January 1943. The company was organized similar to, but slightly smaller than, a standard Marine infantry company. It was assigned to the V Amphibious Corps in August 1943 and expanded to a battalion in April 1944. In August 1944, the battalion again became an asset of the Fleet Marine Force, Pacific, supporting the three Marine amphibious corps in the final operations of the war.[82]

The prewar Marine Corps had maintained a scout company in its two existing divisions. This company was equipped with light tanks and later with scout cars. These companies later became part of the first divisional tank battalions that the Marines formed in early 1942 and were retained when new divisions were created. The company as then configured had 3 scout car platoons (12 vehicles) and a scout platoon with 4 jeeps and 4 motorcycles.[83]

During the war, the scout companies evolved organizationally. Jeeps replaced the scout cars before any of the companies deployed to combat, giving the company 32 of the small utility vehicles. In 1943, the scout companies were placed directly under the division headquarters, and in 1944, they were redesignated reconnaissance companies. At the same time, the jeeps were eliminated, and from then on, the companies depended on rubber boats and foot movement to conduct reconnaissance. The divisions often used the reconnaissance companies to secure small islands near larger islands that were being assaulted.[84]

The 1st Marine Division formed a small scout and sniper detachment in September 1942 while on Guadalcanal. Operationally, the detachment combined with a line Marine unit, the 3d Battalion, 2d Marines, to form a de facto reconnaissance element in the division's final weeks on the island. In response to the success of the detachment, the division subsequently formed a scout and sniper platoon in each of its regiments, a concept that the Marine Corps adopted in all its regiments by April 1943. The platoons conducted reconnaissance patrols, secured regimental flanks, and served as artillery observers. Marine regiments organized separate from any division contained an additional reconnaissance platoon, equivalent to the divisional reconnaissance company, in addition to its scout and sniper platoon.[85]

Summary

At the end of the war, the US Army conducted a detailed analysis of its reconnaissance operations and organizations. In general, observers believed that the mechanized cavalry units in the European theater in World War II were less capable of performing the reconnaissance mission than they were of performing the combat missions that horse cavalry had previously performed. Ironically, while these units were particularly designed to conduct reconnaissance, postwar after-action reviews revealed that the actual missions to which they were often assigned were primarily combat missions and that the organizational structure of the units made them ineffectual when conducting reconnaissance missions.[86]

In addition, analysis indicates that these reconnaissance units at all levels spent only a small proportion of their time conducting reconnaissance operations. Therefore, a majority of US Army observers thought that the World War II mechanized cavalry units needed to focus less on conducting reconnaissance and more on providing a mechanized version of the former horse cavalry. As a result, most of these critics believed that the units needed to be expanded in personnel and equipment to provide "a light, fast and hard hitting combat force" capable of performing the spectrum of missions formerly done by horse cavalry and actually accomplished by reconnaissance units in World War II: offensive and defensive combat, mobile reserve, rear area security, security and counterreconnaissance, and reconnaissance.[87]

Throughout the war, US Army reconnaissance units depended on the ¼-ton utility vehicle, the jeep, as its primary means of transportation for scouts. The jeep was small, light, and capable of cross-country movement. It also could be armed with various weapons, including machine guns and light antitank weapons. However, the jeep was vulnerable in combat to enemy small-arms fire. In US Army cavalry group and squadron reconnaissance sections and platoons, jeep-mounted scouts were teamed with reconnaissance troops mounted in the M8 light armored car. The M8 had a long range (up to 350 miles) and could move fast on highways (55 mph). It was also armed with a 37-mm cannon and a .30-caliber machine gun.[88]

The M8 was one of several wheeled armored vehicles that the US Army used in World War II. Another was the smaller M3 scout car. The M3, a four-wheeled vehicle capable of speeds up to 50 mph and a range of 250 miles, was used by reconnaissance troops of the infantry divisions. The M8 was the basic armored car used in cavalry groups and squadrons. It was a six-wheeled vehicle armed with a 37-mm gun.[89]

In the Army's reconnaissance organizations, the armored cars and scout jeeps were supported by a truly combined arms team at the squadron level. Each squadron included a light tank company and an assault gun troop. The light tank used in this role was the M3/M5 Stuart tank. It weighed 14.7 tons, double the weight of the M8, and was equipped with the same 37-mm gun. Each US Army tank battalion also contained a company of Stuarts, which, when employed, became the

Figure 32. An M8 armored car in Paris, August 1944.

battalion's reconnaissance element rather than a supporting element as in the mechanized cavalry units.

Although supported by armored elements, US Army reconnaissance in World War II was primarily an affair of unarmored jeeps and lightly armored wheeled scout cars. Although often used in combat roles throughout the war, the reconnaissance elements were not equipped or designed for such operations on an extended basis.

The Experiences of Other Armies
The French

The previous discussion in this chapter of the 1940 campaign shows the French Army's use of its reconnaissance assets during the war. The French deployed a mix of mechanized and hybrid horse, mechanized, and motorized reconnaissance units at the army, corps, and division levels. A cavalry corps of three light mechanized divisions (*DLM*s) provided the reconnaissance and counterreconnaissance assets for the Allied main effort in Belgium. This corps engaged a German panzer corps near Gembloux. While causing the Germans extensive losses, the concept of the corps operational employment meant that, once the infantry forces of the French First Army were in place along the Dyle River, the corps had to retreat into the main position and have its assets dispersed among the infantry. The Germans, working under a different concept, kept their armored forces together and used them as a strike force that maintained the initiative despite the losses incurred at Gembloux.

Elsewhere, the French deployed hybrid light cavalry divisions (*DLC*s) to screen and reconnoiter forward of the positions of their infantry corps. These divisions combined horse, mechanized, and motorized elements under one command. The *DLC* was to discover the German dispositions and delay the German advance until the French could prepare countermeasures. In this mission, these units failed. Even in the restricted terrain of the Ardennes, the Germans, moving fast and bypassing opposition whenever possible, managed to reach the Meuse River and cross it in 3 days. The *DLC*s also failed to discover the extent of the German armored deployment in the Ardennes. The French High Command, therefore, did not realize the location of the enemy's main effort until the panzers were across the Meuse, and then, there was nothing the French could do about it.

The British

In 1940, the British primarily depended on a combination of light tanks and scouts mounted in Bren armored personnel carriers to conduct reconnaissance operations. The mechanization of scouts was a trend the Germans also adopted later. After the failure of the 1940 campaign, the British removed light tanks from the reconnaissance role in infantry divisions. Armored cars, formerly only found in the corps-level reconnaissance regiment, replaced the tanks. The reconnaissance squadron of the infantry division reconnaissance regiment later in the war contained a combination of armored cars, scouts in Brens, and a truck-mounted motorized infantry platoon. The armored division later in the war contained a reconnaissance regiment that combined three squadrons of medium-tank assault guns with a squadron of armored cars.[90]

British operational employment of its reconnaissance assets was a mixed bag during the war. The jeep-mounted Long Range Desert Group quite successfully provided theater-level reconnaissance in North Africa in 1941–43. Two army-level armored car regiments virtually fought a separate war with the German reconnaissance battalions throughout the campaign, particularly during the long retreat to Tunisia in late 1942 to early 1943. During the retreat, the British reconnaissance units were never able to penetrate the German counterreconnaissance screen sufficiently to allow the British to successfully outflank Rommel's retreating forces. Nevertheless, when the British used their deliberate methods of combined arms coordination that were the hallmark of Field Marshal Bernard Montgomery's command style, their reconnaissance assets, particularly those containing tanks, performed their tasks as well as similar elements in other armies.[91]

The Soviets

The German invasion in June 1941 caught the Soviets in the middle of organizational changes based on an analysis of the 1940 French campaign. The German strike forced organizational change to take place as improvisation. Many of the prewar mechanized units were destroyed in the early battles. It was not until after the German repulse at Moscow in December 1941 that the Red Army was able to begin fielding new-style tank and mechanized corps. By 1943, the Soviets had begun fielding corps-sized tank armies to spearhead offensives. Each tank army contained a motorcycle-mounted reconnaissance regiment and three subordinate corps, each with a reconnaissance battalion equipped with armored cars and truck-mounted scouts. Subordinate tank and mechanized brigades also contained small armored car elements.[92]

Operationally, later in the war, the Soviets depended greatly on deliberate attacks as their primary offensive action. Before 1944, the reconnaissance elements of the attacking forces performed detailed, deliberate long-range scouting. To save time, starting in early 1944, Red

Army units organized a reconnaissance echelon consisting of company- and battalion-sized units as the lead part of the deliberate attack. This echelon's purpose was not only to find the German positions but also to seize the German outpost lines. German defensive doctrine called for these advance positions to be lightly held so that the weight of the Soviet attack would not hit the main battle line directly. The Soviet transformation of its reconnaissance elements into the lead fighting echelon negated this German technique, allowing the Soviet main attack echelon to concentrate on the German main defenses.[93]

The Red Army also pursued deep battle, the exploitation of penetrations created in the German defensive lines. For this purpose, the Soviets used forward detachments, combined arms units designed to sprint ahead of the main force and seize key terrain or to disrupt the German retreat. Forward detachments typically were built around tank brigades, although forward detachments themselves were often echeloned with a tank corps following the lead tank brigade. Forward detachments were fighting rather than reconnaissance organizations, and they usually contained only their organic reconnaissance elements when conducting such missions.

Summary

In World War II, all armies deployed reconnaissance units at least up to battalion level. The British, French, and Americans used larger organizations specifically to conduct operational reconnaissance to support field armies and corps. The Germans thought they only needed such forces in the North African theater, in which case the command removed reconnaissance battalions from divisions and employed them separately. Elsewhere, when the Germans needed an operational-level force to conduct reconnaissance or security operations, they used whole mobile divisions. Such divisions then reverted to less-specialized combat operations on the completion of the reconnaissance or security mission.

The French fielded division-sized reconnaissance units and, generally, only used them in this role even when their superior armament gave them advantages over their German opponents. The British used battalion-sized regiments at the corps and army levels, while the Americans utilized the regiment-sized cavalry group at the corps (and sometimes field army) level. In the American case, the shortage of operational units and the mobility of the mechanized cavalry usually resulted in field commanders using these assets in nonreconnaissance roles, particularly at the higher levels.

With the demise of horse cavalry reconnaissance units, the debate shifted to that of equipping the mechanized or motorized replacement elements. While the armored car was almost universally adopted because of its on-road speed, range, and ability to mount heavy weapons, other equipment for scouts varied from the American use of the jeep and the early war German employment of the motorcycle to the British adoption of the armored and fully tracked Bren carrier and the extensive German use of the half-track later in the war. Assault guns were also almost universally given to reconnaissance units to support the scouts. The British and Americans also provided tanks to support their reconnaissance troops, usually at the squadron level.

The Germans started the war with light, primarily motorized reconnaissance units. By the end of the war, although still retaining the armored car with its light armor, German scouts were mounted in armored half-track carriers. On the other hand, the Americans maintained large scout forces mounted in light, unarmored jeeps. However, these scouts were supported by light tanks.

Postwar American critiques of reconnaissance units still stressed the importance of the jeep/armored car combination while pressing for the use of mechanized cavalry units by design in nonreconnaissance roles. To give this light unit more staying power, these observers proposed the replacement of the light tanks with an infantry company mounted in half-tracks and a battery of 105-mm howitzers also mounted on half-tracks.[94]

World War II was the first major war fought with ground reconnaissance units without horses. Prewar theory and organization looked to the new mechanized cavalry as merely a vehicular replacement for animal transportation. However, unarmored or lightly armored units depending on machine guns and motorcycles soon proved to be too light to survive on the battlefield, particularly in extended campaigns. Such units soon required augmentation or reequipping. Most combatants soon developed combined arms reconnaissance units, retaining light vehicles, such as jeeps, but combining them with half-tracks, light tanks, heavy armored cars, and self-propelled guns into an organization both nimble and survivable. US Army analysis of wartime experience postulated the creation of even heavier reconnaissance units in the postwar period, a prospect unfulfilled due to demobilization.

Notes

1. Peter McCarthy and Mike Syron, *Panzerkrieg: The Rise and Fall of Hitler's Tank Divisions* (New York: Carroll & Graff), 28–29, 124.
2. Ibid., 28–29.
3. Niklas Zetterling, *Normandy 1944: German Military Organization, Combat Power and Organizational Effectiveness* (Winnipeg, ON: J.J. Fedorowicz, 2000), ch *"Infanterie-Divisionen."*
4. Helmut Ritgen, *The 6th Panzer Division, 1937–45* (London: Osprey, 1982), 12–13. The 1st Light's mission was facilitated by the attachment of a panzer regiment to the division.
5. Williamson Murray, "The German Response to Victory in Poland," *Armed Forces and Society* 7 (Winter 1981): 287–289; Robert M. Kennedy, *The German Campaign in Poland (1939)* (Washington, DC: US Army Center of Military History, 1988), 133; Richard DiNardo, "Germany's Panzer Arm: Anatomy and Performance" (PhD diss., City University of New York, 1988), 112–113.
6. Military Intelligence Service, US War Department. "Information Bulletin Number 1, German Armored Car Reconnaissance," 20 December 1941, http://www.lonesentry.com/manuals/armored-car/index.html (accessed 10 September 2007) (hereafter referred to as "German Armored Car Reconnaissance"). This document mentions organizations known as army reconnaissance battalions that "were available to each army in the field for the close reconnaissance mission." However, such organizations are not mentioned in any other available sources. Since the Germans had great difficulty in fielding reconnaissance battalions for the infantry divisions mobilized or created between August 1939 and May 1940, their existence is dubious. US military intelligence probably misevaluated similarly designated Luftwaffe air reconnaissance units with nonexisting ground units. See Heinz Guderian, *Panzer Leader*, trans. Constantine Fitzgibbon (Washington, DC: Zenger, 1952), 486, 498, 511.
7. In the early campaigns of the war, each German panzer corps had a dedicated Luftwaffe air reconnaissance element consisting of one or two units of a type known as army reconnaissance squadrons (*Staffeln*). The squadrons were usually further subtasked among the panzer divisions with a single division commander typically having direct control over about three aircraft (a flight or *Schwarm*). See Guderian, *Panzer Leader*, 511; Hermann Rothe and H. Ohrloff, "7th Panzer Division Operations," *The Initial Period of War on the Eastern Front, 22 June–August 1941: Proceedings of the Fourth Art of War Symposium, Garmisch, FRG, October 1987*, ed. Colonel David Glantz (London: Frank Cass, 1993), 389.
8. Karl-Heinz Frieser with John Greenwood, *The Blitzkrieg Legend: The 1940 Campaign in the West* (Annapolis, MD: Naval Institute Press, 2005), 240–246, 282–283. The British also led their advance into Belgium with reconnaissance troops, led by the BEF's only armored car regiment, the 12th Lancers. See Jean-Paul Pallud, *Blitzkrieg in the West: Then and Now* (London: After the Battle, 1991), 95–97.

9. Frieser, 240–246, 282–283; Pallud, *Blitzkrieg in the West*, 160–166; Ernest May, *Strange Victory: Hitler's Conquest of France* (New York: Hill and Wang, 2000), 480–483.

10. Jeffrey Gunsburg, "The Battle of the Belgian Plain, 12–14 May 1940: The First Great Tank Battle," *Journal of Military History* 56 (April 1992): 227–228, 230–231, 235, 237, 241.

11. Frieser, 226, map B5, after page 224. The French used all five of their *DLC*s in this maneuver as well as two North African *Spahi* horse cavalry brigades.

12. N. Leulliot, "The Divisions Légères de Cavalerie (DLC-Light Cavalry Divisions) Part 1: Organisations," *France 1940*, http://france1940.free.fr/oob/oob.html (accessed 24 September 2007); Frieser, 128, 142–143, 235; Pallud, *Blitzkrieg in the West*, 79–80; May, 485; Robert Doughty, *The Breaking Point: Sedan and the Fall of France, 1940* (Hamden, CT: Archon, 1990), 82–88, 92, 100.

13. Frieser, 101, 114–116.

14. Florian K. Rothbrust, *Guderian's XIXth Panzer Corps and the Battle of France: Breakthrough in the Ardennes, May 1940* (Westport, CT: Praeger, 1990), 50, 53–66; Frieser, 115; Guderian, 99.

15. Ibid.; Doughty, 220, 224. Guderian also used the 2d Infantry Division (Motorized) in this role later in the campaign. See Guderian, *Panzer Leader*, 502–503.

16. Frieser, 163, map C3 after page 322. For a detailed description of the organization and tactical employment of motorcycle units in the German Army, see H.J. von Hoffgarten and Edel Lingenthal, "11th Panzer Division Operations," *The Initial Period of War on the Eastern Front, 22 June–August 1941: Proceedings of the Fourth Art of War Symposium, Garmisch, FRG, October 1987*, ed. Colonel David Glantz (London: Frank Cass, 1993), 318–325.

17. Frieser, 119–121; Rothbrust, 53–55; May, 486; Doughty, 43–44, 51–52.

18. Pallud, *Blitzkrieg in the West*, 206–208, 214. Guderian, 100; Rothbrust, 66.

19. Freiser, 228–229, map C3 after page 322.

20. Ibid., 126–127.

21. Ibid., 129–130, 133–134; Pallud, *Blitzkrieg in the West*, 206–208, 214; Guderian, *Panzer Leader*, 100; Rothbrust, 60.

22. Frieser, 129–130, 133–134; Pallud, *Blitzkrieg in the West*, 206–208, 214; Rothbrust, 60; Doughty, 67.

23. Frieser, 129–130, 133–134, map B3 after page 224, 226; Pallud, *Blitzkrieg in the West*, 206–208, 214. Guderian, 100; May, 486–487; Doughty, 62–64.

24. Ibid.

25. Guderian, *Panzer Leader*, 486; Pallud, *Blitzkrieg in the West*, 336. In the latter work, an armored car from the 2d Panzer Division's 5th Armored Reconnaissance Battalion is shown sitting on an English Channel French beach.

26. Hans von Luck, *Panzer Commander: The Memoirs of Colonel Hans von Luck* (New York: Dell, 1991), 39; Frieser, 275–277.

27. Frieser, 281–285, map C13 after page 322.
28. Pallud, *Blitzkrieg in the West*, 176, 208, 317, 320, 325, 359. Later, mobilized German infantry division reconnaissance battalions contained no horse cavalry. Often, bicycles replaced the horses in such units.
29. "German Armored Car Reconnaissance" provides two vignettes of such operations, one with the armored reconnaissance battalion of the 9th Panzer Division leading the movement of one of the division's motorized infantry regiments. The other vignette recounts a reconnaissance raid by the 1st Panzer Division's reconnaissance battalion 35 miles east of the division's axis of advance.
30. Horst Scheibert, *Panzer Grenadier Division Grossdeutschland*, ed. Bruce Culver, trans. Gisele Hockenberry (Warren, MI: Squadron/Signal, 1977), 23; Military Intelligence Service, US War Department, "Information Bulletin No. 18, The German Armored Division," 15 June 1942, http://www.lonesentry.com/manuals/german-panzer-division.index.html (accessed 10 September 2007) (hereafter referred to as "German Armored Division"), ch 1; The Dupuy Institute, "The Historical Combat Effectiveness of Lighter-Weight Armored Forces," Final Report (McLean, VA: Dupuy Institute, 2001), 26; Matthew A. Dooley, "Ignoring History: The Flawed Effort to Divorce Reconnaissance From Security in Modern Cavalry Transformation" (MMAS thesis, US Army Command and General Staff College, 2006), 30–31.
31. Perett, 21–23; Tessin, 173, 242; Dooley, 29–30.
32. Perett, 23–24; Dooley, 33–38. Armored reconnaissance battalions often varied slightly from the standard presented due to equipment and personnel availability.
33. Peter Chamberlain and Hilary Doyle, *Encyclopedia of German Tanks of World War Two: A Complete Illustrated Directory of German Battle Tanks, Armoured Cars, Self-Propelled Guns, and Semi-Tracked Vehicles, 1933–1945* (London: Arms and Armour Press, 1993), 162, 196. The *SdKfz 251* looked similar to the *SdKfz 250*, but it had two more road wheels in its tracks and a larger cargo capacity.
34. Perett, 12, 25, 40; Dooley, 38.
35. Perett, 12–14, 40; Chamberlain and Doyle, 198–199, 202.
36. DiNardo, 116–117.
37. Lee Niehorster, *German Army Panzer and Panzergrenadier Divisions, 1943–1944*, World War II Organization and Equipment—Book 1 (Brooklyn: Enola Games, 1982), 24; Dooley, 39.
38. Pier Paolo Battistelli, *Rommel's Afrika Korps: Tobruk to El Alamein*, Battle Orders No. 20 (London: Osprey, 2006), 29–31.
39. Ibid., 21, 31, 35, 37, 38–41.
40. Luck, 98–99; Perett, 27–28, 30–34. Hans-Otto Behrendt, *Rommel's Intelligence in the Desert Campaign, 1941–1943* (London, William Kimber, 1985), 71, 73, 99. During the 1942 advance into Egypt, Luck's 3d Armored Reconnaissance Battalion was detached from its parent unit (21st Panzer Division) and placed at the Siwa Oasis covering the German panzer army's right flank during the El Alamein campaign. See Luck, 109, 115.

41. Luck, 95, 100, 117–120. Samuel Mitchum, *Rommel's Desert War: The Life and Death of the Afrika Korps* (New York: Stein and Day, 1982), 40–41, 44, 72–73, 103–106, 147–149, 177; Behrendt, 34.

42. Ibid. During the retreat, Luck's battalion frequently sparred with two British army-level reconnaissance regiments, the 11th Hussars and the 1st Kings Dragoon Guards, and the special operations unit, the Long Range Desert Group.

43. Luck, 141–142, 144.

44. Heinz Guderian, "III Panzer Corps Operations, "*The Initial Period of War on the Eastern Front, 22 June–August 1941: Proceedings of the Fourth Art of War Symposium, Garmisch, FRG, October 1987*, ed. Colonel David Glantz (London: Frank Cass, 1993), 315; Perett, 24–26; Rothe and Ohrloff, 388; Luck, 76–77.

45. Luck, 73; Perett, 24–26; Horst Zobel, "3rd Panzer Division Operations," *The Initial Period of War on the Eastern Front, 22 June–August 1941: Proceedings of the Fourth Art of War Symposium, Garmisch, FRG, October 1987*, ed. Colonel David Glantz (London: Frank Cass, 1993), 241, 243; Hoffgarten and Lingenthal, 327–332. In the 7th Panzer Division, the motorcycle and reconnaissance battalions were merged under one commander from July to December 1941. See Luck, 74.

46. Gerd Niepold, "Conclusions From the German Perspective," *The Initial Period of War on the Eastern Front, 22 June–August 1941: Proceedings of the Fourth Art of War Symposium, Garmisch, FRG, October 1987*, ed. Colonel David Glantz (London: Frank Cass, 1993), 471; Zobel, 393; A.D. von Plato and R.O. Stoves, "1st Panzer Division Operations," *The Initial Period of War on the Eastern Front, 22 June–August 1941: Proceedings of the Fourth Art of War Symposium, Garmisch, FRG, October 1987*, ed. Colonel David Glantz (London: Frank Cass, 1993), 145.

47. Horst Ohrloff, "XXXIX Motorized Corps Operations," *The Initial Period of War on the Eastern Front, 22 June–August 1941: Proceedings of the Fourth Art of War Symposium, Garmisch, FRG, October 1987*, ed. Colonel David Glantz (London: Frank Cass, 1993), 180; Perett, 24–26; Plato and Stoves, 133, 145, 147, 149; Rothe and Ohrloff, 389; Luck 71, 81.

48. Earl F. Ziemke and Magna E. Bauer, *Moscow to Stalingrad: Decision in the East* (Washington, DC: US Army Center of Military History, 1987), 375, 482; Paul Carrell, *Hitler Moves East, 1941–1943: The Nazis' Surprise Attack on the Russo-German Border*, trans. Ewald Osers (New York: Ballantine, 1971), 565–566.

49. George Nafziger, *The German Order of Battle: Infantry in World War II* (Mechanicsburg, PA: Stackpole, 2000), 31, 43, 141.

50. US War Department, Technical Manual (TM-E) 30-451, *Handbook on German Military Forces* (Washington, DC: War Department, 1945), I-83, II-84; Nafziger, 32.

51. TM-E 30-451, *Handbook on German Military Forces*, II-84.

52. Ibid.; Zetterling, ch "*Infanterie-Divisionen*"; Bruce Quarrie, *The Ardennes Offensive VI Panzer Armee Northern Sector*, Order of Battle Series No. 4 (London: Osprey, 1999), 40–41, 81.

53. A good example of this from the Fifth Panzer Army was the Panzer *Lehr* Division. The divisional reconnaissance battalion, under Major Gerd von Fallois, was formed into a task force (*kampfgruppe*) consisting of the reconnaissance battalion, reinforced with a company each of panzergrenadiers, tanks, antitank guns, and engineers. The *kampfgruppe* led the leftmost (southernmost) column of the division and, at most points in the advance, was in front of the other divisional elements. See Jean Paul Pallud, *Battle of the Bulge: Then and Now* (London: After the Battle Magazine, 1984), 77, 255, 363, 365.

54. Quarrie, 28, 32, 35; Bruce Quarrie, *The Ardennes Offensive V US Corps & XVIII US (Airborne) Corps Northern Sector*, Order of Battle Series No. 5 (London: Osprey, 1999), 55–57. The 1st SS Division's reconnaissance battalion is featured prominently in a series of famous photographs taken during its initial advance to the west. See Pallud, *Battle of the Bulge: Then and Now*, 154–159.

55. Quarrie, *The Ardennes Offensive VI Panzer Armee Northern Sector*, 65, 67, 70–71, 74–76; Quarrie, *The Ardennes Offensive V US Corps & XVIII US (Airborne) Corps Northern Sector*, 88–89.

56. In the two armored divisions that retained the older "heavy" organization, an armored reconnaissance troop was at the regimental level. See US Forces, European Theater, General Board, "Organization, Equipment and Tactical Employment of the Armored Division," Study No. 48 (Bad Nauheim, GE, 1945–46) (hereafter referred as the General Board, "Armored Division"), app. 1; Major Richard Runde, "The Intelligence and Reconnaissance Platoon" (MMAS thesis, US Army Command and General Staff College, 1994), 20–23; Christopher R. Gabel, *Seek, Strike, and Destroy: US Army Tank Destroyer Doctrine in World War II*, Leavenworth Papers No. 12 (Fort Leavenworth, KS: Combat Studies Institute, US Army Command and General Staff College, 1985), 21, 25, 45.

57. Matthew D. Morton, "Men on 'Iron Ponies': The Death and Rebirth of the Modern US Cavalry" (PhD diss., Florida State University, 2004), 232, 339; James Sawicki, *Cavalry Regiments of the US Army* (Dumfries, VA: Wyvern Publications, 1985), 118; Shelby L. Stanton, *Order of Battle, U.S. Army, World War II* (Novato, CA: Presidio, 1984), 312–313.

58. Ibid.; US Forces, European Theater, General Board, "Tactics, Employment, Technique, Organization, and Equipment of Mechanized Cavalry Units," Study Number 49 (Bad Nauheim, GE, 1945–46) (hereafter referred as General Board, "Mechanized Cavalry Units"), app. 3, 15; Stanton, 5–6.

59. General Board, "Mechanized Cavalry Units," app. 3, 16. The only exception to the concept of cavalry groups being placed under corps control was General George Patton's use of the 6th Cavalry Group as the information service for the Third Army headquarters for 179 days in 1944. See the previous reference in this note and John J. McGrath, *Crossing the Line of Departure: Battle Command on the Move: A Historical Perspective* (Fort Leavenworth, KS: Combat Studies Institute Press, 2006), 106.

60. General Board, "Mechanized Cavalry Units," app. 22; Morton, 337.

61. Morton, 337; General Board, "Mechanized Cavalry Units," app. 4, 4.

62. General Board, "Mechanized Cavalry Units," 5–6.

63. General Board, "Mechanized Cavalry Units," 7, app. 3, 9. Special operations in this context included rear area security and mobile reserve missions. See General Board, "Mechanized Cavalry Units," app. 5, 2.

64. Ibid., app. 3, 9.

65. John B. Wilson, *Maneuver and Firepower: The Evolution of Divisions and Separate Brigades* (Washington, DC: US Army Center of Military History, 1998), 169, 192; Ron Klages and John Mulholland, "Number of German Divisions by Front in World War II," http://www.axishistory.com/index.php?id=728 (accessed 12 October 2007). The US population in 1940 was 132 million. The German population was 79.4 million. See US Bureau of the Census, "Statistical Abstract of the United States, 1940," http://www2.census.gov/prod2/statcomp/documents/1941-02.pdf (accessed 12 October 2007); "1940 Population Estimates for European Countries," *Population Index* 8 (April 1942), 78–82.

66. Hugh Cole, *The Ardennes: Battle of the Bulge*, United States Army in World War II, The European Theater of Operations (Washington, DC: US Army Center of Military History, 1965), 137–139.

67. Ibid., 139, 145–147.

68. Ibid., 142; Quarrie, *The Ardennes Offensive VI Panzer Armee Northern Sector*, 51–53.

69. Cole, 146–148.

70. Ibid., 149.

71. Ibid, 149–150.

72. Ibid., 161–164, 281; Quarrie, *The Ardennes Offensive VI Panzer Armee Northern Sector*, 51–53.

73. General Board, "Mechanized Cavalry Units," app. 6.

74. The equivalent units in the heavy armored divisions (2d and 3d Armored Divisions) were called an armored reconnaissance battalion. See General Board, "Mechanized Cavalry Units." 6.

75. Morton, 338.

76. General Board, "Armored Division," app. 1.

77. Morton, 346–347.

78. General Board, "Mechanized Cavalry Units," 8, app. 4, 2, app. 14, 15.

79. Morton, 202, 204, 208–209, 287; General Board, "Mechanized Cavalry Units," 8, 21, app. 13, app. 5.

80. Morton, 208–209; Runde, 20–22.

81. David Myers, compiler and ed., *Unit Organizations of World War II: Tables of Organization and Equipment (T.O.E.)* (Milwaukee, WI: Z&M Enterprises, 1983), 14; James Sawicki, *Tank Battalions of the US Army* (Dumfries, VA: Wyvern, 1983), 16; Gabel, 21, 45, 47; US War Department, Table of Organization and Equipment No. 5-15, *Headquarters and Headquarters and Service Company, Engineer Combat Battalion* (Washington, DC: War Department, 13 March 1944), sec 1. Towed tank destroyer battalions maintained two reconnaissance platoons in their headquarters company rather than a separate company.

82. Gordon Rottman, *US Marine Corps World War II Order of Battle: Ground and Air Units in the Pacific War, 1939–1945* (Westport, CT: Greenwood Press, 2002), 182.

83. Ibid., 184.

84. Ibid.

85. Ibid., 183–184.

86. Morton, 3–4, 10–11; General Board, "Mechanized Cavalry Units," 9.

87. General Board, "Mechanized Cavalry Units," 13.

88. Morton, 353; *The American Arsenal: The World War II Official Standard Ordnance Catalog of Artillery, Small Arms, Tanks, Armored Cars, Artillery, Antiaircraft Guns, Ammunition, Grenades, Mines, Et Cetera* (Mechanicsburg, PA: Stackpole, 1996), 75.

89. *The American Arsenal*, 66, 75.

90. Myers, 28, 30–31.

91. Luck, 124–125; Jonathan M. House, *Toward Combined Arms Warfare: A Survey of 20th-Century Tactics, Doctrine, and Organization*, Research Survey Number 2 (Fort Leavenworth, KS: Combat Studies Institute, US Army Command and General Staff College, 1984), 95–96.

92. House, 100–103; Myers, 76–78.

93. House, 122–123.

94. General Board, "Mechanized Cavalry Units," app. 10.

Chapter 4

Reconnaissance Units and Operations, 1945–2005

Introduction

After World War II, mechanization expanded greatly, particularly among the forces of the North Atlantic Treaty Organization (NATO) and the Soviet bloc. The mechanized forces were generally expected to be used only on postulated Cold War battlefields. During the Cold War, mechanized battles were only fought in the series of Arab-Israeli conflicts between 1956 and 1973. Meanwhile, the United States participated in two nonmechanized wars in Korea and Vietnam, while the Soviets used mechanized forces in the rugged terrain of Afghanistan. The development of the helicopter in the 1950s and 1960s produced a new dimension for debate in the organization of reconnaissance units. In addition to helicopters, armored vehicle and weapons technology continued to improve with the fielding of better tanks and armored fighting vehicles. Since the end of the Cold War, US forces have fought in two major campaigns involving reconnaissance units in Iraq. After the last of these, the US Army conducted an organizational restructuring that included a major transformation of reconnaissance forces. This chapter examines these issues and their relation to the historical development of reconnaissance units between 1945 and 2005.

Reconnaissance and the Israeli Defense Force

The Israeli armed forces fought four wars with hostile neighboring Arab powers between 1948 and 1973. In the last three, the Israeli Defense Force (IDF) deployed motorized and mechanized reconnaissance forces in various configurations. The Israeli experience is important because IDF reconnaissance unit design was based on practical experience. Additionally, differing from the US and German experiences in World War II, Israeli reconnaissance forces spent much of their time conducting reconnaissance operations in 1956, 1967, and 1973. Figure 33 shows the Sinai theater of operations where the actions discussed in this work took place in 1956, 1967, and 1973.

Reconnaissance Unit Organization to 1973

The Israeli Defense Force fought the 1948–49 War of Independence with a primarily infantry force. The earliest IDF reconnaissance units were composed of infantry scouts in jeeps from the Nahal local defense organization. As the IDF developed as a military organization in the 1950s, it remained mostly an infantry force, but after receiving a hodgepodge of foreign equipment, it began fielding several armored brigades. The

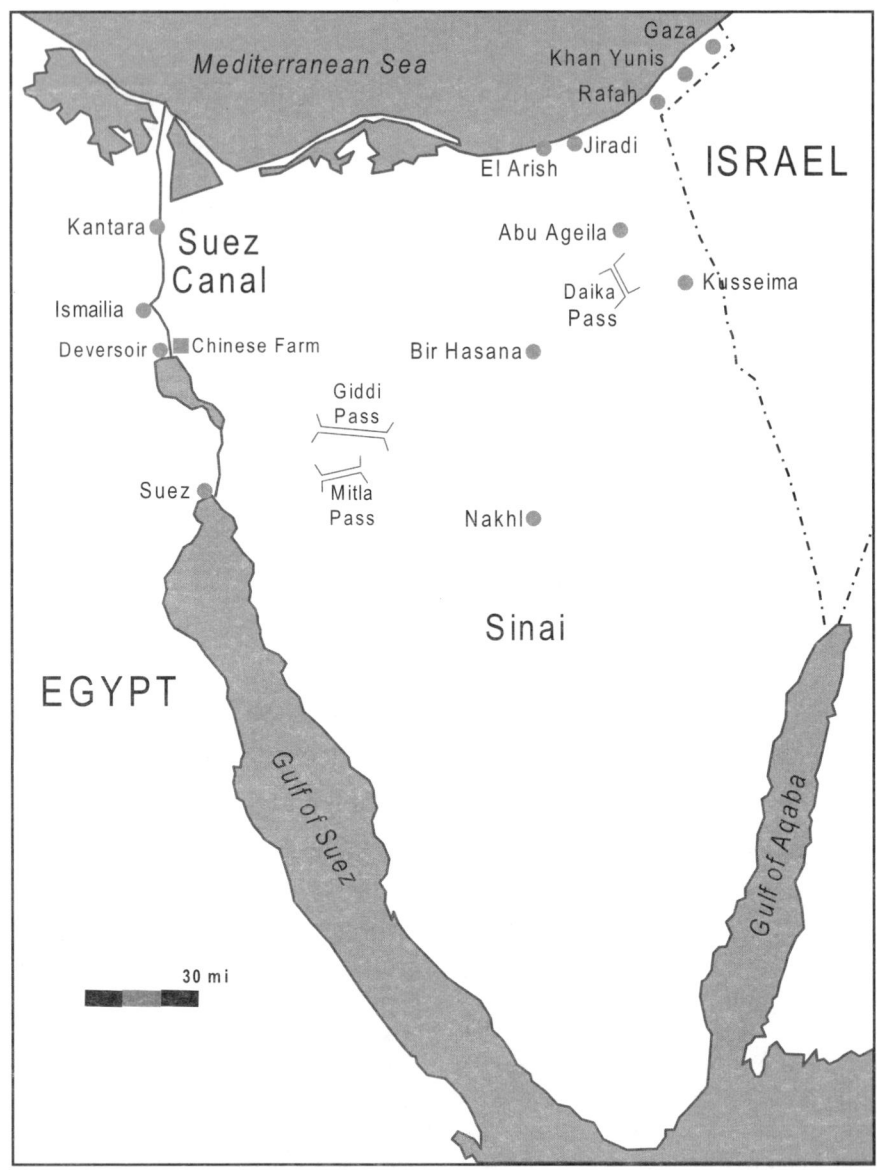

Figure 33. The Sinai theater of operations, 1956 and 1967.

infantry brigades and the early Israeli armored brigades contained a scout company mounted on jeeps as the reconnaissance element. Although the Israelis used division task force headquarters for operations in both 1956 and 1967, the brigade remained the basic operational unit of the IDF until 1973.[1]

By 1956, the scout jeeps in the reconnaissance companies in both infantry and armored brigades were equipped with US antitank recoilless rifles and machine guns. For the October–November 1956 Sinai campaign, the IDF fielded three armored brigades, six infantry brigades, and a paratrooper brigade. Two division task force headquarters controlled the bulk of these forces. However, in 1956, almost all reconnaissance assets were at the brigade level. These jeep companies played a key role in the 1956 Sinai campaign.[2]

Before the 1956 campaign, the IDF had received a number of French AMX-13 light tanks, which were designed for reconnaissance. However, in 1956, the Israelis used them as main battle tanks, partially equipping a tank battalion in the 7th Armored Brigade with the light tanks and supporting paratroopers. Reconnaissance units remained exclusively equipped with jeeps. Occasionally, commanders teamed the AMX-13s with the jeep units.[3]

After leading the brigade's two-pronged advance into the Sinai, the 7th Brigade's reconnaissance company played a decisive role on 30 October 1956 in the key action at Abu Ageila in the central Sinai sector. The company managed to maneuver through deep sand and discover that the key Daika Pass was held only by a small force of Egyptian engineers who fled when the Israelis arrived. The company secured the pass, allowing combat elements of the brigade to pass through and surround the Egyptian defensive position.[4]

Throughout the 100-hour campaign, brigade reconnaissance companies, sometimes split into platoon-sized forces, led IDF advances, both armored and infantry. For example, the 4th Infantry Brigade, operating as part of the action at Abu Ageila, made extensive use of its scouts in advance of its movement on the Egyptian position at Kusseima. This same brigade subsequently detached its reconnaissance company, reinforced with one infantry company mounted on half-tracks and another in busses, to the southwest to link up with paratroopers at Nakhl. While the bus company could not negotiate the sandy terrain, the other two companies joined the paratroopers within several hours.[5]

The 27th Armored Brigade, which assaulted Rafah at the western edge of the Gaza Strip, organized its subordinate battalions into three tank-mechanized infantry task forces, each of which contained a platoon from the brigade reconnaissance company. As this operation was a deliberate assault against entrenched enemy infantry, the jeep platoons did not play a major role. After the Egyptian positions withdrew from Rafah, the 27th Brigade immediately advanced to the west into the Sinai, leading its

Figure 34. Israeli AMX-13 light tank.

advance to the Suez Canal with a task force that was equipped with AMX-13 tanks.[6]

After the success of the 1956 campaign, the Israeli authorities decided to convert the IDF into a primarily armored and mechanized force. This transformation took place in the years between the 1956 and 1967 conflicts. Tanks were upgraded with the Israelis obtaining their first modern tanks, British Centurions and US M48 Pattons. Additionally, the IDF expanded along with the Israeli population from roughly 190,000 to 250,000, with 70,000 of this force earmarked for the Sinai as opposed to 45,000 in 1956. Although brigades still remained the basic units, the IDF armored corps began focusing on divisional operations after 1956. Peacetime exercises began including the employment of divisional headquarters.[7]

Divisions were still considered to be somewhat informal task forces working under theater commands to control the operations of several brigades. Of the four division task forces used by the IDF in 1967, only Brigadier General Ariel Sharon's division in the central Sinai sector had reconnaissance assets attached to it. This battalion-sized command contained a mixture of AMX-13 tanks, jeep-mounted scouts, and half-track mounted mortars.[8]

Sharon used his force to cover the left (southern) flank of his advance on Abu Ageila. Near the end of the campaign, Brigadier General Yisrael Tal, commanding the *Ugdat ha'Plada* or Steel Division in northern Sinai, created a division-level reconnaissance force called Granit Force from his brigade's reconnaissance forces and various other units and sent it westward to Kantara and the Suez Canal. At the canal, reconnaissance troops equipped with recoilless rifles teamed with tanks to envelop and destroy an Egyptian force just east of the canal.[9]

Division commanders primarily depended on the reconnaissance companies of their brigades to conduct such operations. Brigade reconnaissance companies were upgraded between 1956 and 1967. While the jeeps with machine guns and 106-mm recoilless rifles remained the mainstay, forming a platoon each, a platoon of half-tracked armored personnel carriers now became part of the company. The half-tracks mounted a combination of antitank guns, .50-caliber machine guns, and 20-mm cannons.[10]

As part of Tal's division, the 7th Armored Brigade's 643d Reconnaissance Company led the assault on Khan Yunis in the Gaza Strip at the start of the Sinai campaign. This company's experience offers a good example of using brigade reconnaissance elements in the 1967 war (figure 35). As the reconnaissance unit for the only regular armored brigade in the IDF at the time, it played a prominent role in Tal's operations. For combat operations, the company commander, Captain Ori Orr, usually reorganized his platoons into three combat teams each with a mix of half-tracks, machine-gun jeeps, and 106-mm jeeps. The 7th Brigade opened hostilities in Tal's sector by an attack in a single column with its battalions lined up one after the other, with one of Orr's teams leading, supported by a tank battalion. The bulk of the reconnaissance company followed the tanks. Colonel Shmuel Gonen, the brigade commander, used a single column so the reconnaissance troops could clear a path through Egyptian minefields. The brigade had the mission of penetrating the Egyptian and Palestinian defensive belt at a relatively weak point and then swinging south to outflank the rest of the fortified positions. The column broke into the Egyptian positions in an urban area. While some fighting continued near Khan Yunis, the bulk of the brigade turned to the southwest in two battalion columns. Supported by two tanks, Orr's company, minus a team leading a follow-on battalion's advance, moved to the tactically important Rafah Junction, south of Rafah, as the brigade movement's lead element. The reconnaissance unit drove into the middle of an Egyptian position at the crossroads and was ambushed by elements of an enemy armored

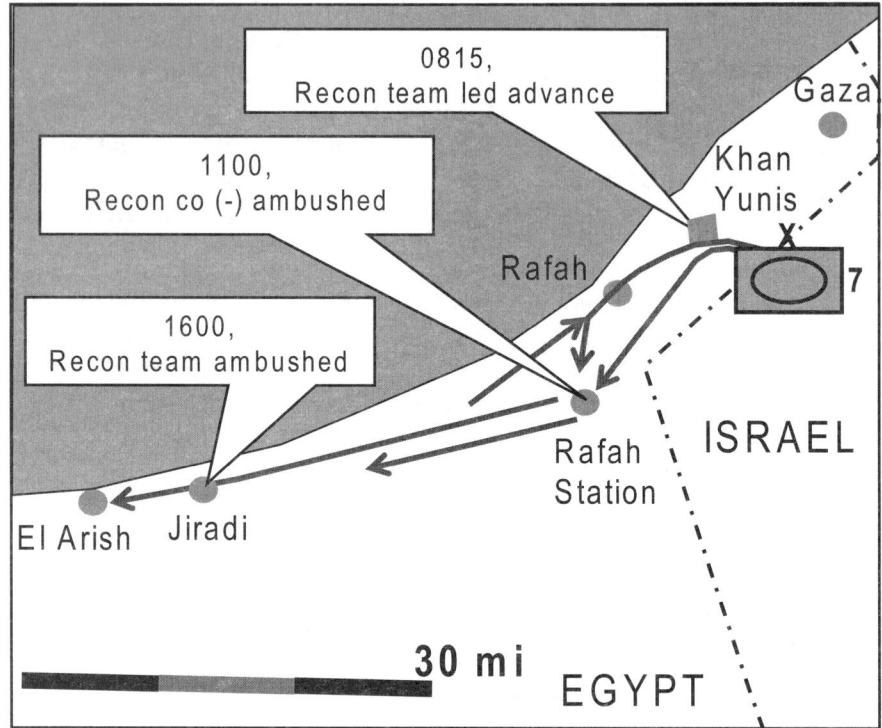

Figure 35. IDF 643d Reconnaissance Company, 5 June 1967.

brigade. Orr aggressively counterattacked and, after heavy casualties and close combat, compelled the Egyptians to retreat. The rest of the 7th Brigade, along with elements from Tal's other brigades, attacked the junction position from the north and south.[11]

The brigade then broke through the enemy defenses and turned west. The reorganized reconnaissance company led the advance of several columns. The fastest column, under the brigade's deputy commander, Lieutenant Colonel Baruch Harel, shifted its light reconnaissance team to the middle of the column, letting the tanks lead. As the column advanced toward El Arish, it passed through an area of rugged terrain near a railroad station called Jiradi. The Egyptians were defending this area in strength but were so stunned by the sudden appearance of Israeli tanks more than 30 miles inside Egyptian territory that they let the tanks pass. By the time the reconnaissance team passed through, the Egyptians had regained their composure and opened fire and destroyed the scout jeeps. The reconnaissance survivors dismounted and hid behind sand dunes while the rest of Harel's column fought through the Egyptian position and continued to El Arish. Brigade commander Gonen soon came up and organized a deliberate attack against the Jiradi position by the time the next tank battalion arrived. The battalion forced its way through to El Arish, with its commander getting killed in the process. But the Egyptians still held their position, and Gonen used his armored infantry battalion in a midnight attack, which finally ejected the Egyptians from the position.[12]

When the IDF Southern Command brought into action a third divisional force between those of Tal and Sharon to exploit Sharon's breakthrough at Abu Ageila, the lead brigade led with its reconnaissance company. On the morning of 6 June, Gonen's brigade, the spearhead of Tal's division, was at El Arish, halfway to the Suez Canal. While Tal sent out the Granit Force to Kantara, the 7th Brigade spent the next 2 days fighting through Egyptian positions on the central Sinai axis. On the evening of 8 June, Tal decided to send the remnants of Orr's company, reinforced with two tank platoons and an artillery battery, to the canal as the spearhead of the advance of the division's main body. Orr's task force successfully reached the canal opposite Ismailia shortly after midnight on 9 June. The reconnaissance troopers watched the last of the Egyptian tanks cross the canal over a bridge. Orr moved northward along the canal and linked up with Granit Force halfway between Ismailia and Kantara. This effectively ended the Sinai campaign of 1967.[13]

The IDF 1973 Armored Reconnaissance Battalion and Company

Up until 1967, divisions in the IDF had been expedient organizations. By 1973, however, seven armored divisions were organized for wartime mobilization. Each division contained an organic reconnaissance battalion. The new battalion organization, as well as the preexisting brigade reconnaissance company, was heavier than the units used in the 1967 war.

An analysis of the operations of reconnaissance forces in the 1967 war led to a reassessment of the composition of reconnaissance forces. One of the IDF's major lessons from the 1967 battles was that reconnaissance forces were too light to survive on the battlefield. Units equipped with jeeps, half-tracks, and light tanks took heavy losses in action at places like Rafah Junction and Jiradi. The AMX-13 tank was too lightly armored and gunned for both a main battle and a reconnaissance role and was completely phased out of the IDF inventory. Units equipped with jeeps took heavy losses when encountering unavoidable firefights. Therefore, between 1967 and 1973, the IDF upgraded its reconnaissance units at the brigade and division levels. For the most part, the IDF replaced antiquated World War

II half-tracks with modern US M113s (Zeldas in Israeli terminology), fully tracked armored personnel carriers (APCs). In the most dramatic shift, main battle tanks replaced jeep-mounted recoilless rifles.[14]

As a result, by 1973, each IDF armored brigade fielded an armored reconnaissance company consisting of a platoon of main battle tanks and two platoons of scouts mounted in M113 APCs or half-tracks. The divisional reconnaissance battalion (figure 36) contained three reconnaissance companies, each with a mix of tanks and scout APCs. The battalion also included a scout company with jeeps and a maintenance and medical platoon.[15]

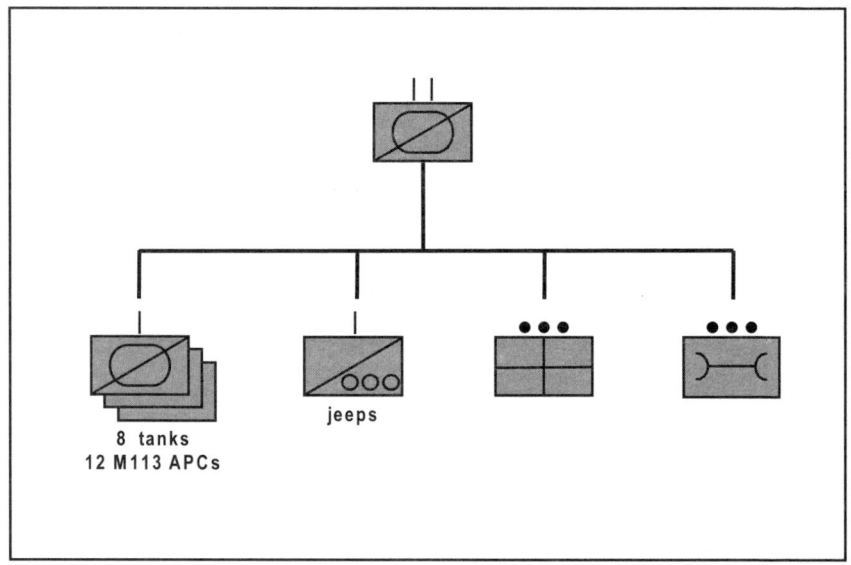

Figure 36. IDF armored reconnaissance battalion, 1973.

In the 1973 Yom Kippur War, various commanders used their reconnaissance units in different ways. Major General Avraham Adan, commander of an armored division on the Sinai front, fought the whole war without his divisional reconnaissance battalion. It was detached to an ad hoc task force defending the extreme northern sector of the front and never returned to divisional control. The 7th Armored Brigade in the Golan used its scouts to flesh out the strength of its mechanized infantry battalion.[16]

One unit, the 87th Armored Reconnaissance Battalion of Major General Ariel Sharon's 143d Armored Division, played a conspicuous role in the operations in the Sinai (figure 37). The IDF organized the battalion in the reserve in May 1973, and it participated in a division-level exercise before the war began. After the Egyptians commenced hostilities, the unit mobilized and then moved to the Sinai theater on its own tracks. During the disastrous series of IDF maneuvers on 8 October, the 87th Battalion remained behind to hold a key position on the southern flank of Adan's division while Sharon moved his forces to the south and back. The battalion fought alone against a large Egyptian attack, in which

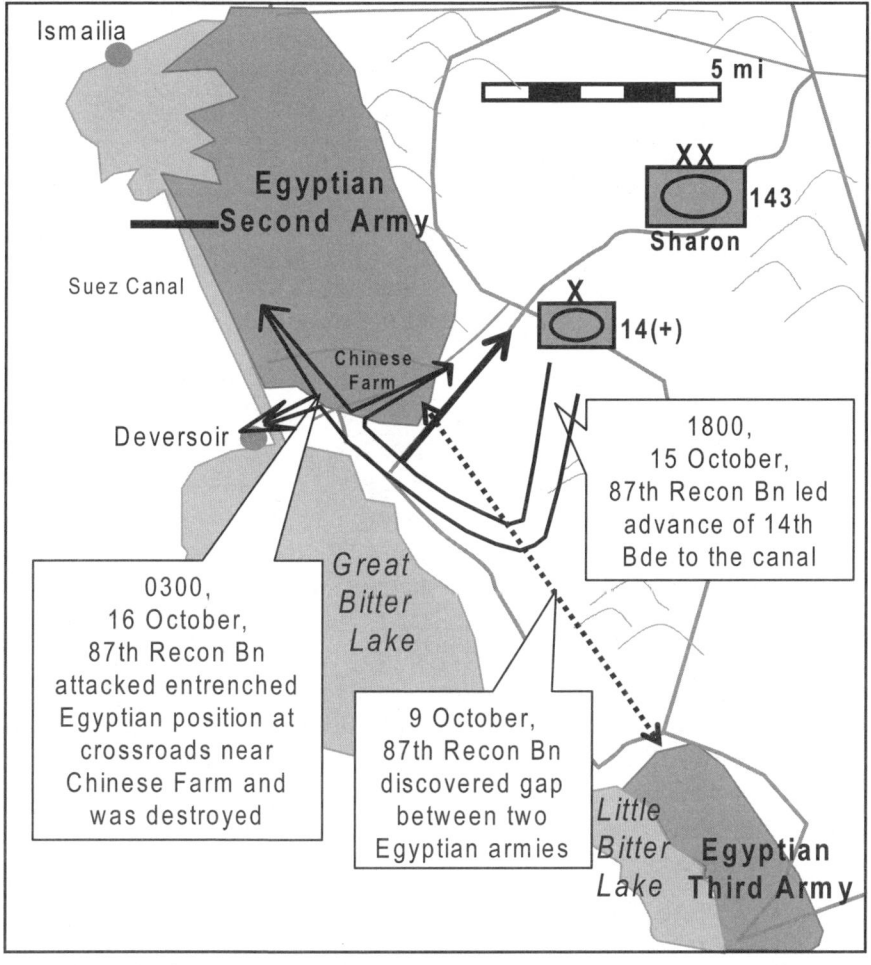

Figure 37. IDF 87th Armored Reconnaissance Battalion in the 1973 Yom Kippur War.

the battalion commander was killed by mortar fire, until Sharon's forces returned to repulse the attackers.[17]

The battalion was then withdrawn behind the front to reorganize. The new battalion commander was Major Yoav Brom. Under Brom, the battalion spent the evening of 9–10 October scouting the Egyptian positions opposite Sharon's division. During this mission, Brom discovered that the enemy bridgeheads on the east bank of the Suez Canal were not joined to each other (figure 37). The battalion was able to reach the shore of the Great Bitter Lake without encountering any Egyptians. The Egyptian Second Army in the northern portion of the Sinai had an open southern flank.[18]

On 14 October, the Egyptians launched a frontwide armored attack. The 87th covered the flank of Sharon's division and participated in the repulse of the attack.

Immediately following this success, the Israelis put into motion their complicated plan for crossing the Suez Canal. This operation used the gap discovered on the 9th to send Sharon's division to secure a crossing site opposite Deversoir, where the canal flowed into the Great Bitter Lake. Sharon's units would send paratroopers across to the far bank while securing the general area of the crossing for follow-on troops from Adan's division. Sharon reinforced his lead unit, the 14th Armored Brigade, to eight battalions, with the 87th first in the column.[19]

The advance began at 1800 on 15 October. Brom led the column along the route he had taken 6 days earlier. By 2100, the column had reached the canal at the crossing site without making any contact with Egyptian forces. Brom's battalion advanced along the east bank of the canal and covered the northern flank of the crossing site. Meanwhile, to the east, several Israeli tank battalions were fighting for their lives to secure a key crossroads in the midst of the defensive positions of the Egyptian 16th Infantry and 21st Armored Divisions. After a series of failed assaults, at 0300 on 16 October, the 14th Brigade ordered Brom to assault the same objective. As the first Israeli paratroopers crossed to the west bank of the Suez Canal, Brom attacked. The 87th advanced from west to east, a new direction for the Egyptian defenders. However, the results were the same. Multiple volleys of rocket-propelled grenade (RPG) and small-arms fire annihilated the reconnaissance unit. Brom was killed within 30 yards of the crossroads when his tank was destroyed.[20]

The remnants of the battalion fought for survival through the night. The Israelis finally took the crossroads the next morning. The 14th Brigade distributed the survivors of the 87th among the various tank battalions of the brigade. For the remainder of the war, the unit ceased to exist. Directly after the cease-fire, the 87th was reestablished, equipped with APCs and jeeps, some equipped with the tube-launched, optically tracked wire-guided (TOW) antitank missile system. After IDF forces were withdrawn from the Sinai in 1982, the battalion was disbanded.[21]

Since 1973

As in the case of the 87th Battalion, after the 1973 war, the IDF disbanded its divisional reconnaissance battalions even though it expanded its divisional forces. Reconnaissance emphasis returned to the brigade level where the reconnaissance company was expanded to a battalion. However, the battalion still only controlled a single reconnaissance company. The bulk of the unit consisted of an antitank company, an engineer company, and a signal company.[22]

In addition to unit reconnaissance organizations, the IDF also raised a number of small elite reconnaissance detachments known as *sayeret* units. These forces, usually of battalion strength, were more akin to US Army Ranger or long-range patrol units than conventional reconnaissance organizations. *Sayeret* units operated directly under the high command or theater commander's orders. By the 21st century, each IDF infantry brigade had its own *sayeret* unit, while the conventional brigade reconnaissance battalion increasingly trained on special operations techniques and counterinsurgency.[23]

The Soviet Experience

After World War II, the Soviets maintained large land forces for more than 40 years. During the Cold War, the Red Army was only used operationally in several eastern European incursions (Hungary 1956, Czechoslovakia 1968) and in Afghanistan from 1979 to 1989. A look at Soviet reconnaissance unit operations, therefore, by necessity is primarily concerned with doctrinal and organizational developments.

Organizational Structure

After 1945, the Soviets eventually motorized and mechanized their entire army and eliminated all remaining horse cavalry units. By the 1970s, almost every operational element rode in a wheeled or tracked armored vehicle. In addition, large reconnaissance units disappeared from the Soviet force structure. By 1984, the Red Army had no reconnaissance units larger than battalion size. Tank and motorized rifle divisions contained a reconnaissance battalion. Tank and motorized rifle regiments contained a reconnaissance company. At levels above division, the only reconnaissance unit deployed was a long-range reconnaissance company.[24]

The basic operational units in the Soviet Army during the latter part of the Cold War were tank and motorized rifle divisions. Each division contained a reconnaissance battalion equipped with 12 BMP armored fighting vehicles, 12 BRDM armored cars, and 6 tanks. Figure 38 shows the organizational structure of this unit. The battalion had a headquarters and service company and four reconnaissance companies. Two of the companies contained two reconnaissance platoons, each equipped with three BMP armored fighting vehicles with scouts and a tank platoon of three tanks. The third reconnaissance company was equipped with two platoons (three vehicles each) of BRDM wheeled scout cars and a motorcycle platoon (24 cycles). The fourth company was a radio/radar reconnaissance unit. This company had specialized radio and radar interception equipment mounted on trucks and operated out of the division rear area. By the late 1980s, the Soviets had added a fifth company, a long-range reconnaissance unit of five teams, to the divisional reconnaissance battalion.[25]

The BMP was a fully tracked armored fighting vehicle with a turret-mounted 73-mm gun and Sagger antitank guided missile launcher. Apart from a three-man crew, the BMP also carried up to nine scouts. The

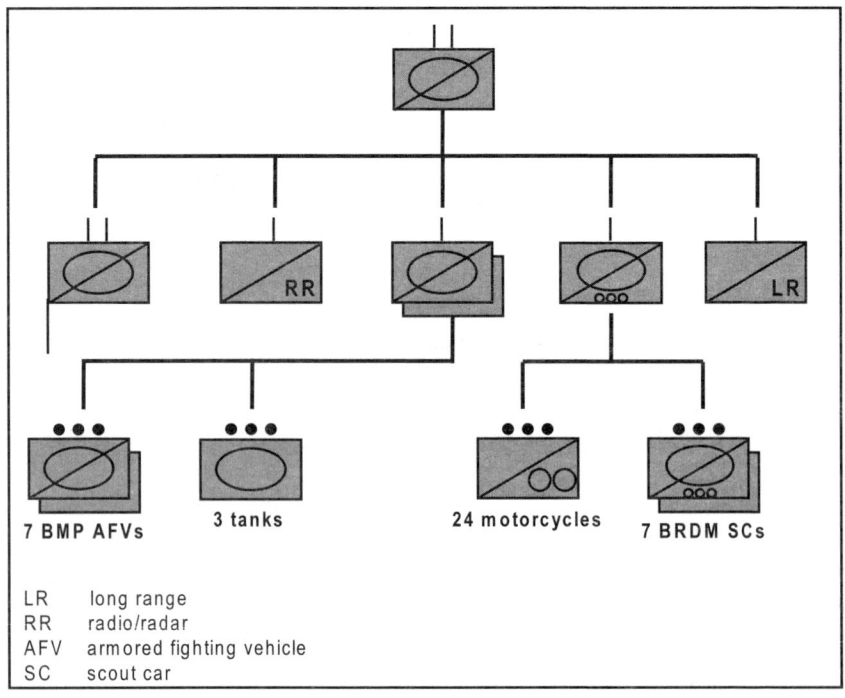

Figure 38. Soviet divisional reconnaissance battalion.

BRDM was a four-wheeled armored vehicle with two turret-mounted machine guns and a crew of four scouts. The BRDM had superseded the motorcycle in the longer range reconnaissance role, with the motorcycles being retained for courier-type duties.[26]

The two tank platoons in the reconnaissance battalion formerly contained PT-76 light amphibious tanks that the Soviets used in the reconnaissance role from the mid-1950s to the late 1970s. The Soviets designed this vehicle using the same chassis later found on the BMP, based on World War II experience. Red Army analysts believed there was a need for a light tank capable of conducting river crossings and supporting reconnaissance operations. The PT-76 mounted a 76-mm gun. The light tank's shortcomings, primarily its light armor and lack of firepower, resulted in it being replaced in the reconnaissance role with a heavier tank in the 1980s. By 1988, most Soviet reconnaissance battalions contained main battle tanks (usually the latest model T-72s) similar to those found in divisional tank regiments.[27]

Every motorized rifle and tank regiment in the Soviet Army also contained a reconnaissance company. The company had a platoon each of BMPs and BRDMs and a section of three motorcycles (figure 39). The Red Army leadership planned to use its reconnaissance battalions and companies as part of larger formations that were part of the regimental and divisional combat formations.

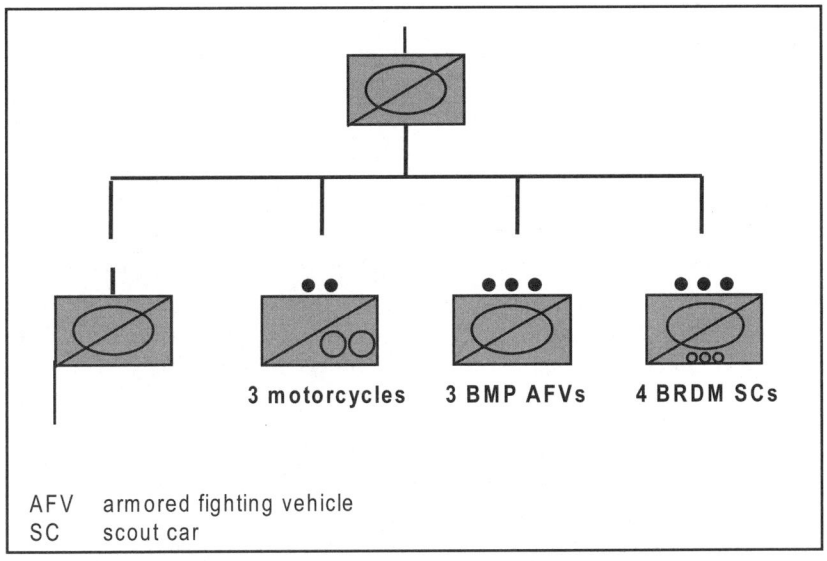

Figure 39. Soviet regimental reconnaissance company.

Figure 40. Soviet reconnaissance vehicles: the PT-76 light tank (left), BRDM-22 (right).

At the field army level (roughly equivalent to a US corps), the Soviets fielded a long-range reconnaissance company. Each divisional battalion also contained such a company. These elite units were lightly armed and had a range from 30 to 200 miles in front of friendly forces to either attack a high-priority target or to develop information without a fight. Companies from second-echelon divisions conducted the shallower missions, while army assets were tasked with the more distant assignments.[28]

Operational Employment

The Soviets did not design or intend to use their reconnaissance units for any missions except reconnaissance. Emphasis was on scouting not fighting. Retaining motorcycles in the reconnaissance role reflected this viewpoint. Scouts were trained to act aggressively and fight only if the enemy element was itself conducting reconnaissance and/or was smaller than the Soviet force. While scout forces could dismount, the ubiquity of armored vehicles made mounted scouting the norm.[29]

Throughout the Cold War, the Soviets maintained a large mass army based on conscription. With the bulk of the force consisting of short-term nonprofessionals, the Red Army developed two interlinked concepts—formations and echelons—to implement its operational doctrine. For most types of operations, particularly offensive ones, the Soviets organized their forces into formations based on general functions. The formations were then echeloned into several attack waves.[30]

The basic building block of the Soviet offensive formation was the division. In a march formation, a division formed several functional elements: a forward detachment, flank security forces, the main body, and the rear body. If the division was advancing on several axes, each column would have these elements. The forward detachment was the lead element and was a task-organized combined arms force usually consisting of about one-third of the column's combat power. Each forward detachment contained a reconnaissance detachment that advanced in front of it. Although the Soviets did not field reconnaissance units above the division level, the primary use of divisional reconnaissance battalions was in the operational role, similar to that of the Wehrmacht. In Soviet doctrine, the divisional reconnaissance battalion usually advanced in front of each divisional column about 1 to 2 hours march (up to 30 miles) in front of the main body. The battalion's scout cars were considered capable of longer range reconnaissance, out to 60 miles, and were to be so employed. Regimental reconnaissance companies preceded the main bodies of their regiments by up to 15 miles, spread out across the 6- to 10-mile-wide regimental sector.[31]

Behind these frontmost reconnaissance detachments, each forward detachment placed an element called the combat reconnaissance patrol (CRP) to its immediate front, roughly 3 to 6 miles to the front. Despite its name, the CRP did not consist of reconnaissance troops but, typically, a combined arms force of tanks and motorized infantry of about company size taken from the units forming the forward detachment. An advancing Soviet force of division size would have deployed three echelons of reconnaissance elements (excluding any long-range reconnaissance units): the divisional reconnaissance element (out to 30 miles), the regimental reconnaissance element (out to 15 miles), and the forward detachment's CRP (out to 6 miles). The purpose of the Soviet reconnaissance echeloning was that Red Army theorists expected the meeting engagement—chance contact between two moving forces—would be the most common action in future warfare. Accordingly, the main purpose of reconnaissance operations was to discover the enemy's dispositions before the meeting engagement.[32]

On the defense, the Soviets used similar techniques to the offense, with reconnaissance detachments in front of a combined arms forward detachment taken from second-echelon defending divisions and regiments. The reconnaissance screen was to be between 18 and 30 miles in front of the main defensive positions and about 10 miles in front of the forward detachment.[33]

At regimental level and above, the Soviets appointed a chief of reconnaissance, a position that combined the US Army roles of that echelon's S2 intelligence officer and reconnaissance unit commander. The chief controlled all the intelligence and reconnaissance assets at the particular level.[34]

Throughout the Cold War, Soviet forces executed their doctrine several times. The most prominent of these were the 1968 Warsaw Pact invasion of Czechoslovakia and the 1979–89 war in Afghanistan. In the former case, the Soviets successfully concealed the buildup for the invasion from both NATO and the Czechs. However, the advance into Czechoslovakia and subsequent operations were mostly roadbound. The 1979 movement into Afghanistan and the 1988–89 withdrawal were both well-executed operations. However, the heavily mechanized nature of the Soviet Armed Forces in that conflict meant that most forces were tied to large bases and roads. Reconnaissance operations in Afghanistan during the war were generally considered to be minimally effective in the early phases. The Soviet forces were not organized or designed to conduct counterinsurgency operations. However, after 1984, the Soviets increased their emphasis on tactical reconnaissance by expanding the number of specialized reconnaissance units in the theater. However, this increased effectiveness did not affect the overall combat situation. By 1986, the insurgent forces were equipped with US-supplied Stinger surface-to-air missiles. This weapon system negated the Soviet air advantage. The Soviet forces in Afghanistan were composed of only a small portion of the total strength of the Soviet military establishment and were given the limited mission of assisting the Marxist government. They withdrew from the country in an orderly fashion in 1988–89.[35]

Summary

The Soviets fielded heavy mechanized forces while still retaining armored cars and motorcycles into the 1980s. Their reconnaissance forces included main battle tanks and other armored vehicles, each armed with guns of a caliber of 76-mm and above. Nevertheless, Soviet doctrine postulated that reconnaissance units were not intended to fight but to gather information. Soviet theory received only minor application in real-world scenarios, none of which fitted the situation for which the forces had been designed.

Reconnaissance Units in European Armies

All the major European armies fielded reconnaissance units of at least battalion size in the postwar and Cold War periods. In this section, the structure of the reconnaissance units in the British, French, and German Armies, NATO's major armed forces, is examined.

The British Army

As developed out of World War II changes, the British cavalry as an arm represented both armored (tank) and armored reconnaissance units. Cavalry units could be configured in either type of structure. The cavalry had three branches, the Household Cavalry, units with lineage to the traditional royal horse guard units; the Royal Armoured Corps, which included the traditional cavalry regiments of the army and the Royal Tank Regiment; and the Yeomanry, which included reserve-style Territorial forces.[36]

The basic reconnaissance unit of the British Army in the 1980s was the armored reconnaissance regiment, a battalion-sized unit usually assigned to a division. While there were different organizational structures, all active British armored reconnaissance units consisted primarily of light, fully tracked armored vehicles. At the height of the Cold War, the structure of the first-line British armored reconnaissance regiments stationed in Germany is shown in figure 41. The regiment had three reconnaissance squadrons.[37]

Two of the regiment's squadrons were designated as medium reconnaissance units. Medium reconnaissance, in the context of the

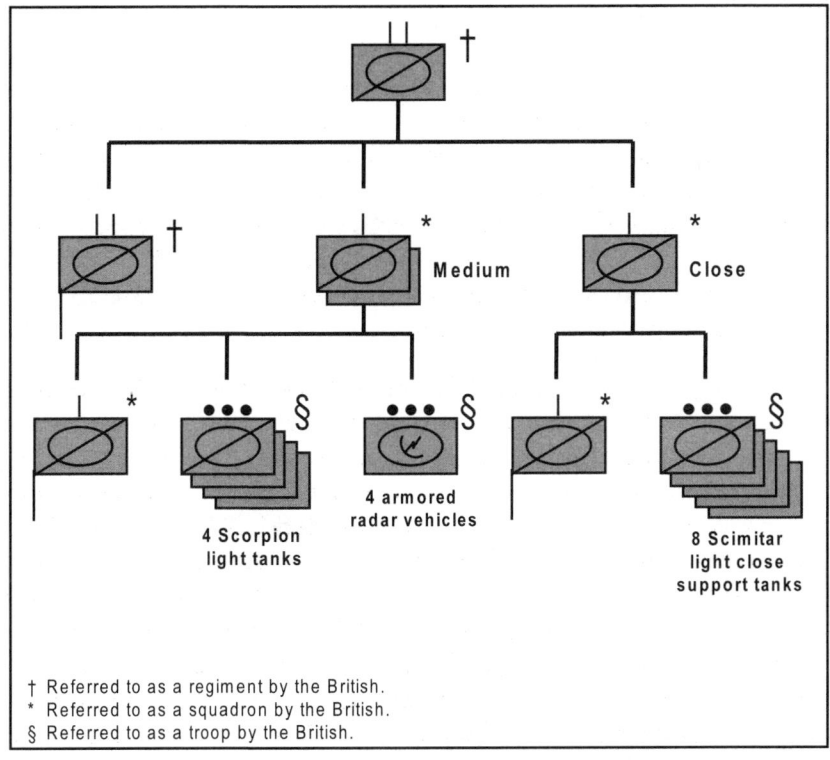

Figure 41. British first-line armored reconnaissance regiment, 1983.

Figure 42. British reconnaissance vehicles: Scimitar (left), Scorpion (right).

terminology used in this special study, was a combination of tactical reconnaissance at the division or brigade level and operational reconnaissance, as necessary, to support both division and higher operations. The medium reconnaissance squadrons were equipped with the Scorpion light tank that was armed with a 76-mm cannon. The squadron also contained a survey troop with radar sets mounted in armored personnel carriers. These units were designed to support the division's two maneuver brigades or the division as a whole.[38]

The remaining squadron was designated as a close reconnaissance unit. As such, the squadron did not operate as a unit but provided reconnaissance troops for the battalion-sized combined arms battle groups the brigades habitually formed from their assigned armored regiments and mechanized infantry battalions. Close combat troops were primarily equipped with the Scimitar light tank. The Scimitar mounted a 30-mm gun. The Scimitar was similar to the Scorpion then used in the medium squadrons, except that the latter had a larger (76-mm) main gun.[39]

For service in Operation DESERT STORM in 1990–91, the British Army originally deployed an armored brigade, then a whole armored division (the 1st (UK) Armoured Division) to Saudi Arabia to participate in the ground campaign. A battalion-sized armored reconnaissance regiment, the 16/15th Queen's Royal Lancers, was found at division level. This organization contained three organic and one attached company-sized reconnaissance (or sabre in contemporary British usage) squadrons. By 1990, the British had switched the roles of the Scimitar and Scorpion. Each squadron contained three platoon-sized reconnaissance troops equipped with four Scimitars, an antitank guided missile (ATGM) troop using the Swingfire ATGM mounted on four Spartan APCs, and a support troop with infantry on four Spartan APCs.[40]

Uniquely, the British assigned their divisional reconnaissance regiment to the division artillery group. In theory, the regiment was tasked with finding long-range targets for the 203-mm cannon and multiple rocket launcher batteries. The British command considered the regiment's armored vehicles to be too slow and lightly armored and gunned to provide effective reconnaissance in front of the tanks and mechanized infantry. Before the end of the campaign, the unit was to provide rear area security for the division's support units.[41]

The 1st Armoured Division's three battalion-sized armored (tank) regiments each contained a company-sized reconnaissance troop. By 1990, the Scorpion had replaced the Scimitar in the close reconnaissance role, and the troop had eight Scorpion light tanks armed with 76-mm cannons. These troops remained with their parent units during the campaign.[42]

The 1980s-era British reconnaissance units in Germany were heavy on light armored vehicles with small (three-man) crews and light on scouts who could dismount in rough terrain. In DESERT STORM, adding a mechanized infantry troop to each squadron gave the unit this capability.

Figure 43. French reconnaissance vehicles: AMX-10 (left), Panard ERC-90 (right).

The French Army

The French Army also sent a division to Operation DESERT STORM. An examination of the reconnaissance elements of this specially organized expeditionary task force (*6e Division Légère Blindée* (*6e DLB*)) illustrates the state of reconnaissance in the French Army at the end of the Cold War. The *6e DLB* had six battalion-sized maneuver combat units, two of which were reconnaissance elements. These were the *1er Régiment Étranger de Cavallerie* (*1 REC*) and the *1er Régiment de Spahis* (*1 RS*). Each regiment contained 3 company-sized squadrons, an equipment inventory of 36 AMX-10RC armored cars, and 12 HOT ATGM systems mounted on

141

wheeled APCs. The AMX-10RC was a medium armored car mounting a 105-mm cannon on a turret.⁴³

In addition to the larger units, there were two separate company-sized reconnaissance squadrons (1/*Régiment Husards de Parachutistes* (*RHP*) and *2/RHP*), each equipped with 12 Panhard ERC-90 armored cars and 2 truck-mounted Milan ATGM systems. The ERC-90 was a six-wheeled armored car mounting a 90-mm cannon. Two of the 3 battalion-sized motorized infantry regiments in the division each also had a supporting armored car squadron of 12 AMX-10RCs.⁴⁴

Figure 44. German reconnaissance vehicles: Fuchs (left), Luchs (right).

The German Army

The new German Army, the *Bundeswehr*, was established in 1955 with units organized in a pattern similar to the US Army's contemporary armored division structure. However, almost immediately, the Germans restructured their army, replacing combat commands with self-contained brigades under division headquarters. With minor tweaks, this structure remained until the end of the Cold War. During this period, the Germans maintained reconnaissance units at the division and brigade levels. These units primarily depended on a mix of tanks, APCs, and armored cars as their major equipment items.⁴⁵

Each *Bundeswehr* division included an armored reconnaissance battalion. Similar to the latter days of the Wehrmacht, these battalions did not have cavalry unit designations, although most maintained formal cavalry traditions from the imperial army and the interwar *Reichswehr*. The West Germans began forming the first battalions in 1956, with the first class of conscripts training in 1957.⁴⁶

The original battalion organization was a force of one heavy and two light reconnaissance companies equipped with a mix of US M41 light tanks and a German-modified version (*SPz kurz*) of the French Hotchkiss APC armed with a 20-mm cannon and a crew of five scouts. Starting in 1966, the Germans phased out the M41s and replaced them with either the new German Leopard I or US M48 Patton main battle tanks. The Hotchkiss vehicles were replaced later with a combination of a reconnaissance variant of the *Bundeswehr*'s standard Marder infantry fighting vehicles and Luchs and Fuchs armored cars. The Luchs became the standard reconnaissance vehicle (*Spähpanzer or SPz*) in the *Bunderswehr* and was a eight-wheeled armored scout car with a 20-mm cannon and a four-man crew. The Fuchs was a six-wheeled APC (*Transportpanzer* or *TPz*) that carried infantry support personnel for reconnaissance units.[47]

Figure 45 shows the German battalion organization in the mid-1980s. This unit contained a large headquarters company, three reconnaissance companies, and a mechanized infantry company. The reconnaissance

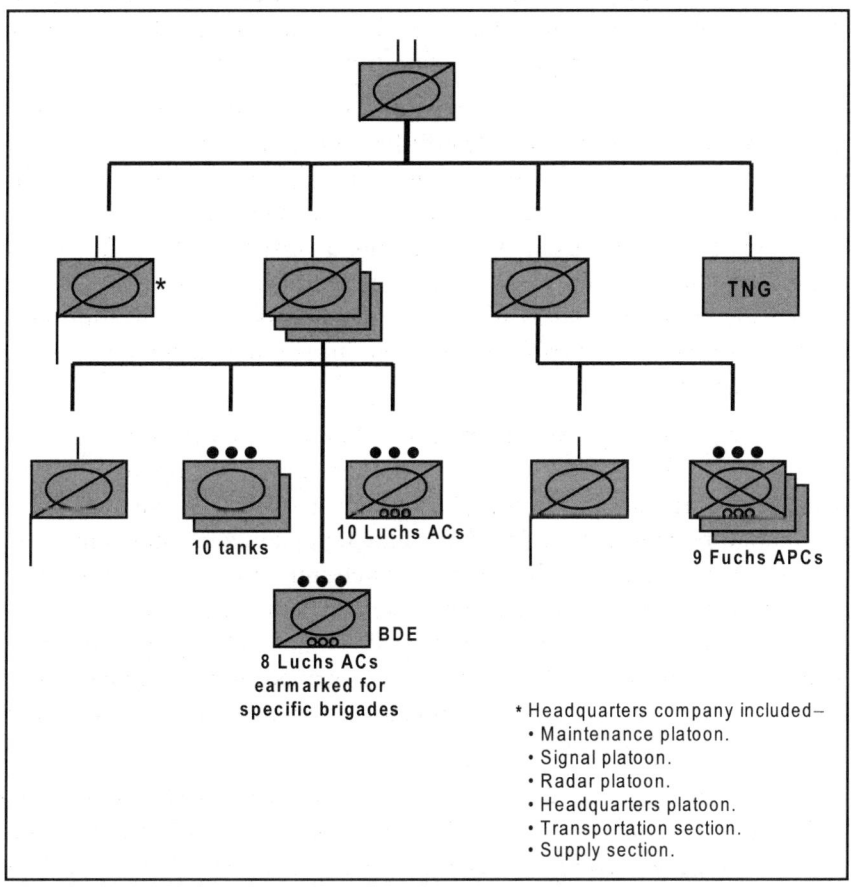

Figure 45. West German panzer reconnaissance battalion, 1985.

143

companies were a mix of tanks and armored cars. The mechanized infantry company contained a platoon to support each reconnaissance company. The platoons were usually mounted in Fuchs wheeled APCs but sometimes in US-made M113 APCs or Marders. While a combined arms unit at the battalion level, the German structure clearly emphasized the use of the tank in the reconnaissance role. In the early 1990s, most reconnaissance battalions upgraded their tanks to the latest German model, the Leopard II.[48]

For most of the Cold War, the *Bundeswehr* fielded scout units in each combat brigade. From 1959 to 1961, these units were of company size. From 1961 to 1982, each brigade contained a scout platoon in its headquarters company (*Spähzug der Brigadestabskompanie*). After 1982, the brigade scout platoons were made part of the divisional armored reconnaissance battalion. This remained the status quo from 1982 until the organizational reforms at the end of the century. These platoons originally had their scouts mounted in Hotchkiss APCs. Starting in 1982, the Luchs replaced the Hotchkiss in the platoons earmarked to support brigades.[49]

Since the *Bundeswehr* organizations were never tested in combat, there is no example of whether the proliferation of tanks in reconnaissance units would have affected their operational employment. However, with the end of the Cold War, the Germans transformed their reconnaissance philosophy into one based on lighter units. From 1995 to 2004, the *Bundeswehr* underwent several waves of reorganization. Starting in 1995, the Germans replaced tanks in all their reconnaissance units with more Luchs. By 2004, the *Bundeswehr* divided up its reconnaissance into two classes of units.[50]

The first category, the Intervention Force (*Eingreifkräfte* or *EK*), consisted of divisions and supporting forces earmarked for intervention operations or operations requiring heavy forces. An *EK* division contained a divisional reconnaissance battalion and reconnaissance companies in its heavy (panzer) brigades. The *EK* divisional unit contained 3 companies, each equipped with 12 of the newly fielded Fennek armored cars and 2 small wheeled scout cars similar to the high-mobility, multipurpose wheeled vehicles (HMMWVs) and an unmanned aerial vehicle (UAV) drone platoon. The *EK* brigade company contained four Fenneks, two scout cars, and a drone platoon.[51]

The second *Bundeswehr* category was the Stabilization Force (*Stabilisierungskräfte* or *SK*). *SK* units were generally lighter and designed for peacekeeping and stability operations. Instead of a divisional reconnaissance battalion, each brigade had its own battalion. *SK* brigade battalions had two reconnaissance companies with eight Luchs, eight Fennek armored cars, two scout cars, and a drone company.[52]

Operational Reconnaissance Units

Except for units designed to be broken up to support divisions, the British, French, and Germans did not field reconnaissance units above the division level. However, it is clear that, as with the World War II Wehrmacht, these armies considered that the divisional reconnaissance battalions/regiments fulfilled this role as necessary or whenever aerial reconnaissance needed to be supplemented from the ground.[53]

The American Experience, 1945–2005

Postwar to Vietnam, 1945–63

The US Army ended World War II with extensive experience in fielding reconnaissance units at all levels of command. While the postwar US Forces, European Theater (USFET), General Board recommended extensive revisions to organizations based on wartime experience, most changes actually made between 1945 and 1958 were just tweakings of the World War II organizations. The infantry division retained its reconnaissance troop, now called a reconnaissance company, and the armored division retained its reconnaissance squadron. The two biggest changes were the conversion of the cavalry group into the armored cavalry regiment and the fielding of the Pentomic division to replace the World War II-type infantry division.

Cavalry doctrine shifted after World War II. In general terms, the Army believed that mechanized cavalry units had been too light for the missions they actually performed. Wartime doctrine stressed reconnaissance. However, revised doctrine in the postwar period stressed the security (or counterreconnaisance) role over reconnaissance. The revised doctrine stressed the need for such units to fight to conduct security and reconnaissance missions if necessary. To provide the units with the ability to do so, light tanks and armored infantry were universally added to reconnaissance platoons.[54]

In the postwar era, weapons and vehicle technological advances continued to enhance reconnaissance unit capabilities. The World War II-era armored cars and half-tracks were soon replaced with a new family of light tanks and armored personnel carriers. As the Cold War extended over several decades, the Army developed specially designed cavalry vehicles. However, scouts continued to use the jeep as their primary vehicle until the M114 fully tracked armored command and reconnaissance vehicle (ACRV) was fielded in 1964.[55]

Figure 46. US Army light tanks: M3/M5 Stuart (left), M41 Walker (right).

During the war, the US Army used light tanks extensively in tank battalions. The tank used was the M3/M5 Stuart, which was thinly armored and mounted a tiny 37-mm main gun. It soon proved ill-suited in the main battle role and was relegated to a reconnaissance role in tank battalions. This tank was also used in reconnaissance squadrons and battalions. Mechanized cavalry units deployed light tanks in companies at the reconnaissance squadron level in both the armored division and cavalry group. After the war, a section of tanks was also at the reconnaissance platoon level.[56]

An improved light tank, the M24 Chaffee, with a 75-mm main gun, began replacing the Stuart in cavalry units in late 1944. The Chaffee was, in turn, replaced by the M41 Walker Bulldog during the Korean War. The M41, which was also used by the *Bundeswehr*, mounted a 76-mm main gun. The Bulldog was replaced in the early 1960s by a combination of the M48 Patton main battle tank and the M551 Sheridan light tank.[57]

Fully tracked and covered armored vehicles replaced the wartime half-track starting in the immediate postwar period. With an infantry squad added to each reconnaissance platoon after the war, this squad was mounted in such vehicles, initially the huge M44s and later the M59 APCs. Organizational changes removed the infantry from reconnaissance organizations in 1963, but at the same time, the scouts, formerly mounted in jeeps, received the M114, an armored vehicle specially designed for reconnaissance duties.[58]

Immediately after World War II, the Army inactivated almost all of its nondivisional mechanized cavalry forces. Some units were absorbed into the US Constabulary, a cavalry-like military police force established in Germany for occupation duties. The divisions that remained still contained their organic reconnaissance elements. The primary lesson of the war was that reconnaissance units were generally too light in firepower for the missions they actually performed. However, in the era of rapid demobilization, little happened immediately to apply these lessons to the force structure.[59]

In the early postwar period, the Armored Force, with its cross-branch and temporary wartime expedient structure, was converted into the branch-specific Armor branch by the merging of the corps of officers detailed to the Armored Force with those who remained in the Cavalry branch. The process was officially completed in 1950. During the same period, the Army replaced the term "mechanized cavalry" with "armored cavalry."[60]

By early 1948, with demobilization complete, only a single armored division (the 2d) and no armored cavalry units remained in the US Army force structure. However, later in the year, with the Berlin Blockade signaling the formal beginning of the Cold War, the Army started reactivating large reconnaissance units in the form of armored cavalry regiments (ACRs). By the end of 1948, four ACRs were formed. For most of the Cold War, the Army maintained five ACRs. With the European buildup concurrent with the Korean War, the Army also increased the number of operational armored divisions from one to four.[61]

The Armored Division, 1945–63

The postwar armored division retained most of the characteristics of the light World War II structure until 1963. Some support units routinely attached to the division during the war became organic elements, while the infantry and tank components were slightly increased. The division kept its unique combat command headquarters structure. Based on the lessons of the war, the divisional reconnaissance squadron, retitled a battalion from 1947 to 1958, added armored infantry and light tanks at the platoon level, while losing its assault gun battery and armored cars (figure 47). Adding punch to the reconnaissance organization, the tank company at battalion level was upgraded in equipment from light to medium tanks, identical to those found in tank battalions.[62]

The battalion retained the same basic structure until 1958 when the infantry division converted to the Pentomic structure. While the armored division reconnaissance battalion retained the same basic elements as it previously had, force developers reconfigured it into a new unit, now referred to as the "armored cavalry squadron." Instead of integrating combined arms at the platoon level, the tanks, scouts, armored infantry, and mortars were consolidated into separate platoons at the troop level. This gave each troop two light tank platoons, an armored infantry platoon, and a scout platoon. The two mortars were upgraded to 4.2-inch (107-mm) models mounted on an armored carrier (M82) and placed together in a section assigned to the scout platoon. This change was short lived. Since the armored cavalry troops in the contemporary armored cavalry regiment and Pentomic infantry division still integrated its arms at the troop level, for standardization purposes, the Army converted the troops in the armored division back to the previous structure (figure 47). US armored divisions retained this organization until 1963.[63]

The Pentomic Division

Despite the General Board's recommendation that the infantry division's reconnaissance element be increased in size to a squadron, the postwar infantry division retained the wartime reconnaissance troop, which was redesignated a company in 1948. At that time, the company's organization

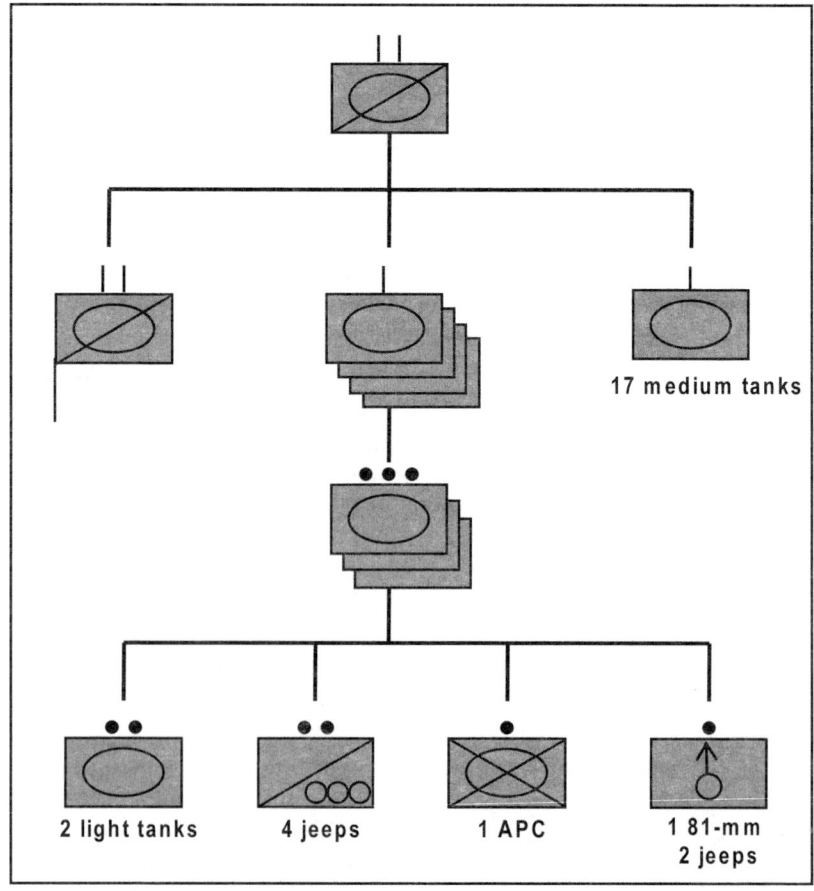

Figure 47. US Army armored division reconnaissance battalion, 1948.

was adjusted. While the jeep remained the primary scout vehicle, two M24 light tanks replaced the three scout cars in each reconnaissance platoon, and each platoon added an armored infantry squad mounted in a fully tracked armored vehicle (M44).[64]

This company structure remained in place during and after the Korean War until the Army converted its infantry divisions to the Pentomic structure in 1958. The Pentomic organization replaced the three divisional infantry regiments with five smaller battle groups. Lost in this transformation were the three regimental intelligence and reconnaissance (I&R) platoons. However, under Pentomic, the division's reconnaissance company was expanded into an armored cavalry squadron. The new squadron consisted of three troops organized similar to the World War II armored division's troop (figure 30, page 105). While the Pentomic organization routinely arranged its elements into fives, the squadron contained only three troops. By design, this left the squadron with too few troops to support all the battle groups at the same time. This meant such support was to be on an exceptional basis.[65]

Battalion-Level Reconnaissance Units

In World War II, one of the four line companies in each tank battalion was equipped with light tanks. While not originally envisioned as such, by the end of the war, this company was the battalion's de facto reconnaissance element. Postwar reorganizations replaced the light company with a reconnaissance platoon containing a section of two light tanks and a scout section with jeeps. The armored infantry battalion received an identical platoon. In the 1957 reorganization of the armored division, these platoons lost their tanks, and the scout section was expanded to platoon size. The 1957 armored division reorganization provided each combat command headquarters with its own jeep-mounted scout section.[66]

The Armored Cavalry Regiment, 1948–63

When large cavalry units reemerged in the US Army, starting in 1948 with the activation of the 3d Armored Cavalry Regiment, the new organization reflected the lessons of World War II. It contained three organic battalions, compared to the group's two attached squadrons (figure 48). This increased the combat power of the new organization by a third over that of its predecessor. Each battalion had three reconnaissance companies, a medium tank company, and a howitzer battery of six 105-mm self-propelled cannons, which represented firepower upgrades from light tanks and 75-mm guns in the World War II organization. The presence of this battery was the only organizational difference between the ACR

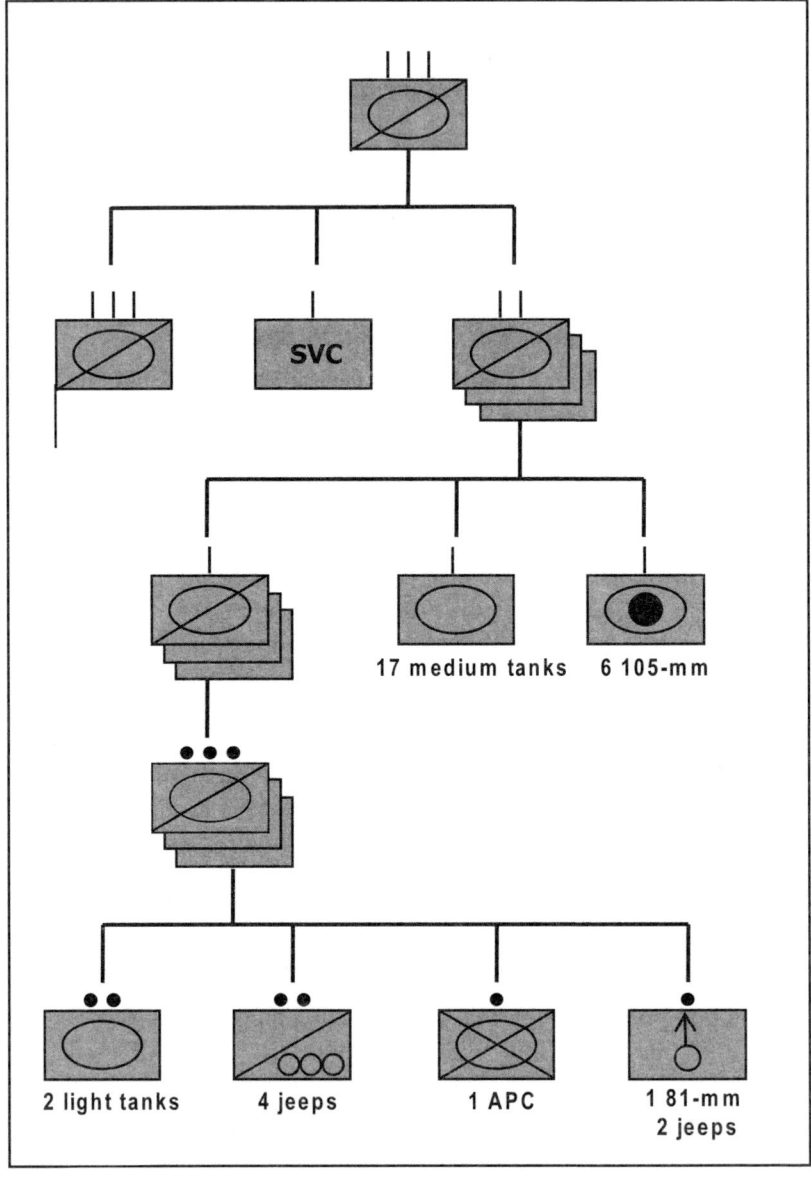

Figure 48. US Army armored cavalry regiment, 1948.

battalion and the postwar armored division battalion. In the troop, light tanks replaced armored cars in each platoon, initially with a section of two tanks, later increased to three. The troop also gained an armored infantry squad mounted in an APC.[67]

The Army provided armored cavalry regiments initially at the field army level, but ultimately, each corps had its own ACR. The major Army command in Germany, the Seventh Army, augmented its three ACRs with an armored infantry and armored field artillery battalion each for several years in the 1950s. Each ACR was initially given a mission of screening in front of one of the Seventh Army's infantry divisions in the nascent planning for the defense of West Germany.[68]

In December 1952, three ACRs (initially the 2d, 6th, and 14th) assumed responsibility for military security along the intra-German border. This was a peacetime mission that US Army ACRs continued until the end of the Cold War in 1989. Under war planning, the ACRs had specific defensive delaying lines to defend in front of the infantry and armored divisions.[69]

In the same reorganization in 1960 that reestablished squadron and troop designations, a small aviation company was added to each ACR. During the 1961 Berlin Crisis, the Army sent a fourth ACR to Germany, which assumed a reserve role. After the crisis passed in 1963, one ACR was withdrawn, with a second redeploying to the United States in 1968, leaving Germany with two ACRs for the remainder of the Cold War. In 1965, German troops assumed some of the US border patrol duties.[70]

The European ACRs set up an extensive system of observation posts and patrols along the border, typically with a sector and observation post for each squadron. Each ACR also maintained between three and six border camps. As necessary, corps commanders attached divisional armored cavalry squadrons to support or supplement the efforts of the ACRs, either on a rotating basis or semipermanently.[71]

US Army Reconnaissance Units, 1964–2003

ROAD Reorganization

From 1962 to 1964, the Army again reorganized its major combat units in a program called Reorganization Objective Army Division (ROAD). ROAD abandoned the Pentomic concept and adopted the armored division structure, with some tweaks, on an Armywide basis. Combat commands were redesignated brigades, and the number of maneuver battalions was increased to 9 or 10 per division. Division types were expanded to include a new mechanized infantry division as armored infantry was now redesignated. Except for the two specialized ROAD divisions (airborne and airmobile), each division (armored, mechanized infantry, infantry, collectively know as heavy divisions) contained a common base of divisional support units. The specific type of division was determined primarily by the mix of maneuver battalions.

In the division base, each ROAD division contained either an armored cavalry squadron (in the heavy divisions) or a new organization, the air cavalry squadron in the airmobile division. The airborne division had a light version of the standard divisional armored cavalry squadron.

The ROAD armored cavalry squadron contained three ground troops and an air cavalry troop. The three ground troops resembled the pre-ROAD armored cavalry troop, with the integration of scouts, tanks, infantry, and mortars at the platoon level (figure 49). When the Army deployed the M114 armored reconnaissance vehicle and M551 Sheridan tank in the 1960s, these vehicles replaced the jeeps in the scout section and the tanks in the tank section. The infantry squad's vehicle was the newly fielded M113 armored personnel carrier. In later years, both the Sheridans and M114s were replaced by M60 tanks and M113 APCs respectively.[72]

The air cavalry troop was a new organization, placing a newly developed series of utility and observation helicopters into the reconnaissance role. Similar to the integrated nature of the ground troop, the air troop combined observation helicopters, infantry, and rocket-firing helicopters in one organization. The troop had two combat platoons, an aeroscout platoon, and an aerorifle platoon. The aeroscout platoon had two light sections, each equipped with four OH-6A Cayuse light observation helicopters and a heavy section flying four UH-1B Huey utility helicopters. The OH-6A was later replaced with the OH-58. The aerorifle platoon contained four UH-1D troop carrier helicopters in its headquarters to carry its four infantry squads. The platoon also contained a weapons section that deployed four UH-1B Hueys armed with 2.75-inch rocket launchers. The weapons section was later reequipped with the AH-1G Cobra attack helicopter and expanded to platoon size. The three elements of the troops were known colloquially as the white (aeroscout), blue (aerorifle) and red (aeroweapons) teams.[73]

The biggest changes to the ROAD armored cavalry squadron took place primarily at the armored cavalry platoon level. The first change from the structure shown in figure 49 was the replacement of the M114s in the scout section with M113 APCs in 1973, followed by the deletion of the mechanized infantry and mortar squad in 1975. In 1978, the Army replaced the light Sheridans with main battle tanks (M60s). This left a platoon with a scout section of four M113s and a tank section of three M60s. The platoon headquarters also had an M113 and an M60 tank.[74]

In many ways, commanders considered the ROAD armored cavalry squadron to be an extra maneuver battalion rather than an exclusively reconnaissance unit. Unlike mechanized infantry and tank battalions, which required the cross-attachment of companies and platoons between battalions to create combined arms task forces, the divisional squadron

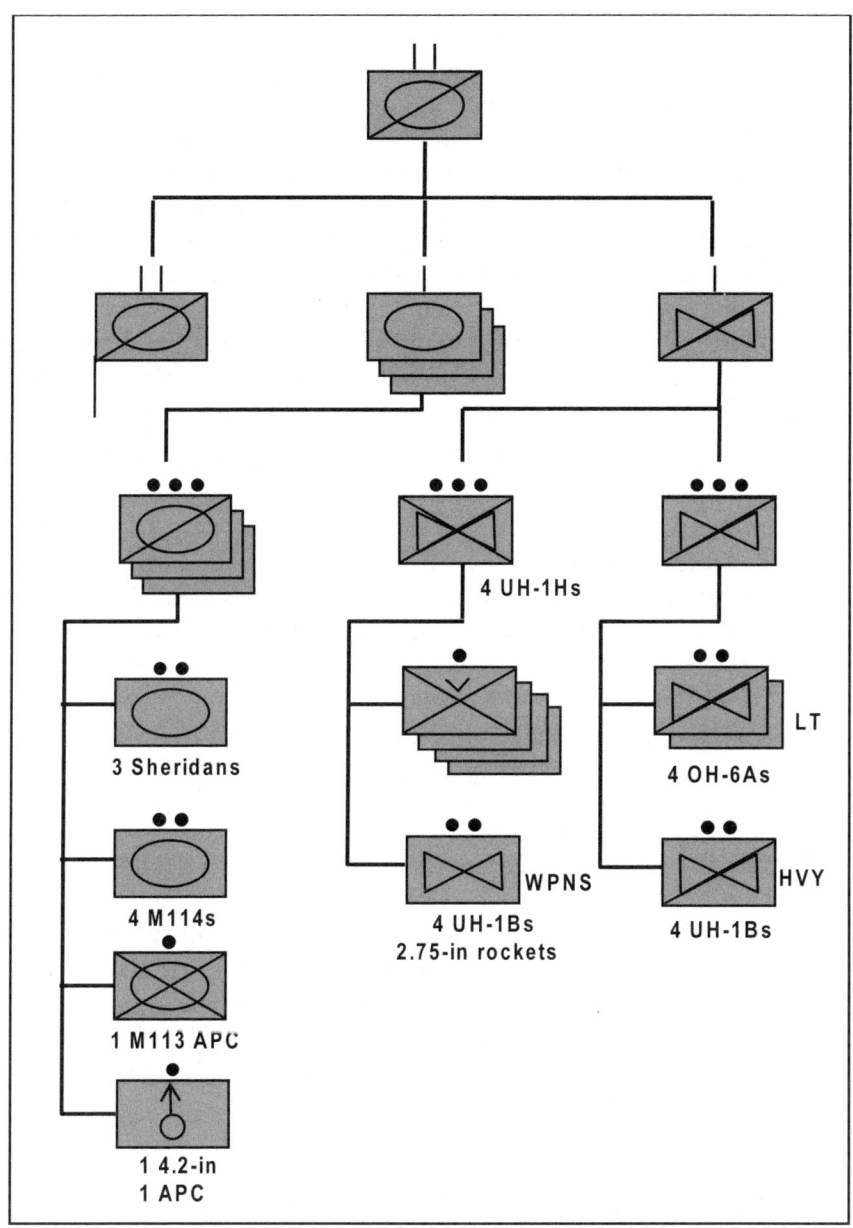

Figure 49. US Army ROAD divisional armored cavalry squadron, 1968.

contained combined assets down to the platoon level. This organizational feature and the fact that the unit reported directly to the division headquarters made it a convenient asset for commanders to use as a reserve or as an extra maneuver force.[75]

Under the ROAD reorganization, the Army fielded a new kind of unit—the airmobile (later air assault) division. The airmobile division was basically an infantry division with enough helicopter assets to carry and support one-third (that is, a brigade) of the division's combat elements. The helicopter assets were primarily assigned to an organic aviation group. The airmobile division's organic reconnaissance unit was an air cavalry squadron with three air cavalry troops and one ground troop. The air cavalry troops had an aeroscout platoon, an aerorifle platoon, and an aeroweapons platoon with similar equipment as the air cavalry troop in the armored cavalry squadron. The ground troop consisted of two jeep scout platoons equipped with machine guns and 106-mm rifles. While in Vietnam, one platoon replaced its jeeps with amphibious armored cars.[76]

Originally, the first airmobile division had an old World War II airborne designation (11th Air Assault). But immediately before deployment to Vietnam, it was redesignated the "1st Cavalry Division (Airmobile)." Although, structurally, the division was an infantry unit with helicopters, the cavalry designation often led to later confusion concerning the nature and role of the organization. When the Army created a second airmobile division in Vietnam, it used a former airborne division, the 101st. After the war, the 1st Cavalry Division transitioned through a test organization to an armored division structure, while the 101st remained in the airmobile configuration, which was redesignated "air assault" in 1974.

Battalion Scout Platoons

Each ROAD tank, mechanized infantry, and infantry battalion contained a scout platoon equipped initially with jeeps. When fielded, the M114 replaced the jeeps in the armored and mechanized infantry battalions. After the Army phased out the M114 vehicle, the M113 APC replaced it. By 1978, battalions in Germany contained scout platoons organized into two scout sections, with each section having four M113s, two of which mounted a TOW ATGM system. The platoon leader and platoon sergeant also had their own M113s.[77]

New Equipment

Since the Korean War, Army research and development (R&D) worked on producing a new series of armored vehicles specifically designed for reconnaissance units. After many delays, R&D fielded the M114 armored command and reconnaissance vehicle and the M551 Sheridan armored reconnaissance/airborne assault vehicle in 1968. In Vietnam, units modified the new M113 APC (which had replaced the M114 in units in Vietnam) into the armored cavalry assault vehicle (ACAV).

Figure 50. An M114 vehicle in Vietnam showing its difficulty with cross-country mobility.

The M114 was a vehicle similar to the M113 APC but with a lower silhouette and longer body. It was in the US Army's inventory between 1964 and 1973 and replaced jeeps in heavy battalion scout platoons and in armored cavalry squadrons. The M114 also was the command vehicle in mechanized infantry platoons and companies. In these roles, some M114s deployed to Vietnam, but due to operational deficiencies, ACAVs soon replaced them in Southeast Asia. The M114 was deficient in cross-country mobility caused by the vehicle's overhanging front hull, and it had limited troop-carrying and firepower capabilities. The M114 had a three-member crew and room for one more passenger. Outside of Vietnam, the M114 was universally replaced in the early 1970s by the M113 APC.[78]

The M551 Sheridan was a light tank. Its main armament was a unique 152-mm gun-missile combination. The missile was the Shillelagh, an infrared guided antitank missile that could hit a target out to 2,000 meters. The Sheridan was groomed to replace all the tanks in armored cavalry and airborne units. The Army fielded it starting in 1968, and it was used in Vietnam primarily with the 11th ACR. In the cavalry role, the M60 tank gradually replaced the M551 starting in 1978.[79]

The ACAV was designed specifically for counterinsurgency operations in Vietnam. It was a modified M113 APC. At the main weapons station, the M2 .50-caliber machine gunner was protected by the addition of an armored gun shield. For additional firepower, the ACAV also mounted two

Figure 51. M551 Sheridan firing a Shillelagh missile.

M60 7.62-mm light machine guns on mounts with gun shields out of the vehicle's rear hatch on the left and right sides. In Vietnam, the ACAV's primary use was to conduct counterinsurgency operations. The ACAV modifications were not adopted outside of Southeast Asia, and after US troops withdrew from the area, the ACAV concept was abandoned.[80]

Vietnam

Vietnam was the first combat test of the ROAD armored cavalry squadron and the armored cavalry regiment, which was not used in the Korean War. During the Vietnam conflict, the Army deployed six armored cavalry squadrons, one air cavalry squadron, and one ACR to Southeast Asia. Almost immediately after the change to the ROAD structure, US Army troops began moving to Vietnam.

Between 1965 and 1972, the Army sent to Southeast Asia one armored cavalry regiment, seven divisional armored cavalry squadrons, and eight troops supporting separate brigades. There were also several nondivisional squadrons and troops. Divisional squadrons substituted M113 APCs for the M114s before deployment.[81]

The troops in the divisional squadrons were frequently parceled out to subordinate brigades and used separately. At times, the tanks in the cavalry troops were withdrawn and maintained at a centralized location as US commanders initially attached a stigma to using tanks in Vietnam. Later, both the tanks and armored cavalry units in general were used extensively for road security and convoy protection operations.[82]

The ROAD armored cavalry squadron was a hybrid unit, combining ground and air (helicopter) assets under one headquarters. However, the air cavalry troops were frequently detached to the division's aviation

Figure 52. A troop of M48 tanks and ACAVs in Vietnam.

battalion. This dichotomy between the ground and air elements in cavalry units became an ongoing theme. In future operational employments, particularly after the air element in the squadron was increased in the 1980s, higher commanders frequently separated the air element from the ground element and operated each separately.[83]

The 11th Armored Cavalry Regiment deployed to Vietnam in September 1966, remaining there until March 1971. Before deployment, the ACAV version of the M113 replaced the M114s and M48 tanks found in each troop, although the regiment retained its M48s found at squadron level. Sheridans replaced those tanks in 1969. From the start, the US Military Assistance Command, Vietnam (MACV), the US theater command in Vietnam, considered the use of the 11th ACR in Vietnam not as a reconnaissance or security unit but as a highly mobile, firepower-intensive general-purpose maneuver unit. Therefore, common missions for the regiment included road clearance and security. As was the case with the divisional squadrons, the subordinate units were often detached to other units, and the ACR itself was attached to the 1st Cavalry Division (Airmobile) for an extended period in 1969 and 1970.[84]

As operations continued, the 11th ACR played a major role as a main combat element. In Operation CEDAR FALLS, II Field Force, Vietnam (II FFV), cordoned off a large section of the enemy-infested Iron Triangle area northwest of Saigon in Tay Ninh Province near the Cambodian border. The 11th ACR, along with a brigade each from the 1st and 25th Infantry Divisions, spearheaded the advance through the Triangle, pushing the enemy toward the troops forming the cordon.[85]

The cavalry troopers also played a leading role in the advance into Cambodia in May and June 1970. In that operation, the regiment attacked north 25 miles to Snuol, reaching the Cambodian town in 2 days. The armored cavalry regiment surrounded Snuol and conducted a coordinated two-squadron attack against its North Vietnamese defenders. The Communist forces fled in small groups. Snuol proved to be a large enemy logistical hub. The Cambodian operation proved to be MACV's largest operation involving armored cavalry forces in the Vietnam War.[86]

Unlike the operations of the 11th ACR, the 1st Cavalry Division's air cavalry squadron, the 1st Squadron, 9th Cavalry, played a leading role in the division's operations while functioning in a reconnaissance role. A former 1st Cavalry Division commander later commented that "practically every major engagement was started with a contact by the 1st Squadron, 9th Cavalry [1-9th Cav]. . . ."[87]

The Ia Drang campaign in November 1965 presents a good example of the 1-9th Cav's operational employment as the 1st Cavalry Division's reconnaissance element. In October, based on intelligence indicators of a North Vietnamese buildup there, the newly arrived airmobile division was shifted to Pleiku Province in the western Central Highlands of South Vietnam. In addition to covering the division's movement into the area, the 1-9th Cav received the mission to locate the enemy. The squadron conducted an area reconnaissance and then a reconnaissance in force along the border with Cambodia at the extreme western edge of the division's area of operations. Typically, the 1-9th Cav operated on a troop basis, with each troop sending its aeroscouts out in observation helicopters. When the scouts spotted enemy positions or were fired on, the troop commander landed his aerorifle platoon to investigate and develop the situation. If the enemy was found in force, an infantry battalion would replace the cavalry. Sometimes, the squadron combined its three aerorifle platoons for dismounted operations. In the opening stages of the Ia Drang campaign, the 1-9th Cav found large enemy forces both in its area reconnaissance and in the reconnaissance in force along the border. The division and brigade commanders based their subsequent tactical decisions on the cavalry squadron's information, deploying large forces by helicopter in the vicinity of enemy concentrations.[88]

During the US involvement in South Vietnam, the Army of the Republic of Vietnam (ARVN) created its own armored cavalry regiments. The first units were formed in 1963 and originally consisted of one armored reconnaissance squadron and two mechanized rifle squadrons. Following the French custom, the regiments were battalion size and the squadrons company size. The reconnaissance squadron was equipped with a troop (platoon) each of World War II-era M24 Chaffee light tanks, M8 armored cars, and the new M114. The mechanized rifle squadrons had M113 APCs. Initially, the ARVN deployed one ACR for each of its four corps-sized tactical zones. The ARVN expanded this force to 6 regiments in 1964 and to 18 by 1972. At the end of this expansion, one ACR was in each ARVN division. M113s eventually replaced the M114s and the armored cars. Korean War-vintage M41 light tanks supplanted the M24s.[89]

As with US armored cavalry in Vietnam, ARVN cavalry forces primarily operated as mobile main battle and route security forces rather than reconnaissance units. In the late stages of the war, nondivisional armored cavalry units were often combined with nondivisional armored units to form brigade- and division-sized task forces. These task forces fought in some of the ARVN's biggest battles after the withdrawal of US forces.[90]

In Vietnam, both the Americans and the South Vietnamese primarily used armored cavalry units as combat maneuver forces. Air cavalry troops and squadrons performed most reconnaissance missions, especially early in the US deployment when enemy air defense was limited. Armored cavalry units devoted most of their time to route security missions, clearing roads and protecting the camps and movements of logistical units.[91]

Long-Range Reconnaissance and Patrol Units

During the US deployment to Vietnam, the Army formed a number of company-sized long-range reconnaissance and patrol (LRRP) units, initially informally and later formally under the designation "ranger." Usually, there was one such company per division or separate brigade. The US Marines, Israelis, and Soviets also fielded such units. Universally, such units were light infantry in composition and usually depended on helicopters for their combat insertions. Sometimes, these units also used specialized ground transportation equipment. While some of the operations of LRRP units could be considered reconnaissance in nature (usually at a strategic or operational level), most of their activities fit better in the category of special operations.[92]

LRRP units saw extensive service in the counterinsurgency/low-intensity environment of Vietnam, but the use of such units later in a conventional role at the operational and tactical levels in Operation DESERT STORM proved to be problematic. While most corps and divisions used such forces before the start of the ground campaign to determine enemy dispositions and placed several teams deep behind lines with long-range radios, at least one senior commander did not use his long-range assets because he feared the survivability of the unit and wanted to use other means to acquire the same information. As of 2004, such units remained a component of several US light divisions and as corps troops.[93]

The Armored Cavalry Regiment Since 1964

The ROAD restructuring did not affect the armored cavalry regiment. However, in 1965, an air cavalry troop replaced the aviation company at the regimental level. In 1988, this troop was expanded into an aviation squadron as part of the Army of Excellence (AOE) reorganization, with the mix of observation, attack, and transportation (utility) helicopter troops (figure 53), although AH-1 and OH-58A/C attack helicopters substituted for the AH-64s in some units.[94]

The AOE study examined the roles and missions of Army cavalry units in relation to the expected operational environment and the new equipment

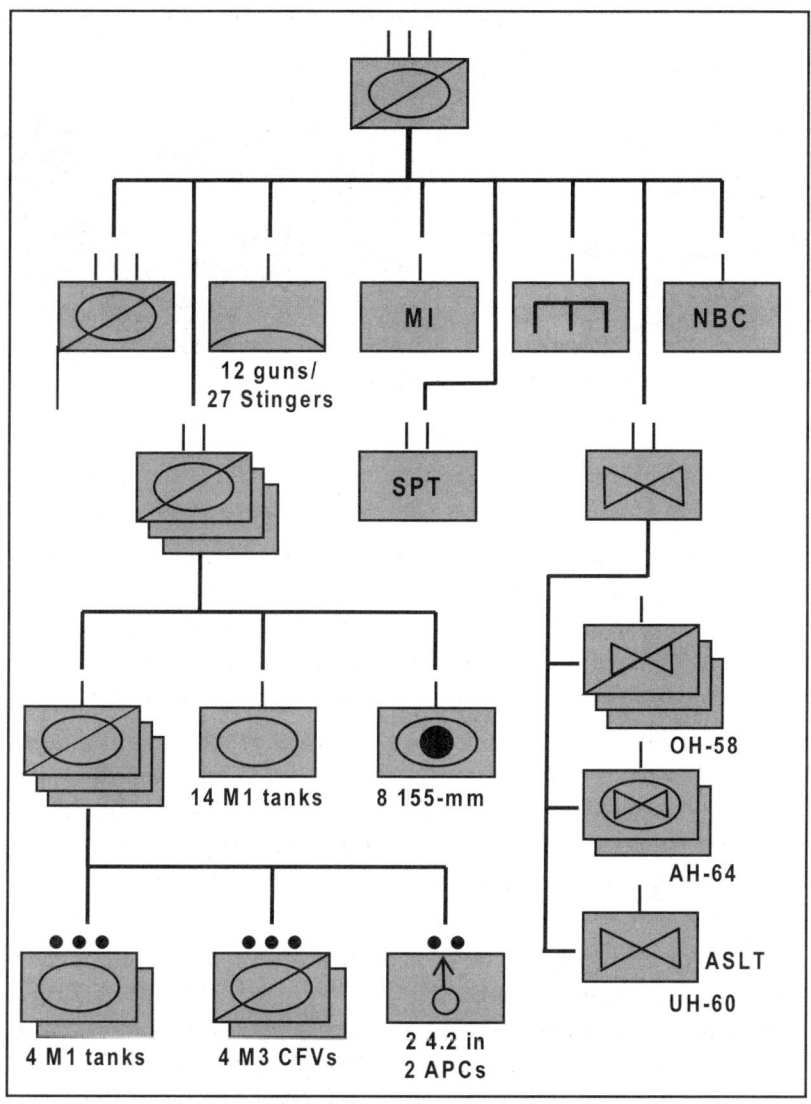

Figure 53. US Army AOE armored cavalry regiment, 1988.

being fielded in the 1980s. This equipment included the M1 Abrams tank and the M3 Bradley cavalry fighting vehicle (CFV). The acronym RCRS (reconnaissance-counterreconnaissance-surveillance) summarized the missions the Army expected of its cavalry units in the mid-1980s at the battalion, division, and corps levels. In this concept, the focus of the armored cavalry regiment was on the counterreconnaissance/operational reconnaissance mission. The ACR's projected main wartime role was to act

Figure 54. American reconnaissance vehicles: M3 CFV (left), HMMWV (right).

as the corps covering force in Europe with divisional cavalry organizations under Division 86/AOE primarily organized for reconnaissance.

The structure of the AOE armored cavalry regiment reflected both this operational consideration and the fielding of new equipment while providing continuity with the previous ACR structure (figure 48, page 150). The AOE regiment retained its three ground squadrons, which were organized as combined arms mixes of scouts, tanks, and artillery.

The ACR received additional support assets in the form of company-sized air defense artillery, military intelligence, and engineer units as well as the aviation squadron as previously mentioned. This squadron contained three troops equipped with the OH-58 scout helicopter, two AH-64 Apache attack helicopter troops, and a troop of UH-60 Blackhawk troop carrier helicopters.[95]

The major change in the AOE reorganization was the reorganization of the armored cavalry platoon. The final version of the ROAD platoon (H-series table of organization and equipment (TOE)) was a mix of main battle tanks and scouts mounted in M113s. With the fielding of the M1 tank and M3 CFV, Army planners consolidated similar systems at the troop level. Accordingly, AOE reorganized the troops to include two tank platoons (for tanks), two scout platoons (four CFVs), and a mortar section (two 4.2-inch mortars, later replaced by 120-mm mortars) mounted on the mortar carrier version of the M113.[96]

The ACR organization received tweaks throughout the 1990s, primarily in its aviation squadron, where the mix of aviation troops was changed several times. As of 2006, the squadron consisted of three AH-64 Apache troops and a UH-60 utility helicopter troop. Otherwise, the heavy ACR retained its AOE structure through Operation DESERT STORM and on into the 21st century when the Army began applying the Modular Army structure to other units in 2004.[97]

However, while the armored cavalry regiment kept its longtime structure, the Army converted one of the two ACRs in the Active force structure into a new lighter version in August 1992. Force developers wanted a cavalry regiment that could deploy quickly worldwide on a contingency basis. Therefore, the Army created a new organization, the light armored cavalry regiment (LACR) (later redesignated cavalry regiment (light)). Structurally, the LACR was similar to the standard ACR. The original concept was to replace the M3 CFV with the M113 APC and the M1 tank with a newly developed light tank system known as the armored gun system (AGS). The M113s were soon replaced by HMMWVs, which were supposed to be stand-ins for projected future systems. The AGS was never fielded, and in its place, the LACR used the ubiquitous HMMWV with a TOW ATGM mounted on it.[98]

The light cavalry regiment, as it was fielded, is shown in figure 55. The cavalry troop maintained the 2x2 configuration of the armored cavalry troops with 2 scout platoons equipped with 10 HMMWVs, half armed with the M2 .50-caliber machine gun and half with the Mk-19 automatic grenade launcher system, and 2 antitank platoons equipped with 4 HMMWVs each armed with the TOW ATGM system. As part of the conversion to the new Modular Army structure in 2004, the Army announced that its lone LACR, the 2d Cavalry Regiment (Light), was converting to the Stryker brigade configuration.[99]

The Division 86/AOE Cavalry Squadron

In the late 1970s, in preparation for the fielding of a series of new equipment, including tanks, armored fighting vehicles, attack and utility helicopters, and rocket and air defense artillery, the Army began a series of organizational studies to develop updated organizations to enhance the operational employment of the new equipment. Detailed studies began with the structure of the future heavy division called Division 86. The program was later extended to the whole Army under the name Army of Excellence.

The Division 86/AOE study produced several basic organizational concepts. The most significant of these affecting the cavalry organization was the consolidation of single weapons systems at one level higher than previous practice and the deletion of tanks from the divisional squadron. As with the ACR's troops, the new divisional structure shifted combined arms from the platoon level to the troop level in the division's cavalry squadron.

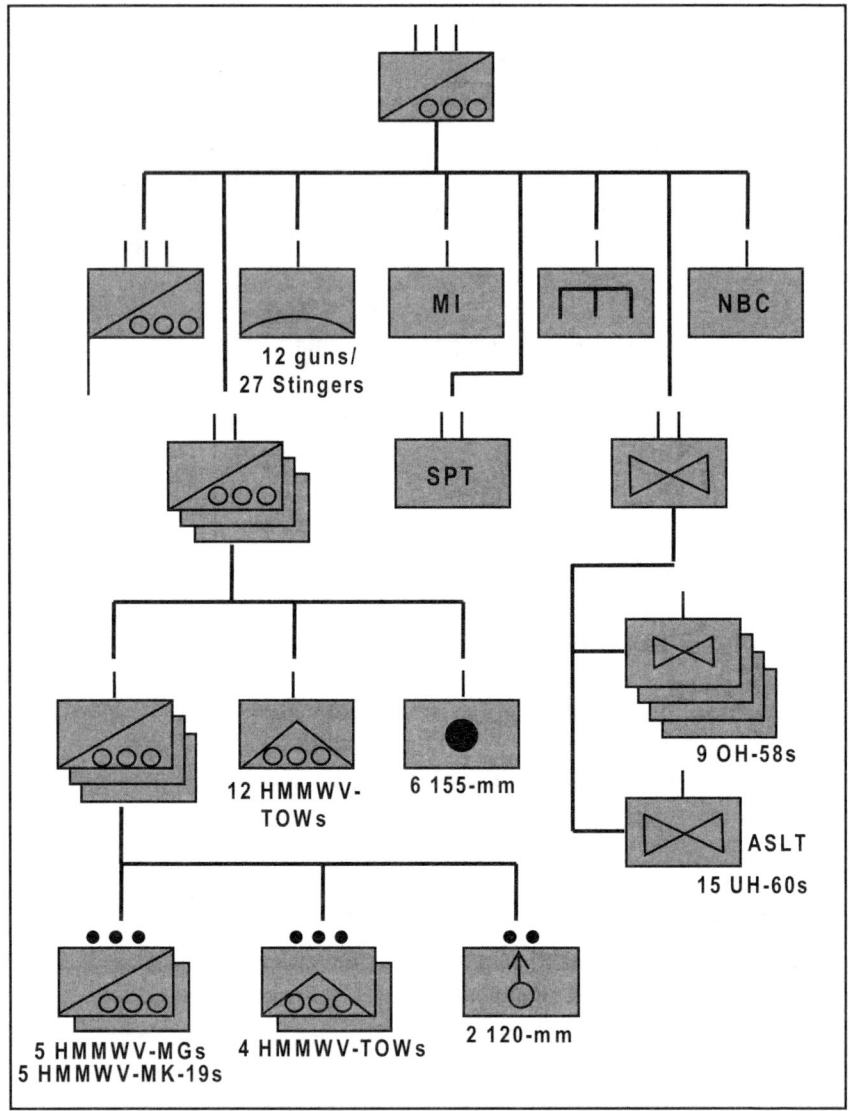

Figure 55. US Army light cavalry regiment, 1997.

Under ROAD, divisional armored cavalry platoons had contained tank and scout sections. The new organization consolidated these elements at the troop level. The new troop consisted of three platoons of six M3 CFVs each and a mortar section with three 4.2-inch mortars mounted in a modified M113 armored vehicle.[100]

The biggest changes were the deletion of one ground troop and the loss of tanks in the remaining troops. The force developers' rationale was that the division would always be operating in proximity to an armored cavalry regiment and would not be required to conduct economy-of-force missions. The presumption was that such missions would routinely fall to the ACR and the divisional squadron would not need the combat power of the tanks. The tankless unit was known as the J-series squadron (figure 56), based on the alphanumeric designation of its TOE.[101]

In addition to ground elements, the J-series squadron also contained two aviation troops, each with a platoon each of observation and attack helicopters. With a mix of aviation and ground assets, the unit was formally redesignated a "cavalry squadron." Army planners originally intended to remove attack helicopters from the squadron, consolidating all the division attack assets into three attack helicopter aviation battalions.[102]

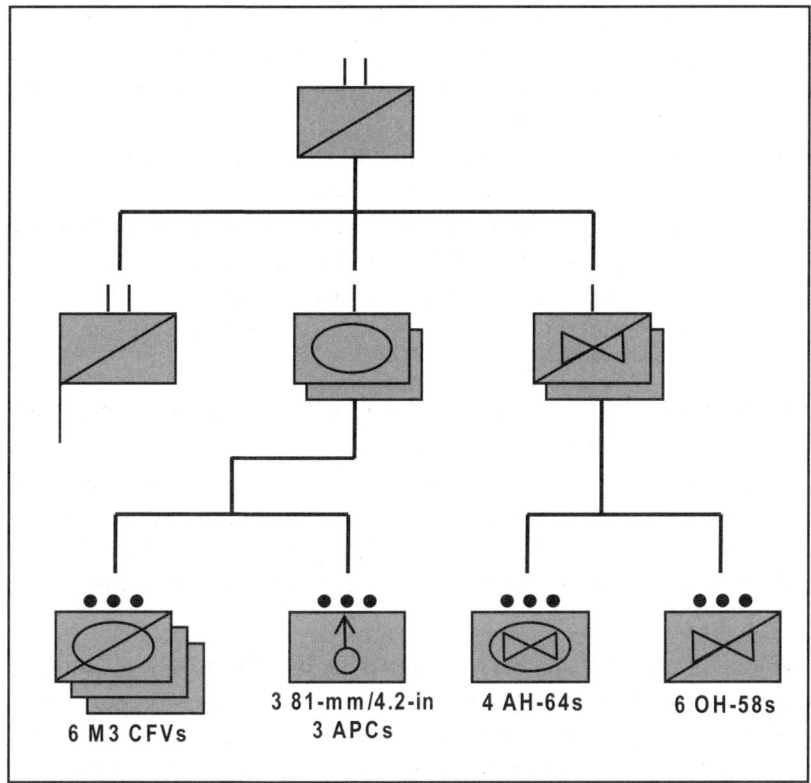

Figure 56. J-series divisional cavalry squadron, armored and mechanized division, 1987.

The increase in air cavalry troops in the divisional squadron was part of a general trend in the Division 86/AOE reorganization: the expansion of aviation assets. This was also reflected in the creation of an aviation squadron in the ACR. Each division also received an aviation brigade. Although the brigade headquarters was formally considered to be a maneuver element, all divisional aviation assets, including logistical ones, were assigned to it. The cavalry squadron, traditionally an organization that reported directly to the division headquarters, was also placed under the aviation brigade. Without tanks, force developers believed this was the best place for the squadron as part of the policy of combining all aviation assets under the brigade. With the squadron so positioned organizationally, the attack platoons were retained. While the cavalry unit was technically a part of the aviation brigade, most division commanders continued to retain the squadron under their direct control.[103]

The loss of tanks remained a controversial move. Although one observer at the end of the 1980s remarked that tanks were permanently out of the division cavalry squadron, this was not the case. Commanders, particularly those in Europe, pushed for their return almost from the start. After DESERT STORM, when the Army adopted the new L-series TOE, tanks returned to the armored cavalry troops of the divisional squadron. The new troop matched the organization of the ACR's 2x2 troop, with two tank and two cavalry fighting vehicle platoons and a mortar section (figure 57). Platoon size was standardized at four vehicles each. For the loss of one CFV platoon per troop and two CFVs in each of the remaining platoons, the troop gained eight tanks. The squadron also regained its third ground troop. The Army retained the L-series squadron until the introduction of the Modular Army in 2004.[104]

In the 1980s, the Army developed a light infantry division as part of the AOE program. This division also contained a cavalry squadron (figure 58). However, the ratio of ground to air troops in this organization was 1 to 2. The squadron contained a single ground troop equipped similar to the LACR with two HMMWV scout platoons and two HMMWV TOW ATGM platoons. The two air troops each contained two platoons of scout/attack helicopters.[105]

Under AOE, the cavalry squadrons in the airborne and air assault divisions also were primarily aviation organizations. The airborne squadron was similarly organized to the light division, with one ground and three air troops. The ground troop had three scout platoons, each consisting of a mix of HMMWVs with machine guns and TOWs. The air troops fielded

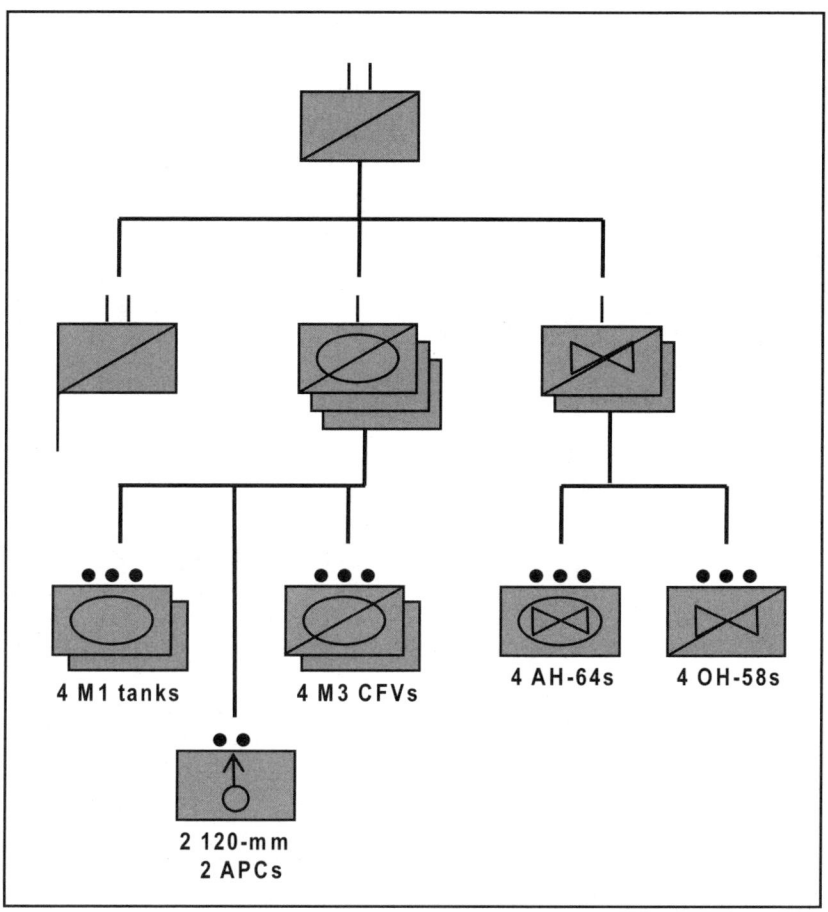

Figure 57. L-series divisional cavalry squadron, armored and mechanized division, 2003

eight OH-58D helicopters. The squadron in the air assault division had four air troops, each with eight OH-58Ds, and no ground troops.[106]

The AOE changes extended the hybrid nature of reconnaissance units. Whereas before World War II such elements had a contrast between horses and motorized or mechanized vehicles, the modern equivalent was the difference between ground and air (helicopter) assets. In principle, the two components were designed to complement each other in the reconnaissance role. In practice, however, except in the ACR, the aviation assets were controlled by the aviation brigade commander and the ground elements directly by the division commander.

167

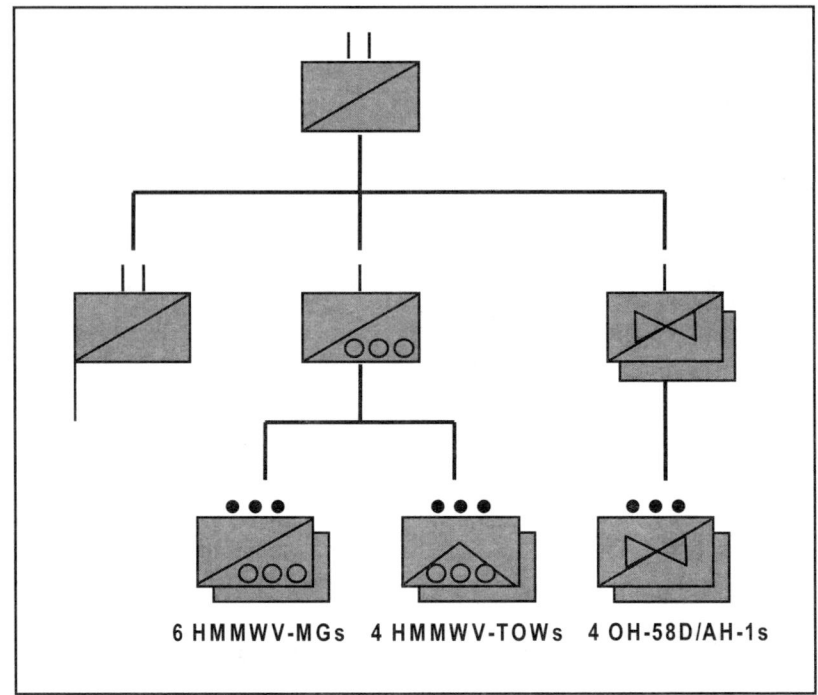

Figure 58. AOE light infantry division cavalry squadron, 1997.

Maneuver Battalion Scout Platoons, Brigade Reconnaissance Troops, and Force XXI

Initially, under AOE, the heavy maneuver battalion scout platoon had six M3 CFVs, replacing the late ROAD-era's three M113s and three improved TOW vehicles (ITVs) (a modified M113 with a turret for the TOW). But before DESERT STORM, the Army began replacing the CFVs with 10 HMMWVs organized into four 2-vehicle sections and a 2-vehicle platoon headquarters. Each section contained a HMMWV with an M2 .50-caliber machine gun and one with the MK-19 automatic grenade launcher.[107]

In the early 1980s, the US Army established the National Training Center (NTC) at Fort Irwin, California. The NTC provided comprehensive field exercises using extensive laser technology and a dedicated enemy force (the opposing force or OPFOR). Most heavy maneuver battalions rotated through the NTC on a regular basis. Army force developers, supported by a 1987 Rand Corporation report, analyzed the results of these rotations and determined that the stealth and speed of the HMMWV, which the OPFOR used, was more important than the survivability and firepower that the cavalry fighting vehicle offered. Unit tests at the NTC supported the viability of a HMMWV-equipped platoon. As a result, and after several tests at the NTC, at Fort Knox, and in DESERT STORM, the Army removed armored vehicles from battalion scout platoons. Chief of Staff General Carl Vuono officially approved a TOE for the new platoon in mid-1991, just before his retirement.[108]

Since 1943 (as the combat command until 1963), the US Army's concept of the divisional brigade was just a headquarters command to which combat battalions and companies were attached on a mission basis. Such attachments could include a reconnaissance troop from the divisional cavalry squadron. Implementation of ROAD and AOE did not change this concept. In the 1990s, because of unit drawdowns and redesignations, the Army began to position brigades separate from their parent divisions. The battalions and companies usually habitually attached to the brigade for training or deployment purposes were usually also positioned at the brigade's location. The brigade with its attachments became known as a brigade combat team (BCT).

After DESERT STORM, the Army began looking to the future with a program called Force XXI. Force XXI was the application of new and projected technology to the AOE structure. It was hoped that digitalized communications would allow for the streamlining of units. As part of the Force XXI reforms, in 1998, the Army added a brigade reconnaissance troop (BRT) to each heavy maneuver brigade.[109]

The lack of an organic reconnaissance element at the brigade level went back to the original concept of the armored division combat command in World War II. The combat command was considered a headquarters to control combat units assigned to it from the division. The division commander provided reconnaissance assets just like he provided tank and armored infantry assets to the command on a mission basis. The organization of the division reconnaissance squadron (figures 30, page 105, and 47, page 148) reflected this, providing four reconnaissance troops. This ensured that, even if a troop was attached to each of three combat commands, there would still be a troop left over under the division commander's control. However, when ROAD updated the combat command concept to three divisional brigades, the new structure of the divisional armored cavalry squadron contained only three ground troops (figure 49, page 153). For the division commander to retain any ground troops under his control resulted in depriving one or more of the brigades of such assets. The AOE organization continued this trend (figures 56, page 165, and 57, page 167).

Army force structure specialists and service school students had long discussed the creation of a brigade reconnaissance unit. There were frequent field tests of the concept at the NTC and Armor School. The original Division 86/AOE structure even included a reconnaissance platoon in the brigade headquarters company. However, the platoon did not survive to make the final version of the organization that was fielded. The brigade remained without a dedicated reconnaissance unit.[110]

However, even after the transformation to the AOE structure, brigade reconnaissance continued to be a topic of interest. Concurrent with the testing done on the organization of the maneuver battalion scout platoon that resulted in the conversion to an all-HMMWV platoon, the Army also tested brigade reconnaissance organizations. NTC rotations often noted the deficiency at the brigade level. But NTC exercises could be considered skewed since brigades often performed in isolation without many of the assets that would have been available to them as part of a larger force, including divisional reconnaissance elements. Nevertheless, in DESERT STORM, where a complete array of units was available, one corps commander subsequently commented specifically on the lack of a brigade reconnaissance asset.[111]

However, the period after DESERT STORM was one of economy and drawdown, so it was not until the experimental Force XXI concept streamlined unit structure that the issue of a brigade reconnaissance unit, now of troop size, reappeared. While the Force XXI changes overall only affected the single Army division being organized under the structure, some of its organizational tweaks, including the creation of the brigade reconnaissance troop, applied throughout the force under a program called Limited Conversion Division XXI (LCD XXI) in 1998. The trade-off for the creation of the BRT was, however, the elimination of one of the four line companies in the tank and mechanized infantry battalion.[112]

As with the contemporary maneuver battalion scout platoon, the BRT was a HMMWV unit. It contained two platoons, each of two sections with two squads/vehicles. Counting the platoon headquarters, there were six HMMWVs per platoon in the troop. Doctrinally, field artillery fire support and combat observation and lasing teams (COLTs) were supposed to augment and support the troop and its platoons.[113]

The BRT only existed in the period from 1998 to 2004 when the Modular Army reorganizations began. During that period, the BRT was tested in training exercises and participated in combat in the 2003 Baghdad campaign. The brigade-centric Modular Army structure eliminated the divisional squadron but, in turn, placed a squadron in each brigade.[114]

The Marines

Marine divisions had contained small company-sized scout elements during World War II. After the war, these units were inactivated and reactivated several times. In 1958, the Marines created a reconnaissance battalion organization in each of its four divisions. These battalions consisted of three companies, each with three platoons. The reconnaissance units were organized similar to Marine infantry units of the same size, with more light automatic weapons. Generally, the battalion was split up with a company supporting each infantry regiment in the division and a platoon supporting each battalion. In amphibious operations, the standardized battalion landing team (BLT) organization included a reconnaissance platoon from the divisional battalion.[115]

In 1991, the Marine Corps initiated a force structure study that looked specifically at reconnaissance units. As a result of this study, the former divisional reconnaissance battalion merged with the divisional armored infantry battalion. This battalion was equipped with the light armored vehicle, the LAV-25. The LAV-25 was a wheeled, amphibious armored personnel carrier that mounted a 25-mm gun and carried nine troops. The Marines broke up the former reconnaissance battalion's three companies, transferring a company each to two infantry regiments and retaining one company in the division's headquarters battalion as a light reconnaissance unit for the division. The new light armored reconnaissance (LAR) battalion contained four LAV-25 companies, each with 25 troop carrier, 4 antitank, and 2 mortar vehicles. These battalions, despite the redesignations, were designed to perform reconnaissance missions and to provide general armored infantry support to Marine infantry units. Therefore, the 1st Marine Division contained two LAR battalions while the lower priority 3d Marine Division had only a company detached from one of the 1st Division's battalions. In 2000, the Corps reactivated its divisional reconnaissance battalions while retaining the LAR battalions as well.[116]

DESERT STORM, 1991

Operation DESERT STORM and the initial phase of Operation IRAQI FREEDOM (OIF) were the major wartime experiences of the AOE organization. In both actions, reconnaissance units played major roles in combat operations and in precombat deployment, screening, and traffic control operations.

For the ground offensive, the US Army deployed two corps, each with an assigned armored cavalry regiment, divisional cavalry squadrons, and battalion scout platoons (figure 59). The VII Corps, tasked with the main effort, had two (later a third was added) armored divisions, a mechanized

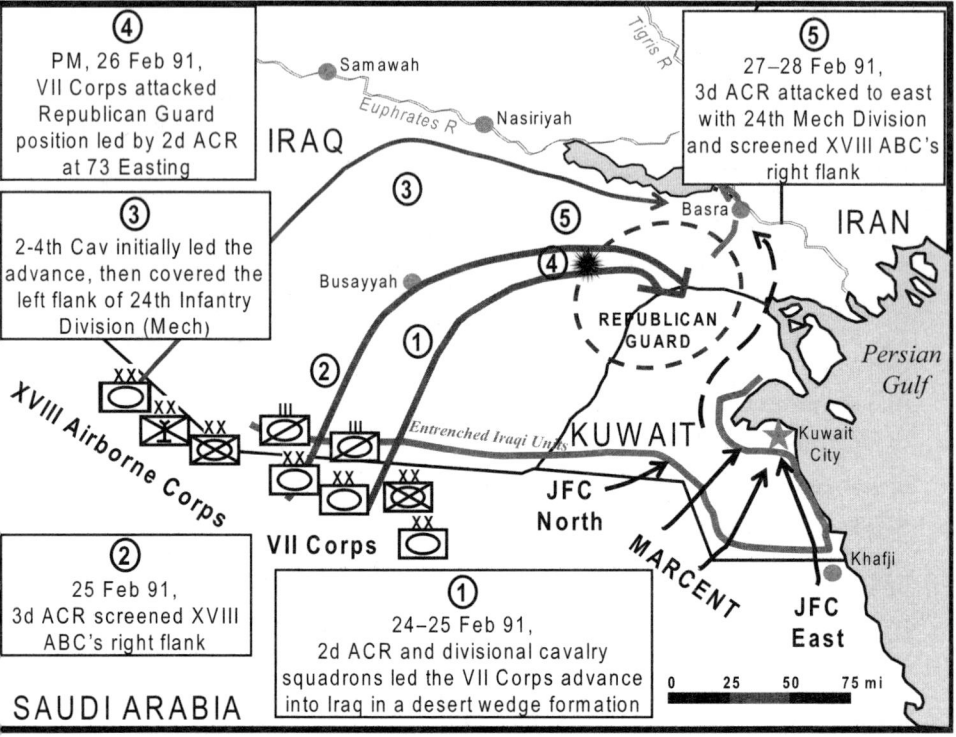

Figure 59. Cavalry forces in Operation DESERT STORM, 1991.

infantry division, and a British armored formation. The XVIII Airborne Corps (ABC) contained a mechanized infantry division, an air assault division, an airborne division, and a division-sized French force.[117]

At the corps level, each corps used its respective armored cavalry regiments based primarily on the firepower and armored punch inherent in the units rather than as purely reconnaissance or security forces. This was particularly true in the XVIII Corps whose forces, apart from the 3d ACR and the 24th Infantry Division (Mechanized), consisted mostly of light infantry elements. Since the corps was on the left of the Coalition forces, it had to cover that open flank. The corps gave the French division, a force with much lighter armor than comparable US mechanized and armored cavalry units, this mission rather than the 3d ACR. After screening the corps movement to its start positions and covering its assembly, in the ground campaign, the 3d ACR initially screened the corps' right flank, maintaining contact with both the advancing units of the VII Corps to the east and the rapidly advancing 24th Division, the XVIII Corps' main effort, on the west. After the 24th had reached its initial objectives, the regiment moved up and covered the division's eastern flank as it advanced on its subsequent objectives. Elements of the 82d Airborne Division then relieved the ACR of this mission, allowing it to join the corps' main effort. The regiment was thereafter placed under the control of the 24th Division where it both covered the corps' right flank, which was adjacent to the VII Corps, and participated in the advance and attack to the east against elements of the Iraqi Republican Guard.[118]

In contrast, the VII Corps commander, Lieutenant General Frederick Franks, initially used his 2d ACR as an advance guard covering force, then as an attacking element. Franks originally intended to conduct a 130-mile movement to contact to the vicinity of where the Republican Guard was thought to be positioned. At that point, the ACR had wanted a three-division strike force. With two of his divisions initially committed to a breach operation against the western end of the fortified Iraqi line, he was left with only two divisions for his fist. Accordingly, the 2d ACR became the third piece. Franks augmented the 2d ACR with attachments, including an entire field artillery brigade, that turned the regiment into a minidivision.[119]

The regiment moved out in front of the corps' two armored divisions and, at first, only fought skirmishes with small Iraqi units. When the advance shifted to the east on the second day, the 2d ACR no longer was in front of the 1st Armored Division, which moved into an attack formation. A day later, the armored cavalry shifted to the southeast, uncovering the 3d Armored Division as well. This was part of a maneuver whereby Franks intended to line up his armored divisions side by side, reinforced with the 1st Infantry Division (Mechanized), to attack the defensive positions of the Iraqi Republican Guard Forces Command (RGFC). With the operational tempo of the maneuver increasing, the 2d ACR in front of the arriving 1st Division continued to advance against the left flank of the Iraqi *Tawakalna* Mechanized Division.[120]

The result was the 2d ACR's Battle of 73 Easting, named after a map grid line, on the afternoon of 26 February. Franks wanted regimental commander Colonel Leonard "Don" Holder to fight to find out the *Tawakalna* dispositions without becoming pinned down in a big fight. Holder advanced with his three ground squadrons on line, meeting the southern half of the Iraqi division's defensive line and an adjacent armored brigade from another division, destroying the armored brigade and partially destroying one of the *Tawakalna* brigades. The 1st Infantry Division then passed through the regiment to continue the attack the next day. The ACR remained in reserve and later reinforced the 1st Division's final attacks on the Republican Guard on the last day of the campaign.[121]

During the brief DESERT STORM ground campaign, both Army corps commanders used their ACRs as security or reconnaissance forces in the initial phase of the advance but later used them as main battle combat forces. Neither commander could afford to hold back the combat power represented by the ACR's mix of tanks and Bradley cavalry fighting vehicles.

In the VII Corps, each armored division advanced in the open desert terrain of southwestern Iraq in a formation known as the desert wedge. Advancing initially behind the 2d ACR, the 1st and 3d Armored Divisions maintained compact formations of about 15 miles across. The ground troops of the divisional cavalry led the advance followed by one brigade, then the other two brigades side by side. The cavalry maintained contact with the 2d ACR and the units on both flanks. As the advance transitioned into an attack, the divisional squadrons shifted to cover the flanks of their respective divisions, primarily maintaining contact with adjacent friendly units.[122]

The cavalry squadron of the 1st Infantry Division (Mechanized), 1st Squadron, 4th Cavalry (1-4th Cav), led the division's advance as its command conducted a large breach operation against the Iraqi defensive line along the Saudi-Iraqi border. The squadron then reinforced the 1st Brigade, which attacked on the left (west) side of the breach sector on the afternoon of 24 February. When the division shifted to the main VII Corps front on 26 February, the squadron led the divisional movement and then screened the division's left (northern) flank as it moved to the east to attack the Iraqi Republican Guard, maintaining contact with the 1st Armored Division's cavalry squadron (4th Squadron, 7th Cavalry), which covered that division's right flank during the advance.[123]

The XVIII Airborne Corps had three divisional cavalry squadrons, each organized differently. The 24th Division's 2d Squadron, 4th Cavalry (2-4th Cav), had one CFV ground troop, one troop with tanks and M113s, and two air troops. The 82d Airborne Division's 1st Squadron, 17th Cavalry (1-17th Cav), consisted of a HMMWV-equipped troop and three air troops. The 2d Squadron, 17th Cavalry (2-17th Cav), 101st Airborne Division (Air Assault), was purely a helicopter unit.[124]

Each of these squadrons was used differently in the campaign. The 2-17th Cav was reinforced with troops from infantry battalion scout platoons in the initial phase of the operation and conducted area reconnaissance missions until the division conducted a series of air assaults, after which it screened the northern flank of the division. The 82d Airborne Division moved up in the latter stages of the campaign by truck, with the 1-17th Cav leading all the movements.[125]

The 24th Division reassigned the 2-4th Cav's air troops to the aviation brigade where they were committed to numerous short-term missions supporting various units throughout the campaign. The division augmented the ground troops with a tank company, engineer company, and a field artillery battery. In the initial phase of operations, one troop was detached to support the brigade on the left (west) of the division sector while the remaining force led the division's main two-brigade effort—the advance into the Euphrates Valley. Similar to the covering force advance of the 2d ACR, the 2-4th Cav led the advance against limited Iraqi resistance. In the second phase of the operation, the squadron covered the division's left flank as it maneuvered into the Euphrates Valley and turned to the east.[126]

DESERT STORM was the first major test of the AOE organization. Ground reconnaissance forces carried out a number of missions. At the corps level, ACRs were used either to lead the advance, or as an additional combat force, or both as in the case of the 2d ACR. At division level, cavalry squadrons were split into air and ground elements, which generally operated separately. Ground elements primarily covered the flanks of the movement and kept divisions tied in with the units to their left and right. Division commanders, as necessary, also used their squadrons as attacking forces, as in the case of the 1-4th Cav.

Operation IRAQI FREEDOM, 2003

Twelve years after DESERT STORM, US Army cavalry forces were again in combat operations in Iraq (figure 60). For the 2003 Baghdad campaign, the Army deployed a single corps (V Corps), which used a lone division for its main effort. No ACRs deployed with V Corps, and basically, two squadrons and a separate troop were available and designed to conduct the reconnaissance and security missions, as follows: the 3d Squadron, 7th Cavalry (3-7th Cav), 3d Infantry Division (Mechanized); the 2-17th Cav, 101st Airborne Division (Air Assault); and Troop A, 1-17th Cav, supporting the 2d Brigade, 82d Airborne Division.

The 3-7th Cav was organized as an L-series squadron with three ground troops that included tanks and two troops of attack/scout helicopters. The 2-17th Cav was organized as it had been in 1991 with four subordinate air troops, each with eight OH-58D Kiowa reconnaissance/attack helicopters. The squadron was assigned to the attack aviation brigade of the 101st Airborne Division. Troop A, 1-17th Cav, also had eight OH-58Ds.

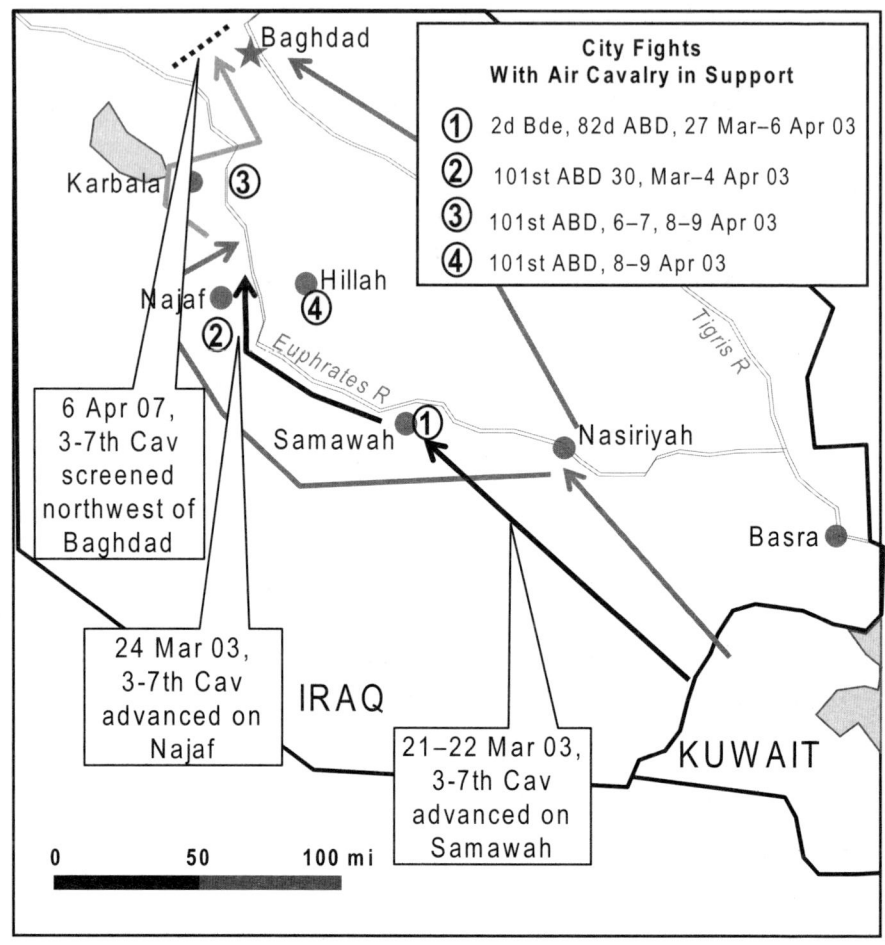

Figure 60. Cavalry units in Iraq, March–April 2003.

The commander of the 3d Infantry Division (Mechanized) chose to use the ground troops of the 3-7th Cav as a separate maneuver element during the campaign. In the initial phase of operations, the squadron led a separate advance onto the Euphrates River city of Samawah. Upon relief by a divisional brigade, the squadron then advanced north along the Euphrates to the Najaf area, securing several vital crossing sites. When the division moved on Baghdad, occupying initially an objective south of the city, then the airport west of the downtown area, the cavalry squadron moved to the northwest and screened that area as maneuver battalions advanced into the center of the city.

Both the 82d and 101st ended up fighting in cities bypassed by the 3d Division in its rapid advance on Baghdad. In these actions at Samawah,

Najaf, Hillah, and Karbala, the divisions used their air cavalry elements as fire support as infantry cleared the cities. The OH-58D proved ideal for such a role, being able to maneuver along city streets and provide immediate support.[127]

From 29 March through 6 April 2003, the 2d Brigade, 82d Airborne Division, fought a clearing battle at Samawah, a city of 120,000 located on the Euphrates south of Najaf. The brigade used its attached air cavalry troop to provide fire support. With the city cordoned off by ground units from the south and east and west, Troop A, 1-17th Cav, covered the northern exits across the Euphrates by fire with its OH-58D Kiowa attack/scout helicopters. When the brigade executed a two-battalion attack on 31 March, air cavalry helicopters attacked enemy vehicles and personnel fleeing the city to the north.[128]

The 101st Airborne Division (Air Assault) fought, in turn, to clear the cities of Najaf, Karbala, and Hillah, all located on or near the Euphrates between Samawah and Baghdad. In each of these operations, the 101st adopted a systematic approach that included fire support from the 2-17th Cav. The combat teams did not seek to take the city building by building. Instead, the advance was aimed at finding the key insurgent centers and destroying them. At Karbala on 6 April, Kiowas flew in support overhead as four battalions of the 2d Brigade systematically cleared out the streets of the city and nests of resistance using a combined arms team centered on the infantry but supported by attached tanks and field artillery. The operation was an overwhelming success, and Karbala was cleared in 2 days.[129]

In the airborne and air assault divisions in OIF 2003, some of the same factors that had affected the Wehrmacht resurfaced. The mobility and/or firepower of the division- and battalion-level reconnaissance units made them more valuable as mobile reserves or mobile strike forces than as reconnaissance units. With the heavier 3d Infantry Division (Mechanized), the long advances and bypassed cities that sapped forces to screen them made the divisional cavalry squadron, with its combined arms force of tanks and CFVs, a more valuable asset as an additional maneuver force than as a reconnaissance or security element.

Modular Army

Stryker Brigades

Even as the US Army was looking at a digitalized division in Force XXI, other factors resulted in the Army supplanting the Force XXI concept with the Modular Army structure beginning in 2004. The Modular

Army had its origins in the attempt to field a maneuver brigade that was air transportable while not being too light to fight once it deployed. After much experimentation, the Army developed an organization known as the Stryker Brigade Combat Team (SBCT) starting in 1999. The brigade was built around the newly developed Stryker, a complexly digitalized, medium-weight wheeled armored personnel carrier. The Stryker came in various configurations, including a reconnaissance vehicle (RV) variant.[130]

The SBCT was designed as a stand-alone brigade, able to operate without a division. Digitization, which had been the major feature of Force XXI, was incorporated extensively into the SBCT structure. The three Stryker infantry battalions retained a reconnaissance platoon containing two reconnaissance sections, each with two RV Strykers. However, it was at the brigade level when the SBCT organization departed from prior reconnaissance structures. Whereas previous brigades had only recently fielded a troop, the SBCT contained a cavalry squadron, known by the acronym RSTA (reconnaissance, surveillance, and target acquisition). The RSTA squadron was considered to be "the primary force for providing combat information to build the knowledge base necessary to achieve a common operational picture." To do this, the unit was equipped with an array of digital and surveillance systems.[131]

The RSTA squadron in the SBCT had a headquarters troop, three reconnaissance troops, and a surveillance troop (figure 61). The reconnaissance troops each had three platoons, each equipped with four RV Strykers and a Stryker-mounted mortar section. The surveillance troop contained elements usually found in military intelligence (MI) units. It included a platoon of four unmanned aerial vehicles supported by 20 troopers; a ground sensor platoon with eight sensor devices; a multisensor platoon with three Prophet systems; and a nuclear, biological, and chemical (NBC) reconnaissance platoon with three Fox NBC armored car systems.[132]

The Army fielded the first SBCT in 2003. The brigade deployed to Iraq for a 1-year rotational tour in November 2003, with subsequent SBCTs following in later rotations. With the success of the Stryker program, the Army decided to convert the 2d ACR, the HMMWV-equipped LACR, to the Stryker configuration. The regiment converted to the new structure in 2005. The SBCT organization, common to all fielded Stryker brigades, contained three infantry battalions, the RSTA squadron, an artillery battalion, an antitank company, and various support elements. To achieve the SBCT structure, the 2d Cavalry's three line squadrons retained their designations but were reconfigured as three infantry battalions. The Army

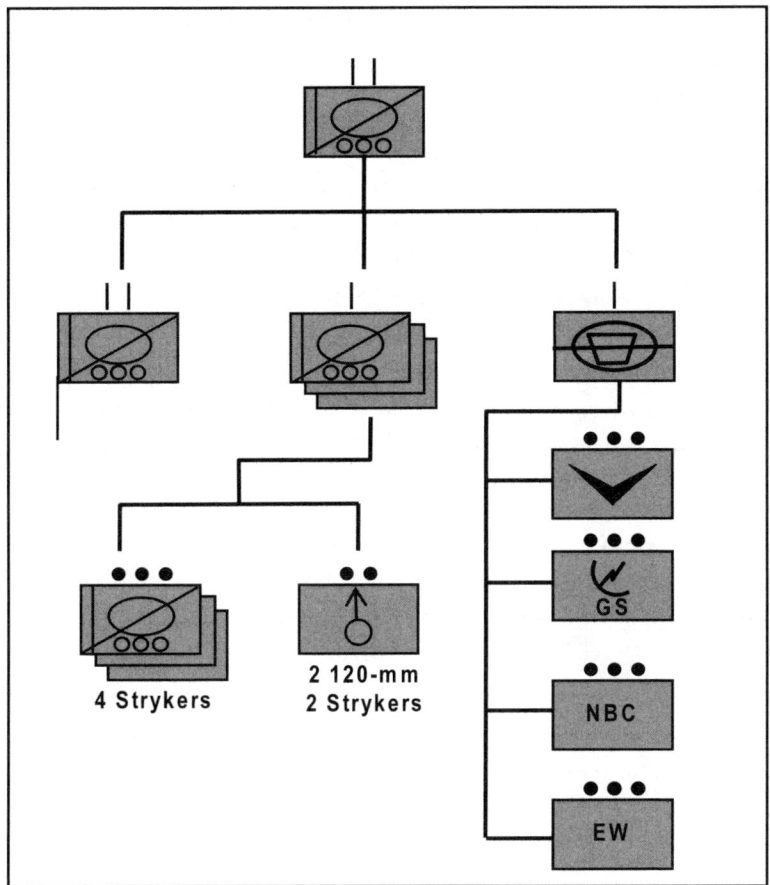

Figure 61. SBCT RSTA squadron, 2003.

attached the RSTA squadron and antitank company with separate cavalry (2d Squadron, 14th Cavalry) and infantry (D Company, 52d Infantry) designations respectively. The conversion of regiment to the SBCT format transformed it into a regimental combat team since these elements did not retain organic regimental designations as had routinely been done in the past.[133]

The conversion of the 2d Cavalry to an SBCT structure showed the Army's line of thinking involving the Stryker brigades. They were self-contained medium brigade packages able to be deployed worldwide alone or as part of a larger unit. In other words, the SBCT resembled historic armored cavalry regiments more than the previous divisional brigades.

The next logical step was the expansion of the SBCT concept to the rest of the Army.

Modular Brigades

The Modular Army was an extension of the SBCT concept to the rest of the Army. Under this concept, starting in 2004, the Army initiated a program to standardize the structure of brigades and expand the existing active maneuver brigades into a number of smaller, self-contained BCTs. Thus, the US Army became brigade-centric rather than, as it had been since World War I, division-centric.[134]

The heavy BCT replaced the armored and mechanized brigades in the Army's force structure. Although the SBCT had three maneuver battalions, the heavy BCT contained only two.[135] Each of these battalions was, however, a combined arms task force containing two tank and two mechanized infantry companies and a scout platoon consisting of three scout sections with three M3 CFVs and five armored HMMWVs in total. Supporting the brigade was a field artillery battalion and a RSTA squadron. Since the BCT contained only two maneuver battalions, both the field artillery and cavalry units reflected this in a reduced number of subordinate elements.[136]

The rationale for including a cavalry squadron in each brigade was the perception of Army Chief of Staff General Peter Schoomaker that the brigade echelon had previously been weak at detecting enemy activities and capabilities. Little or no consideration was given to past operational employment of reconnaissance units.[137]

The RSTA squadron contained three cavalry troops, each composed of two subordinate platoons (figure 62). The platoons were equipped with a combination of CFVs and HMMWVs equipped with surveillance equipment. Each reconnaissance team had two Long-Range Advanced Scout Surveillance Systems (LRAS3s), and for targeting, each platoon had two Lightweight Laser Designator Rangefinder (LLDR) Systems. Each troop also had a UAV system and a dedicated three-man field artillery COLT. The brigade had an MI company to support the RSTA squadron.[138]

The heavy BCT RSTA cavalry squadron combined both tracked and wheeled vehicles into a single organization at the platoon level. In theory, the troop commander and platoon leader could consolidate the vehicles by type or team them together. The first modular squadrons deployed to Iraq in 2005.

The modular design applied to light units as well. The light units included light infantry, airborne, and air assault brigades. Apart from

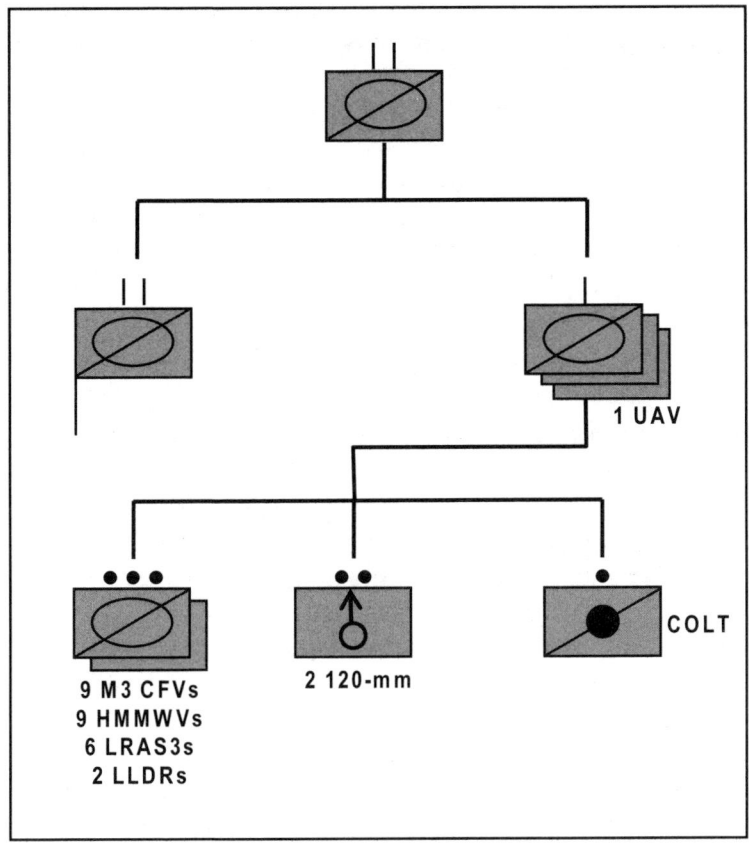

Figure 62. Modular brigade RSTA squadron.

the special capabilities of the latter two organizations, the light modular brigade was standardized as much as possible. The light brigade contained two infantry battalions, each with three infantry companies and a weapons company. The light RSTA squadron was organized with two troops mounted in HMMWVs and equipped heavily with surveillance equipment and a third dismounted troop. The dismounted troop contained 50 scouts trained to operate on foot.[139]

Nonbrigade Units

When the Army adopted the modular design, small units above brigade level were planned to be building blocks to divisional task forces under functional brigade headquarters. This idea was similar to the pooling concept used in World War II. Nevertheless, as of 2007, the 3d ACR retained its AOE structure and place in the force structure.[140]

In general terms, the reconnaissance units above the brigade level were more technically oriented than previous such units. A RSTA brigade, later referred to as a battlefield surveillance brigade (BfSB), would typically be formed to support a division. The division, under modularity, became more of a mission-oriented task force than the fixed organization it had previously been. The BfSB was not expected to conduct combat operations, including traditional cavalry missions such as security operations. Instead, division commanders were to assign such missions, as necessary, to combat BCTs. A typical BfSB organization consisted of a headquarters company, support battalion, and MI battalion. Other elements, such as separate surveillance and reconnaissance battalions, teams, or troops, would be assigned on a mission or task organization basis.[141]

The modular structure began operational testing in counterinsurgency operations in Iraq and in Afghanistan beginning in 2005. Many elements, such as the RSTA squadrons, were usually relegated to infantry-type duty, controlling a geographical sector or providing convoy security. Such operations were not a true test of the organizational structure, but based on previous experience, the use of RSTA units similar to brigade maneuver battalions was not an unexpected development.

Summary

Since World War II, the world's major armies have tackled the twin organizational issues of the levels at which to deploy reconnaissance forces and how to equip them based on a combination of experience, the implementation of technological developments, and the expected operational environment. For many years, the Cold War and its Central Front dominated the equipment and organization of reconnaissance units on both sides of the Iron Curtain. In this atmosphere, only the United States deployed reconnaissance units above the division level, units that also had a unique border guard mission in Germany for several decades.

The NATO allies fielded various reconnaissance vehicles. The British and French favored light tanks and wheeled armored personnel carriers, while the Germans combined main battle tanks and armored cars in their reconnaissance battalions. The Soviet concept of reconnaissance transcended the formation of dedicated reconnaissance units. While the Soviets maintained such units at every level from regiment to division and equipped them with a combination of armored and wheeled vehicles, they organized for attack and defense into formations that had specific reconnaissance or security responsibilities apart from the reconnaissance units. The Red Army used the divisional reconnaissance battalion operationally, placing it far forward of its parent unit to scout. The division and lower units depended on a task-organized combined arms force from its organic units called the combat reconnaissance patrol to conduct tactical reconnaissance. The combat reconnaissance patrol was the lead element of divisional and regimental forward detachments. Outside of Central Europe, the Israeli Defense Force formulated its own ideas on the organization and equipment of reconnaissance forces. After heavy combat losses in the open desert by lightly equipped, but stealthy, reconnaissance units, the IDF made these elements heavier, equipping them with tanks and armored personnel carriers. Ironically, reconnaissance units again suffered heavy losses in 1973 when, because of their increased combat power, they were committed to high-intensity battles such as the Battle of the Chinese Farm.

The American experience since World War II saw reconnaissance units become progressively heavier, with main battle tanks replacing light tanks and tracked armored vehicles replacing jeeps and armored cars. Despite several attempts to remove them from the cavalry force structure, tanks remained an integral part of such units until the Modular Army reorganization and, in fact, continued as a key component in the only remaining armored cavalry regiment even after the implementation of the new structure. With heavier reconnaissance units, American commanders viewed such units as additional maneuver elements and, therefore, so used them in DESERT STORM and in Iraq in 2003.

Later, reconnaissance organizations incorporated advances in helicopter technology. Hybrid air-ground squadrons appeared. But, operationally, these units suffered from the aviation imperative to place all helicopter assets under an aviation commander. This typically resulted in the splitting up of squadrons in combat operations. Only in the armored cavalry regiment, where the regimental commander controlled the aviation and ground assets without a higher aviation headquarters, did such units work together well. Air cavalry squadrons in the air assault division and light divisions provided their worth in Vietnam. However, in the post-Vietnam era, similar to tank-heavy ground squadrons, commanders often used these units primarily for their firepower rather than for their reconnaissance capabilities.

In the 1990s, after tests conducted at the National Training Center, the US Army began to use the HMMWV extensively in the reconnaissance role, even in heavy units. While such a move seemed effective in the NTC exercise environment, in real-life practice, commanders often feared for the survival of such units and gave them rear area security, traffic control, demolition of enemy equipment, prisoner-of-war guard duty, or headquarters guard missions.[142]

The SBCT and the Modular Army concept dramatically changed the echeloning of reconnaissance units in the US Army. While in the past reconnaissance units existed from the brigade level to the corps level, the new brigade-centric force had a squadron organic at the brigade level. Higher level forces were assembled on a mission basis. The RSTA squadron, particularly in the Stryker brigades, had an increasingly technical focus, stressing the use of surveillance and targeting systems formerly retained in less combat-oriented military intelligence units. The increased size of the cavalry unit at the brigade level matched a similar new century move by the German *Bundeswehr* for its units conducting contingency operations. US Army modular doctrine also recognized that many missions formerly conducted by reconnaissance units could also be conducted by maneuver units if necessary. This principle also reflected past German practice.

Notes

1. Gunther Rothenberg, *The Anatomy of the Israeli Army: The Israel Defence Force, 1948–78* (New York: Hippocrene, 1979), 65, 81, 86; Samuel M. Katz, *Fire and Steel: Israel's 7th Armored Brigade* (New York: Pocket Books, 1996), 40; Seth Caron, "The Arab-Israeli Wars, Armies in Conflict, TO&E: Anatomy of a War," *The General* 14 (September–October 1977): 3; Gideon Avidor, "From Brigade to Division," *Military Review* 58 (October 1978): 65–67.

2. Katz, 48–49.

3. Ibid.; George W. Gawrych, *Key to the Sinai: The Battles for Abu Ageila in the 1956 and 1967 Arab-Israeli Wars*, Research Survey No. 7 (Fort Leavenworth, KS: US Army Command and General Staff College, 1990), 25, 42; Rothenberg, 107; Trevor N. Dupuy, *Elusive Victory: The Arab-Israeli Wars, 1947–1974* (Fairfax, VA: HERO Books, 1984), 184.

4. A. Harding Ganz, "Abu Ageila, Two Battles—Part 1: 1956," *Armor* 83 (May–June 1974): 38–39, 41; S.L.A. Marshall, *Sinai Victory* (Nashville, TN: Battery Press, 1985), 103–106; Gawrych, 37, 39, 41–42; Dupuy, *Elusive Victory*,162; Katz, 50.

5. Gawrych, 37–39, 41–42; Dupuy, *Elusive Victory*, 160, 162.

6. Dupuy, *Elusive Victory*, 184, 188–191.

7. Gawrych, 69–71; Avidor, 65–67; Edward Luttwak and Daniel Horowitz, *The Israeli Army, 1948–1973* (Lanham, MD: University Press of America, 1983), 169, 171, 176, 186.

8. Gawrych, 88, 92–94; Dupuy, *Elusive Victory*, 249–250, 253; Chaim Herzog, *The Arab-Israeli Wars: War and Peace in the Middle East* (New York: Vintage Books, 1984), 159; Katz, 48–49; Rothenberg, 100, 159. Several sources cite reconnaissance "regiment" of multiple battalions being assigned to Brigadier General Yisrael Tal's division, commanded by Lieutenant Colonel Uri Barom. However, an analysis of all available sources indicates that Barom actually commanded a tank battalion, an extra unit initially attached to the paratrooper brigade assigned to Tal's division. The confusion results from the common Israeli practice of splitting battalions in half and using each half separately in combat operations. See Shabtai Teveth, *The Tanks of Tammuz* (New York: Viking, 1969), 160. One source indicates that Sharon's reconnaissance force was a preexisting border patrol force. See A. Harding Ganz "Abu Ageila, Two Battles—Part 2: 1967," *Armor* 83 (July–August 1974): 16.

9. Ganz, "Abu Ageila, Two Battles—Part 2: 1967," 19; Herzog, 159; Gawrych, 93; Dupuy, *Elusive Victory*, 249–250, 253, 258; Rothenberg, 141; Luttwak and Horowitz, 255. Katz, 77; Teveth, 218; Granit Force was named after its commander, Colonel Granit Yisrael. The Steel Division was later given the numerical designation 162d Armored Division.

10. Teveth, 133–134; Ori Orr, "Bloody Gaza," *Jerusalem Post Supplement, The Six Day War—30th Anniversary*, 4 June 1997, http://info.jpost.com/1998/Supplements/30years/orr.html (accessed 17 October 2003); Caron, 5; Luttwak and Horowitz, 215.

11. Katz, 78, 82–84, 87; Orr; Dupuy, *Elusive Victory,* 249, 251; Teveth, 132–134, 145–147, 166–167.
12. Dupuy, *Elusive Victory,* 249, 251; Teveth, 187–189; Katz, 93–95.
13. Ganz, "Abu Ageila, Two Battles—Part 2: 1967," 19–20; Teveth, 249.
14. Rothenberg, 100, 158–159; Katz, 48–49; Caron, 3–4.
15. Caron, 5; "The 87th Armored Recon Battalion [IDF]," http://www.87th.org.il/enhistory.html (accessed 3 August 2005). Some divisional reconnaissance battalions may have had only two tank/APC companies instead of three.
16. Katz, 138; John J. McGrath, "Sinai 1973: Israeli Maneuver Organization and the Battle of the Chinese Farm," *An Army at War: Change in the Midst of Conflict: The Proceedings of the Combat Studies Institute 2005 Military History Symposium* (Fort Leavenworth, KS: Combat Studies Institute Press, 2005), 65.
17. "The 87th Armored Recon Battalion [IDF]." The battalion commander killed in action was Lieutenant Colonel Ben-Zion Carmeli. In 1967, Carmeli had commanded the tank company that followed directly behind the 7th Brigade's reconnaissance element at Khan Yunis.
18. Ibid. Brom had been vacationing abroad when the war started.
19. Ibid.; McGrath, "Sinai 1973: Israeli Maneuver Organization and the Battle of the Chinese Farm," 70, 74.
20. McGrath, "Sinai 1973: Israeli Maneuver Organization and the Battle of the Chinese Farm" 74, 77; "The 87th Armored Recon Battalion [IDF]."
21. "The 87th Armored Recon Battalion [IDF]."
22. While most IDF order of battle information is kept in a close-hold status, several Israeli veterans have discussed the status of reconnaissance elements on the Internet. See the archived discussion page for the Wikipedia entry on the IDF: "User Talk: Novlador/Archive 3," http://en.wikipedia.org/wiki/User_talk:Noclador/Archive_3 (accessed 21 October 2007).
23. Ibid.; "Sayeret Matkal," http://www.militaryphotos.net/forums/showthread.php?t+4006 (accessed 21 October 2007); Katz, 61; Luttwak and Horowitz, 178.
24. US Department of the Army, Field Manual 100-2-3, *The Soviet Army: Troops, Organization, Equipment* (Washington, DC: Department of the Army, 1984), 4-8, 4-26, 4-33, 4-101, 4-106, 4-114, 4-115; David Isby, *Weapons and Tactics of the Soviet Army*, new ed. (London: Jane's, 1988), 373.
25. Field Manual 100-2-3, 4-67, 4-68, 4-69; Isby, 373.
26. Field Manual 100-2-3, 5-15, 6-21; Isby, 370.
27. Isby, 381–383.
28. Ibid., 370–371.
29. Ibid., 371–372.
30. Colonel David Glantz, *The Fundamentals of Soviet* Razvedka (Fort Leavenworth, KS: US Army Soviet Foreign Studies Office, 1989), 10–13.
31. Ibid., 11, 23–24; Isby 43–45.
32. Isby, 45–47, 370; Major Bryan Oliver, "The Combat Reconnaissance Detachment in the Meeting Engagement and Defense," *Armor* 99 (July–August

1990): 7; C.J. Dick, "Soviet Battle Drills: Vulnerability or Strength?" *International Defense Review* 18 (May 1985): 663.

33. Isby, 69.
34. Ibid., 369.
35. Ibid., 45, 55, 371.
36. Terry Gander, *Encyclopedia of the Modern British Army*, 2d ed. (Cambridge, England: Patrick Stephens, 1982), 20.
37. Ibid., 25.
38. Ibid., 24–25.
39. Ibid., 24–25, 170.
40. Thomas Dinackus, *Order of Battle: Allied Ground Forces of Operation Desert Storm* (Central Point, OR: Hellgate, 2000), 27-4, 27-9. The attached squadron was from the 1st Queens Dragoon Guards. When the British initially deployed only a single brigade to the Gulf, this squadron was the brigade's attached reconnaissance element.
41. Ibid., 27-4.
42. Ibid, 27-8.
43. Ibid. 28-5. HOT means *Haut subsonique Optiquement Téléguidé*, which translated means high subsonic optical guided.
44. Dinackus, 28-5.
45. Thomas Koch Schulz, *Das deutsche Heer Heute* (Bonn, GE: Mittler, 1987), xxv.
46. "Tradition," *KameradschaftPanzeraufklärungsbataillon 12 e.V.*, http://www.pzaufklbtl12.de/Tradition/tradition.htm (accessed 29 October 2007). For a detailed discussion of the debate over *Bundeswehr* traditions, see Donald Abenheim, *Reforging the Iron Cross: The Search for Tradition in the West German Armed Forces* (Princeton, NJ: Princeton University Press, 1988).
47. "Die Geschichte des Panzeraufklärungslehrbataillons 3," *Freudeskreis der Panzeraufklärer*, http://www.panzeraufklaerungstruppe.de/truppengtg/bataillone/PAB03L/gescchichte.html (accessed 26 October 2007); "Die Gliederung des Panzeraufklärungsbataillon 12 im Wandel der Heersstrukturen," *KameradschaftPanzeraufklärungsbataillon 12 e.V.*, http://www.pzaufklbtl12.de/Geschichte/heeres.htm (accessed 28 October 2007).
48. "Die Gliederung des Panzeraufklärungsbataillon 12 im Wandel der Heersstrukturen;" Matthew A. Dooley, "Ignoring History: The Flawed Effort to Divorce Reconnaissance From Security in Modern Cavalry Transformation" (MMAS thesis, US Army Command and General Staff College, 2006), 40.
49. "Die Geschichte des Panzeraufklärungslehrbataillons 3"; "Panzerbrigade 18—Holstein, 1956–1994," http://www.bundesarchiv.de/php/bestaende_findmittel/bestaendeuebersicht/druckansicht.php?id_bestand=3778 (accessed 29 October 2007); "Die Gliederung des Panzeraufklärungsbataillon 12 im Wandel der Heersstrukturen"; Kenneth L. Boeglen, "Does the Heavy Maneuver Brigade Commander Need an Organic Reconnaissance/Security Organization?" (MMAS thesis, US Army Command and General Staff College, 1992), 84–85.

50. "Gepanzerte Kampftruppen, Panzeraufklärer und Panzertruppenschule Sacchstand und Perspektiven," presentation by the *Bundeswehr*'s Armored Branch Chief on 12 November 2004, www.panzertruppe.com/pdf/pdf%20s-b/struktur_nh.pdf (accessed 29 October 2007); "Die Panzeraufklärer der Bundeswehr," *Die Panzeraufklärer im Internet*, http://www.pzaufkl.de/include.php?path=content/articles.php&contentid=2&PHPKITSID=d868e33dcb939f55858d768008fb07f4 (accessed 29 October 2007).

51. Ibid.

52. Ibid.

53. Gander, 18. Many NATO armies, including the French, British, and Belgian forces, deployed reconnaissance battalions at the corps level. However, these units were all designated for attachment or divisions or brigades. Only the Dutch (battalion) and American (regiment) armies employed separate reconnaissance forces at the corps level in the 1980s. See Andy Johnson and Pat Callahan, "NATO Order of Battle 1989," http://www.scribd.com/doc/37695/NATO-Order-of-Battle-1989 (accessed 26 October 2007); Lutz Unterseher, "Europe's Armed Forces at the Millennium: A Case Study of Change in France, the United Kingdom, and Germany," Project on Defense Alternatives Briefing Report No. 11, November 1999, http://www.comw.org/pda/9911eur.html (accessed 26 October 2007).

54. James Sawicki, *Cavalry Regiments of the US Army* (Dumfries, VA: Wyvern Publications, 1985), 122; Lieutenant Colonel James T. Burke, "Armored Infantry and Recon Unit Organization," *Armor* 65 (July–August 1956): 15; Major Louis A. DiMarco, "The U.S. Army's Mechanized Cavalry Doctrine in World War II" (MMAS thesis, US Army Command and General Staff College, 1995), 133.

55. Captain William O. Boyle, "M114: The Scout's New Vehicle," *Armor* 72 (November–December 1963): 43; Captain Raymond E. Bell Jr., "A New Role for the ACRV," *Armor* 72 (March–April 1963): 49–50.

56. John B. Wilson, *Maneuver and Firepower: The Evolution of Divisions and Separate Brigades* (Washington, DC: US Army Center of Military History, 1998), 249; James Sawicki, *Tank Battalions of the US Army* (Dumfries, VA: Wyvern, 1983), 18.

57. Sawicki, *Cavalry Regiments of the US Army*, 124, 134.

58. R.P. Hunnicut, *Bradley: A History of American Fighting and Support Vehicles* (Novato, CA: Presidio, 1999), 33, 56; Boyle, 45.

59. Sawicki, *Cavalry Regiments of the US Army*, 121; US Forces, European Theater, General Board, "Tactics, Employment, Technique, Organization, and Equipment of Mechanized Cavalry Units," Study Number 49 (Bad Nauheim, GE, 1945–46), 20.

60. Mary Lee Stubbs and Stanley R. Connor. *Armor-Cavalry Part I: Regular Army and Army Reserve* (Washington, DC: US Army Center of Military History, 1969): 74–75; Sawicki, *Cavalry Regiments of the US Army*, 124.

61. Stubbs and Connor, 74. The 1st Cavalry Division was also active, but it was in reality an infantry division. In 1947, the 3d Armored Division was active but as a training unit. It was converted into an operational division in 1955.

62. Wilson, *Maneuver and Firepower*, 227; Lieutenant Colonel William Phelps, Major James Ellingsworth, Captain William C. Jones, Captain Sidney Haszard, and Captain Dandridge Hering, "A Standard Reconnaissance Battalion," Committee 6, Armored Officer Advance Course, 1952–1953 (Fort Knox, KY: US Army Armored School, 1953), 19–20; Burke, 15.

63. Burke, 15–16; Lieutenant Colonel Duane S. Cason, "Introduction to the New Armored Division," *Armor* 66 (November–December 1957): 7; Major Paul M. Fisher and Captain George C. Hoffmaster Jr., "Armored Division Organization and Doctrine," *Armor* 67 (September–October 1958): 8; Sawicki, *Cavalry Regiments of the US Army*, 124; R.P. Hunnicut, *Bradley: A History of American Fighting and Support Vehicles* (Novato, CA: Presidio, 1999), 61–62; Colonel John Beall, "Revisions to ROCAD," *Armor* 68 (March–April 1959): 48–50.

64. US Forces, European Theater, General Board, "Organization, Equipment, and Tactical Employment of the Infantry Division," Study Number 15 (Bad Nauheim, GE, 1945), 11, app 10; General Board, "Mechanized Cavalry Units," app 13, fig m; US Department of the Army, Table of Organization and Equipment (T/O-E) 17-57N, *Reconnaissance Company* (Washington, DC: Department of the Army, 23 January 1948).

65. Beall, 50; "Why Five?" *Infantry* 47 (April 1957): 8; Captain Vernie G. Tosh and Captain James B. Hobson, "Pentomic Infantry Division: Mobility," *Infantry* 47 (July 1957): 35–39.

66. Shelby L. Stanton, *Order of Battle, U.S. Army, World War II* (Novato, CA: Presidio, 1984), 19; Cason, 5–6.

67. Sawicki, *Cavalry Regiments of the US Army*, 122, 124; DiMarco, 132. The ACRs used noncavalry designations for squadrons and troops until 1960.

68. William E. Stacy, *US Army Border Operations in Germany, 1945–1983* (Heidelberg, GE: US Army, Europe, 1984), 61, 85.

69. Ibid, 63, 84, 87.

70. Ibid., 121–122, 124, 126.

71. Ibid., 144, 210–214; "The 1980s," *Armored and Cavalry Units in the European Theater*, http://www.usarmygermany.com/Units/ArmoredCav/ USAREUR_Armd%20Cav.htm (accessed 26 October 2007).

72. US Department of the Army, TOE 17-105, *Armored Cavalry Squadron, Armored Division, Armored Cavalry Squadron, Infantry Division, Armored Cavalry Squadron, Infantry Division (Mechanized)* (Washington, DC: Department of the Army, 15 July 1963); US Department of the Army, TOE 17-107G, *Armored Cavalry Troop, Armored Cavalry Squadron, Armored Division, Armored Cavalry Squadron, Infantry Division, Armored Cavalry Squadron, Infantry Division (Mechanized), Separate Armored Brigade, Infantry Brigade, Infantry Brigade*

(Mechanized) (Washington, DC: Department of the Army, 15 July 1963); US Department of the Army, TOE 17-108G, *Air Cavalry Troop, Armored Cavalry Squadron, Armored Division, Armored Cavalry Squadron, Infantry Division, Armored Cavalry Squadron, Infantry Division (Mechanized), Separate Armored Brigade, Infantry Brigade, Infantry Brigade (Mechanized)* (Washington, DC: Department of the Army, 31 March 1966); Hunnicutt, 232–235. The tank section was originally to contain two light tanks, using a tank that had not yet been developed. In lieu of this tank, the section was issued two main battle M48 Patton tanks, later increased to three.

73. Captain John C. Bahnsen Jr., "Troop D, Armored Cavalry Squadron, ROAD Armored Division," *Armor* 72 (March–April 1963): 33–37; Shelby L. Stanton, *Vietnam Order of Battle* (Washington, DC: US News Books, 1981), 48, 129; TOE 17-108G, *Air Cavalry Troop.*

74. Major General Robert E. Wagner, "Division Cavalry: The Broken Sabre," *Armor* 98 (September–October 1989): 35–36; Brigadier General Phillip L. Bolté (Ret), "Full Circle: The Armored Cavalry Platoon," *Armor* 103 (September–October 1994), 35–37; Jim Pigg, "Why Cav Changed in the '70s," *Armor* 104 (January–February 1995): 3, 50.

75. Major Joseph C. Barto III, *Task Force 2-4 Cav—"First In, Last Out": The History of the 2d Squadron, 4th Cavalry Regiment, During Operation Desert Storm* (Fort Leavenworth, KS: Combat Studies Institute, 1993), 5.

76. Stanton, *Vietnam Order of Battle*, 129; Matthew Brennan, *Hunter-Killer Squadron: Aero-Weapons, Aero-Scouts, Aero-Rifles, Vietnam 1965–1972* (Novato, CA: Presidio, 1990), 273–274; Matthew Brennan, *Headhunters: Stories From the 1st Squadron, 9th Cavalry in Vietnam, 1965–1971* (Novato, CA: Presidio, 1987), 265–266, 268.

77. Captain (P) Mark A. King, "The Battalion Scout Platoon Is Alive and Well," *Armor* 87 (September–October 1978): 35–37.

78. Hunnicutt, 232–235; General Donn Starry, *Mounted Combat in Vietnam*, Vietnam Studies (Washington, DC: Department of the Army, 1978), 37–38, 72.

79. Stanton, *Vietnam Order of Battle*, 130.

80. Starry, 73.

81. Stanton, *Vietnam Order of Battle*, 124–134; Starry, 56–57. One armored cavalry squadron was converted to air cavalry in 1968, and several squadrons left a single troop behind after redeployment.

82. Starry, 57, 106–107.

83. Stanton, *Vietnam Order of Battle*, 125–126; Barto, 3, 11–12. Only in the 11th Armored Cavalry Regiment were air and ground cavalry assets routinely used in unison. See Starry, 221.

84. Stanton, *Vietnam Order of Battle*, 130; Starry, 72–73, 75, 80, 106.

85. Starry, 91; John J. McGrath, *The Brigade: A History: Its Organization and Employment in the United States Army* (Fort Leavenworth, KS: Combat Studies Institute Press, 2004), 67–69.

86. Starry, 170–174.
87. Lieutenant General John J. Tolson, *Airmobility, 1961–1971*, Vietnam Studies (Washington, DC: Department of the Army, 1973), 151.
88. Starry, 58–60; Tolson, 74–75.
89. Starry, 24–25, 28, 30, 33, 37–38; Stanton, *Vietnam Order of Battle*, 275.
90. Starry, 28, 33; Tran Quang Khoi, "Fighting to the Finish: The Role of South Viet Nam's III Armor Brigade and III Corps Assault Force in the War's Final Days, *Armor* 105 (March–April 1996): 19–25.
91. Starry, 221–223.
92. For a detailed discussion of such units, see James F. Gebhardt, *Eyes Behind the Lines: US Army Long-Range Reconnaissance and Surveillance Units*, Global War on Terrorism Occasional Paper No. 10, revised ed. (Fort Leavenworth, KS: Combat Studies Institute Press, 2005).
93. Gebhardt, 127–131, 145; John L. Romjue, *The Army of Excellence: The Development of the 1980s Army* (Fort Monroe, VA: US Army Training and Doctrine Command, 1993), 95. In 1991, the LRRP elements, now referred to as long-range surveillance units (LRSUs) were part of divisional and corps-level military intelligence battalions.
94. Stanton, *Vietnam Order of Battle*, 130; "4th Squadron, 3d Armored Cavalry," http://www.carson.army.mil/4-3frg/index.html (accessed 6 November 2007).
95. Romjue, *The Army of Excellence*, 94–96; John L. Romjue *A History of Army 86, Volume II: The Development of the Light Division, the Corps, and Echelons Above Corps, November 1979—December 1980* (Fort Monroe, VA: US Army Training and Doctrine Command, 1982), 68; Tom Clancy, *Armored Cav: A Guided Tour of an Armored Cavalry Regiment* (New York: Berkley, 1994), 190–191.
96. Major Marc A. King, "2x2: The Regimental Cavalry Troop," *Armor* 90 (March–April 1981): 12–13; Clancy, 188–189.
97. Third Cavalry Museum, *Blood and Steel: The History, Customs, and Traditions of the 3d Armored Cavalry Regiment* (Fort Carson, CO: Third Cavalry Museum, 2006), 56, http://www.hood.army.mil/3d_ACR/docs/history_2.pdf (accessed 6 November 2007); "Unit Designations in the Army Modular Force," US Army Center of Military History presentation to the Association of the US Army (AUSA) Conference, 26 September 2005, www.cascom.army.mil/odct/Documents/AUSA_Briefing_26_Sep_05.ppt (accessed 6 November 2007).
98. Major Mark Little, "The Light Armored Cavalry Regiment—Reconnaissance Force of the Future" (Monograph, School of Advanced Military Studies, US Army Command and General Staff College, 1993), 3, 6, 8; Lieutenant Colonel Kevin Benson, "Whither the 2d Cavalry," *Armor* 106 (January–February 1997): 20–21.

99. Ibid.; "Army Announces Reconfiguration of Fourth Stryker Brigade, Army News Release, 14 May 2004, http://www.globalsecurity.org/military/library/news/2004/05/mil-040514-usar01.htm (accessed 6 November 2007).

100. The rationale for shifting combined arms to the troop level was to decrease the span of control expected of Army lieutenants. See Major Kenneth J. Quinlan, "The Army-of-Excellence Division Cavalry Squadron" (Monograph, School of Advance Military Studies, US Army Command and General Staff College, 1986), 11. At times, some J-series squadrons only contained two ground troops.

101. Romjue, *A History of Army 86, Volume II*, 7; Boeglen, 44.

102. Romjue, *A History of Army 86, Volume II*, 7–8.

103. Ibid., 7–9; Barto, 5. At various times, the aviation brigade was also referred to as the air cavalry attack brigade.

104. Romjue, *The Army of Excellence*, 94–96; Captain George Salerno, "Repairing the Broken Sabre: Overview of L-Series Divisional Cavalry," *Armor* 103 (January–February 1994): 29–34; Department of the Army, TOE 17-285L100, *Cavalry Squadron (AH-1)*/TOE 17-285L200, *Cavalry Squadron (OH-58D) Cavalry Squadron, Division Aviation Brigade, Heavy Division* (Washington, DC: Department of the Army, 1995). The L-series was initially adopted even before DESERT STORM, starting in December 1990 with units that had remained in Germany.

105. US Department of the Army, TOE 17-185L, *Cavalry Squadron, Light Infantry Division* (Washington, DC: Department of the Army, 1997); US Department of the Army, TOE 17-187L, *Cavalry Troop, Cavalry Squadron, Infantry Division (Light)* (Washington, DC: Department of the Army, 1996); US Department of the Army, TOE 1-167A, *Air Reconnaissance Troop (AH-1/OH-58D), Cavalry Squadron, Division Aviation Brigade, Infantry Division (Light)* (Washington, DC: Department of the Army, 1997); Captain Jeff Witsken and Captain Lee MacTaggart, "Light Cavalry in the 10th Mountain Division, *Armor* 99 (July–August 1990): 36–40.

106. US Department of the Army, TOE 1-65A, *Air Reconnaissance Squadron (OH-58D), Division Aviation Brigade, Airborne Division* (Washington, DC: Department of the Army, 1998); US Department of the Army, TOE 17-285L, *Air Reconnaissance Squadron (OH-58D), Division Aviation Brigade, Air Assault Division* (Washington, DC: Department of the Army, 1993).

107. Romjue, *The Army of Excellence*, 95–96; Major Barry Scribner, "HMMWVs and Scouts: Do They Mix?" *Armor* 98 (July–August 1989): 33–38; US Department of the Army, TOE 17-376L, *Headquarters and Headquarters Company, Tank Battalion, Heavy Division* (Washington, DC: Department of the Army, 1997); US Department of the Army, Field Manual 17-98, *Scout Platoon* (Washington, DC: Department of the Army, 1994), 1-1–1-3.

108. Curtis D. Taylor, *Trading the Saber for Stealth: Can Surveillance Technology Replace Traditional Aggressive Reconnaissance?* (Arlington, VA: Institute of Land Warfare, Association of the United States Army, 2005), 3–4; Martin Goldsmith with James Hodges, *Applying the National Training Center*

Experience: Tactical Reconnaissance, A Rand Note (N-2628-A) (Santa Monica, CA: Rand Corporation, 1987), 47, 59, 69; Scribner, 33; "New Scout Platoon Concept Will Test HMMWVs as 'Stealthy' Scouts," *Armor* 98 (March–April 1998): 51; Boeglen, 45, 51–54; First Lieutenant (P) Charles W. Gameros Jr., "Scout HMMWVs and Bradley CFVs: Gulf War Provides a Comparison of Scout Vehicles and MTOEs," *Armor* 100 (September–October 1991): 21.

109. McGrath, *The Brigade*, 104–106.

110. Boeglen, 43–44, 64–71.

111. Boeglen, 51, 102–107; Taylor, 4; Captain Michael Kozlik, "Making a Case for Brigade Reconnaissance Elements," *Armor* 99 (September–October 1990): 12–14.

112. Taylor, 4; McGrath, *The Brigade*, 104–106.

113. McGrath, *The Brigade*, 104–106; Captain Ross F. Lightsey, "Establishing and Using the Brigade Reconnaissance Troop," *Infantry* 90 (January–April 2000): 10–12; US Department of the Army, TOE 17-87F, *Brigade Reconnaissance Troop (HMMWV Mounted)* (Washington, DC: Department of the Army, 1999).

114. McGrath, *The Brigade*, 104–106; "R&S Lessons Learned—Brigade Reconnaissance Troop Employment—Reconnaissance and Surveillance," *Military Intelligence Professional Bulletin* 26 (October–December 2000): 62–63.

115. Lawrence C. Veller Jr., *Never Without Heroes: Marine Third Reconnaissance Battalion in Vietnam, 1965–70* (New York: Ivy, 1996), 3, 5–6, 9–10.

116. Lieutenant Colonel John F. Kelly, "Redesigning Recon," *Marine Corps Gazette* 78 (April 1994): 46–49.

117. Gameros, 23, 25.

118. Charles Lane Toomey, *XVIII Airborne Corps in Desert Storm: From Planning to Victory* (Central Point, OR: Hellgate Press, 2004), 191, 260, 343, 362, 368, 375, 384; 24th Infantry Division (Mechanized), *The Victory Book: A Desert Storm Chronicle* (Fort Stewart, GA: 24th Infantry Division (Mechanized), 1991), 101. The 3d ACR and 1st Armored Division had a fratricide incident across the corps boundary during the advance on 27 February 1991. See Toomey, 384–386.

119. Clancy, *Armored Cav*, 252; Tom Clancy with General Fred Franks Jr. (Ret), *Into the Storm: A Study in Command* (New York: Putnam, 1997), 270; Stephen A. Bourque, *Jayhawk!: The VII Corps in the Persian Gulf War* (Washington, DC: US Army Center of Military History, 2002), 200–201.

120. Clancy, *Armored Cav*, 251; Bourque, 209–210, 251, 252–253, 294; First Lieutenant John Hillen, "2d Armored Cavalry: The Campaign to Liberate Kuwait," *Armor* 100 (July–August 1991): 10–11.

121. Bourque, 327–328, 332–333, 367.

122. Ibid., 208, 210, 257, 332, 338–339; "2d Bde 3 AD History (1st Edition) Operation Desert Shield December 1990 thru 27 February 1991," 3d Brigade, 1st Armored Division, 1991, 5.

123. Stephen A. Bourque and John W. Burdan III, *The Road to Safwan: The 1st Squadron, 4th Cavalry in the 1991 Persian Gulf War* (Denton: University of North Texas Press, 2007), 115, 121–123, 135, 143, 149–150, 143.

124. Barto, 6.
125. Toomey, 330–331.
126. Barto, 11, 44, 47–48, 60, 64–66, 72, 76.
127. Thomas L. Day, *Along the Tigris: The 101st Airborne Division in Operation Iraqi Freedom, February 2003 to March 2004* (Atglen, PA: Schiffer, 2007), 78–79, 81.
128. Karl Zinsmeister, *Boots on the Ground: A Month With the 82d Airborne in the Battle for Iraq* (New York: Truman Tally Books, St. Martin's Press, 2003), 75–76; Gregory Fontenot, E.J. Degen, and David Tohn, *On Point: The United States Army in Operation Iraqi Freedom* (Fort Leavenworth, KS: Combat Studies Institute Press, 2004), 123, 135, 212–213, 277, 280.
129. Fontenot, Degen, and Tohn, 269, 271; Rick Atkinson, *In the Company of Soldiers: A Chronicle of Combat* (New York: Henry Holt and Company, 2004), 217, 235–236, 241, 246; 101st Airborne Division (Air Assault), *Lessons Learned Part I, Operation Iraqi Freedom*, 30 May 2003, 1-161.
130. Mark J. Reardon and Jeffrey A. Charlston, *From Transformation to Combat: The First Stryker Brigade at War* (Washington, DC: US Army Center of Military History, 2007), 3, 9–11.
131. US Department of the Army, Field Manual 3-21.21, *The Stryker Brigade Combat Team Infantry Battalion* (Washington, DC: Department of the Army, 2003), 1-15–1-16; US Department of the Army, Field Manual 3-21.31, *The Stryker Brigade Combat Team* (Washington, DC: Department of the Army, 2003), 1-2.
132. US Department of the Army, Field Manual 3-20.96, *Cavalry Squadron (RSTA)* (Washington, DC: Department of the Army, 2002), 1-4.
133. Reardon and Charlston, 16, 19; US Army Force Management Support Agency, "United States Army Force Structure," Powerpoint briefing, 31 January 2006. The 2d ACR may have syncopated the designations of the new units, as recent press reports mentioned a 4th Squadron, which could only be the RSTA unit. For example, see Kap Kim, "Scout Learns Arabic to Help Platoon, Mission," Army News Service, 4 December 2007, press release http://www.army.mil/-news/2007/12/04/6426-scout-learns-arabic-to-help-platoon-mission/ (accessed 19 December 2007).
134. Gary Sheftick, "Army to Reset Into Modular Brigade-Centric Force," Army News Service, 24 February 2004, http://www4.army.mil/ocpa/read.php?story_id_key+5703 (accessed 9 November 2007).
135. The main reason for the change from three to two maneuver battalions was to increase the number of brigade combat teams available in the force structure without having to add additional maneuver battalions. See William M. Donnelly, *Transforming an Army at War: Designing the Modular Force, 1991–2005* (Washington, DC: US Army Center of Military History, 2007), 40, 43–44, 46.
136. US Army Training and Doctrine Command, Task Force Modularity, *Army Comprehensive Guide to Modularity*, Version 1.0 (Fort Monroe, VA: US Army Training and Doctrine Command, 8 October 2004), 8-1, 8-2, 8-3; Neal A.

Corson, "Combat Effectiveness of the Combined Arms Battalion Scout Platoon" (MMAS thesis, US Army Command and General Staff College, 2005).

137. Donnelly, 43.
138. Ibid.
139. Ibid., 9-3, 9-4.
140. Ibid., 5-1, 5-14, 5-15, 5-16; "United States Army Force Structure."
141. *Army Comprehensive Guide to Modularity*, 5-1, 5-14, 5-15, 5-16; Lieutenant Colonel James J. Mingus, "Finding the Enemy: Bigger Than Recon," *Infantry* 97 (January–February 2006): 7–10.
142. Gameros, 25. A good example of the survivability issue was the order issued by a division commander in the VII Corps in DESERT STORM that prohibited any wheeled vehicles from crossing the line of departure into Iraq until the campaign was over. See "2d Bde 3 AD History (1st Edition) Operation Desert Shield December 1990 thru 27 February 1991," 5.

Conclusions

The lead unit is the recon unit.

General William Wallace, Fort Leavenworth, 2004[1]

Overview

Before World War I, there was no debate over the organization of reconnaissance units. Reconnaissance was one of the functions of horse cavalry. European armies established divisions and corps of cavalry to conduct operational reconnaissance and counterreconnaissance missions. The armies of 1914 attached smaller battalion-sized cavalry units to their infantry divisions to conduct tactical reconnaissance. In the Western Front campaigns of August 1914, for the most part, cavalry failed the combatants in the reconnaissance mission. The French cavalry concentrated on chasing the German cavalry, and both sides were frequently surprised on encountering enemy forces. The airplane quickly replaced the horse as the primary means for operational reconnaissance, while tactical reconnaissance, with the creation of the extended lines of entrenchments, became the province of balloons. While cavalry was used in the Palestine campaign, in most cases, its role was as mounted infantry and not as a dedicated reconnaissance force. When the United States deployed large forces to France, for logistical reasons, few cavalry forces went. The American Expeditionary Force (AEF) conducted combat operations with minimal reconnaissance forces without any apparent ill effects.

During the interwar period, the development of motorized and mechanized vehicles, coupled with the wartime firepower of trench warfare, resulted in a gradual divorce of horse cavalry from the reconnaissance role after a long debate. In World War II, most armies used dedicated motorized or mechanized reconnaissance units. With the disappearance of the horse, the debate turned to that of equipment: light, represented by wheeled vehicles such as jeeps and small scout cars, and heavy, represented by tanks and armored vehicles. The light-heavy debate continues to this day. Cavalry squadrons in the US Army's modular structure retain both armored and wheeled vehicles.

Other aspects of reconnaissance units continue to arise and merit discussion. These areas include the echelonment of units and missions, the use of hybrid units composed of air and ground elements, and whether reconnaissance units are a luxury or a necessity in a force structure with limited maneuver units.

The Light Versus Heavy Debate

The oldest and most long-lasting debate concerning reconnaissance units is that of whether the units should be equipped with light or heavy vehicles. Units with light vehicles represent stealth; those with heavy armored vehicles represent survivability. Aside from theoretical concerns, wartime conditions often dictated how a national army organized its reconnaissance forces. The Germans began World War II as believers in stealth and equipped their units in the light pattern, primarily with motorized vehicles, particularly motorcycles. In the short campaigns at the beginning of the war, where the Germans enjoyed air superiority and attacked using tactical and operational surprise and swift maneuvers, the light reconnaissance forces were effective. However, once the Wehrmacht was involved in an extended campaign in Russia, its reconnaissance assets took heavy casualties. The Germans reduced these elements to minimal levels in nonmechanized units and upgraded the ones in mechanized units, providing them with armored vehicles and, in some cases, tanks. US reconnaissance forces took a similar path of development during the war.

Since 1914, the light-heavy debate has dominated thought on the organization and employment of reconnaissance forces. However, the debate creates a paradox (figure 63) that has kept it alive since World War II. If the forces are too light and, while stealthy, not survivable on the battlefield, or so perceived, commanders tend to use other units for reconnaissance operations. Usually, the choice of a replacement reconnaissance unit has been whatever element is the lead unit in the movement. This has been particularly true in operations with a high operational tempo. Most US Army conventional operations since 1970 have been such maneuvers.[2]

On the other hand, if the reconnaissance force is too heavy or has a mobility or firepower differential equal to that of the bulk of the force of which it is a part, commanders tend to use the reconnaissance element as an additional combat maneuver or support force. This tendency reflects another propensity: commanders almost always feel their commands possess a shortage of combat maneuver units in relation to the missions assigned them. In most recent US Army operations, armored cavalry regiments and divisional cavalry squadrons have been given major combat missions or been attached to subordinate combat organizations to give those units additional combat power.

Additionally, in light infantry units where the reconnaissance elements are often the only organic mobile element, commanders have found this mobility differential to be more important than the need for reconnaissance.

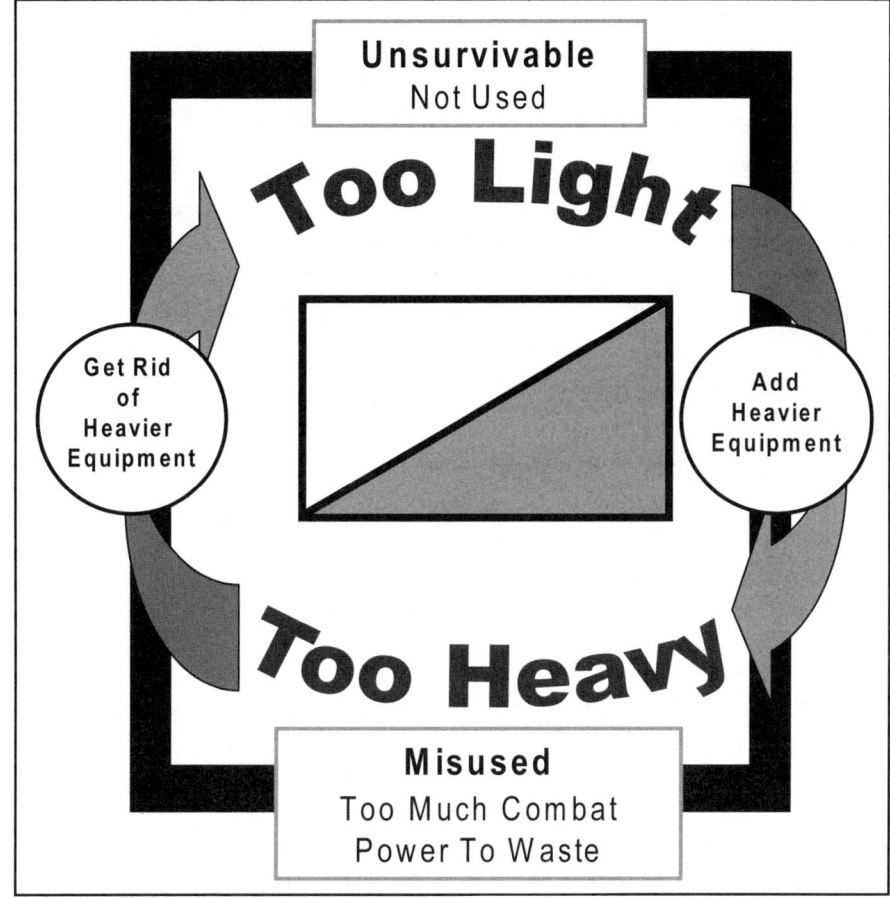

Figure 63. The reconnaissance paradox.

Accordingly, these reconnaissance elements were often used as mobile reserves and counterattack forces. In the 2003 Baghdad campaign, brigade and battalion reconnaissance elements in the 101st and 82d Airborne Divisions were frequently combined with HMMWV-mounted antitank elements into mobile strike forces to reinforce and support the operations of unit infantrymen.

The reconnaissance paradox ensures that most postwar or postexercise analyses of reconnaissance operations repeatedly result in a finding of the misuse of reconnaissance forces. Light forces were not used or were retained in the rear. Mobile forces in light units were used as a mobile reserve or attack forces. Units with a firepower and mobility differential, such as air cavalry troops in light units, often provided fire support to infantry units. Complaints of the misuse of light reconnaissance forces typically led to a reconfiguration of such forces with heavier equipment. Examples of this are the German forces in World War II and US Army forces under the ROAD and right before DESERT STORM.

Commanders of forces containing heavy reconnaissance units, usually including main battle tanks, scouts in armored vehicles, and organic fire support, found such units to be too valuable to use solely in the reconnaissance or security role. But their use as combat forces led to complaints of misuse, often resulting in reequipping the reconnaissance elements with lighter equipment as initially happened in the case of the Division 86 cavalry squadron and later with the maneuver battalion scout platoon.

Several factors, which are recurring themes, may influence the pendulum swing between light and heavy forces. These include the number of available combat units, the creation of hybrid reconnaissance units with subelements of sharply differing mobility or employment characteristics, and the arraying of reconnaissance forces at each organizational echelon.

The Availability of Forces

One issue in the debate on reconnaissance units may be paramount: whether such specialized units are a necessity or a luxury in a force with a limited number of available combat maneuver units. Combat maneuver units by their nature, particularly when organized in a combined arms organization, are general-purpose units capable of performing many different types of missions and roles. Reconnaissance units, while often used in nonreconnaissance roles, are usually organized specifically to conduct reconnaissance operations. When there is a shortage of mobile or firepower-intensive units, or maneuver units in general, commanders have used armored or air cavalry units to alleviate this shortage. In light units, the mobility or firepower differential between dedicated reconnaissance units and the bulk of the combat units in the command has made it difficult for commanders to avoid using them in combat roles.

A good example of this practice is the employment of mechanized cavalry groups in World War II. The US Army raised only a limited number of combat divisions in the war. While these units were usually kept at full personnel strength, their relatively limited numbers forced corps commanders to frequently use cavalry groups, usually augmented with artillery and armor, as stand-ins for nonexistent divisions. On the Ardennes front in December 1944, several mechanized cavalry groups held extensive stretches of frontline trace, while several cavalry squadrons, because of their mobility compared to infantry, were retained at the corps level as mobile reserves rather than conducting security or reconnaissance missions.

The potential impact of the availability of forces may be most telling in the new modular structure of the US Army. The new brigade combat teams, both light and heavy, contain only two maneuver battalions. The ready availability of a third battalion-sized combat unit, the reconnaissance, surveillance, and target acquisition (RSTA) squadron, in the brigade organization makes it almost inevitable that this unit, like its World War II mechanized cavalry predecessors, will spend much of its time on nonreconnaissance missions.

Hybrid Units

Another recurring theme is the organization of hybrid units. The original hybrid reconnaissance units were the horse-mechanized units. Before and during World War II, combatant armies converted all such units completely to motorized or mechanized transportation. Since the development of the helicopter and its application to a reconnaissance role, many reconnaissance units have consisted of a combination of ground and air elements. However, in the US division where additional helicopters existed outside the divisional squadron, the almost universal tendency was to split the ground and air assets and have the reconnaissance helicopter operate either as an independent unit or under the control of the aviation brigade. The original organizational intent of meshing air and ground reconnaissance operations was, therefore, almost never met.

A new version of the hybrid unit is seen in the Modular Army RSTA squadron. This unit combines scouts, who have always been considered combat troops, with surveillance and other military intelligence-style assets that in the past have been considered combat support elements. The Soviets had such a unit in their divisional reconnaissance battalion that contained a radio/radar company. Operationally, this company was always used apart from the rest of the battalion. The RSTA squadron may well find itself routinely split, particularly if the nonavailability of forces results in the scout elements playing a combat role.

Echelonment

Before the development of the military airplane and the decline of the horse, reconnaissance units existed at all levels from tactical to operational. Generals had few other means than horse cavalry at their disposal to find the location of the enemy. The counterreconnaissance imperative often saw opposing cavalry forces cancel out each other in their efforts to defeat the opposing horsemen. As seen in the World War I Hamipré example, the result was often ineffective reconnaissance on both sides. The airplane took over a large portion of the operational reconnaissance mission to the extent that most armies no longer deploy reconnaissance units larger than a squadron.

In opposition to this trend, the US Army has retained the armored cavalry regiment (ACR) as a corps reconnaissance unit since World War II. However, commanders have generally used the ACR more often as an extra combat unit than as an operational reconnaissance asset, particularly in Vietnam and in Operation DESERT STORM. Recent US Army modular doctrinal literature and organizational reorganization initiatives indicate a shift away using dedicated ground units in the operational reconnaissance role. The light cavalry regiment was converted to a Stryker brigade. Despite the continued retention of a single ACR, emerging doctrine for using modular reconnaissance assets above the brigade level stresses technical surveillance activities and states "the RSTA brigade does not conduct offensive or defensive operations, nor does it conduct security operations . . . when the [division] requires [such] operations, it assigns the mission to a BCT. . . ."[3] In other words, general-purpose combat units at higher levels are now expected to conduct missions traditionally assigned to cavalry units.

Conclusion

Before World War I, reconnaissance was the province of horse cavalry. Horse soldiers fell into this role because cavalry could not fight in the main line of battle under normal circumstances. The firepower of massed infantry and artillery, which had developed since the beginning of the gunpowder age, was too great. The cavalry legacy has lasted into the present age, making the assumption that specialized reconnaissance units are a necessity in a modern army. However, the recurring trends and examples of operational employment from World War II to the present indicate that the misuse of reconnaissance forces may, in fact, be merely a miscategorization. The reconnaissance paradox results in claims of misuse no matter how the units are equipped. Are these indicators of the misuse of reconnaissance forces, or perhaps an indicator that reconnaissance, rather than being a specialized mission for specialized units, is one of many missions expected of general-purpose combat units?

Instead of being a function of specialized troops, perhaps reconnaissance is one of many functions of maneuver units similar to attack, defend, or move. Commanders cannot misuse units if they are organized and equipped to perform a variety of functions, of which reconnaissance is but one. So organized, former reconnaissance units will provide more flexible employment similar to the interchangeable modular brigades. As one of many similar units, they will not require augmentation. The heavy-light debate will then become moot or part of a larger discussion over the equipping of general-purpose forces.

The Nature of Reconnaissance

The cavalry legacy often clouds the nature of reconnaissance. Napoleonic infantrymen could not function as cavalry because they did not have horses. The cavalry legacy remained so strong that, even though the AEF fought World War I without dedicated reconnaissance units and no discernible decrease in effectiveness, cavalry still played a large role in US Army interwar force structure and doctrine.

A modern US Army combined arms battalion is, in general terms, similarly equipped to the brigade cavalry squadron. The combined arms battalion, if needed, could perform reconnaissance and security missions. This capability is even greater at higher organizational levels where brigades could perform operational reconnaissance missions if necessary. Doctrine for the new Modular Army even recognizes this as a role for brigades. Light organizations find the mobility of reconnaissance units to be more valuable than their reconnaissance mission.

The clear implication is that the nature of reconnaissance has changed since the days of the horse from a specialized function done by units with unique capabilities to merely one of several functions any combat unit is expected to be able to accomplish. The retention of units designed and organized to perform such missions no longer reflects operational realities. While the Soviets also had reconnaissance units, their doctrine considered it to be a general function conducted by all units as necessary. In offensive actions such as movements to contact and attacks, Soviet units organized with a combined arms advance detachment whose lead elements conducted reconnaissance for the force as a whole. In all recent US Army conventional operations, the most common type of action was movement to contact, a type of operation in which the lead unit, whether cavalry or not, was effectively the reconnaissance element. Similarly in nonconventional operations such as counterinsurgency, where there are no actual front lines, all combat (and even most combat support and some combat service support units) units become de facto reconnaissance units by the nature of the conflict.

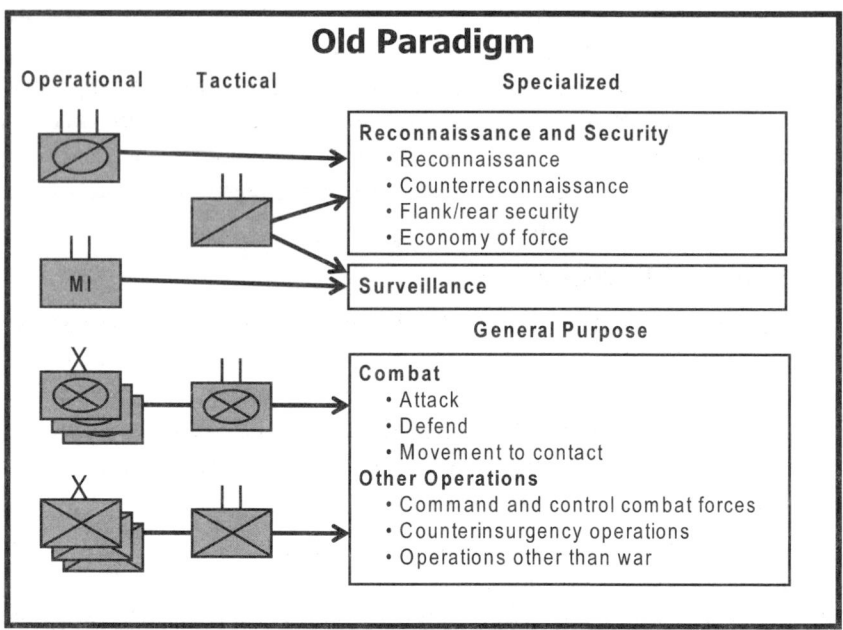
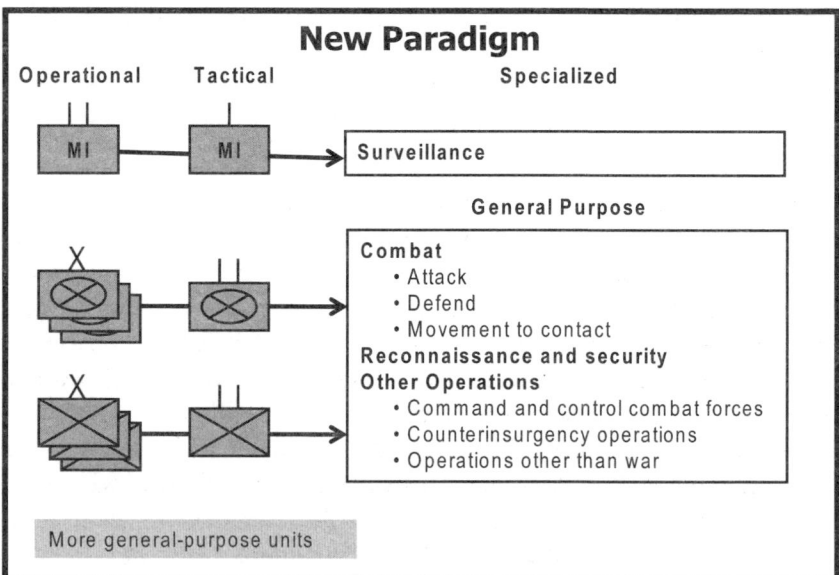

Figure 64. A new paradigm.

Designers of the US Army modular concept have striven to create interchangeable units in the US Army while simultaneously reducing the combat elements in such units and combining combat scouts with technical surveillance troops. Since the demise of horse cavalry, in actual practice rather than in theory, reconnaissance has become a general rather than a specialized combat function. Modularity should be taken one step further by eliminating combat reconnaissance units, allowing for the creation of more general-purpose combat units that could support technical reconnaissance/surveillance activities as necessary while being available to routinely conduct combat operations otherwise.

A historical appreciation of the nature of reconnaissance since World War II creates a new paradigm (figure 64) in the arrangement of reconnaissance and combat tasks. Those reconnaissance tasks requiring routine interfacing with enemy forces rightfully belong with combat tasks that by their nature require such interaction with opposing forces. These, along with the other missions expected of general-purpose combat forces (operations other than war, counterinsurgency), should be bundled together as missions for general-purpose units.

The technical aspects of reconnaissance that do not require routine interface with enemy forces and rely on specialized equipment, such as radars, are usually referred to collectively as surveillance operations. Surveillance operations do require specialized troops. However, the functions of such troops are clearly in the realm of combat support, not combat, and more properly belong in military intelligence support units rather than in combat squadrons.

The replacement of dedicated reconnaissance units with general-purpose maneuver units will yield additional units, addressing all three recurring reconnaissance themes. With more units, commanders will be less likely to perceive a lack of availability of combat forces. The similar organization of such units' design or structure of the force will preclude hybridization, and the modular design of such a force will mean each echelon will have similar assets. Operational utility will replace the reconnaissance paradox.

Notes

1. As quoted at the US Army Combined Arms Center Modularity Conference, Fort Leavenworth, KS, 18 October 2004.

2. One military observer, Major Curtis Taylor, has commented that light reconnaissance unit survivability is directly related to operational tempo. Taylor rightfully contends that commanders are more willing to risk using assets to fight for reconnaissance information when the situation is fast moving. He presumes that, barring a sudden dramatic change of operational tempo, commanders have two choices: to accept heavy casualties in their reconnaissance forces or to use more survivable forces for reconnaissance. See Major Curtis D. Taylor, *Trading the Saber for Stealth: Can Surveillance Technology Replace Traditional Aggressive Reconnaissance?* (Arlington, VA: Institute of Land Warfare, Association of the United States Army, 2005), 13–14.

3. US Army Training and Doctrine Command, Task Force Modularity, *Army Comprehensive Guide to Modularity*, version 1.0 (Fort Monroe, VA: US Army Training and Doctrine Command, 8 October 2004), 5-15, 5-16.

Glossary

A

AAF	Army Air Force
ABC	airborne corps
ABD	airborne division
abn	airborne
Abteilung	A German unit of battalion size
AC	armored car
ACAV	armored cavalry assault vehicle
ACR	armored cavalry regiment
AGS	armored gun system
AOE	Army of Excellence
AEF	American Expeditionary Force
AFV	armored fighting vehicle
APC	armored personnel carrier
AR	artillery regiment (German acronym)
ARB	armored reconnaissance battalion
ACRV	armored command and reconnaissance vehicle
armd	armored
ARVN	Army of the Republic of Vietnam
aslt	assault
AT	antitank
ATGM	antitank guided missile

B

BC	*Brigade de Cavalerie* (French Army cavalry brigade)
BCT	brigade combat team
bde	brigade
BCP	*Battaillon de Chasseurs à Pied* (French Army light infantry battalion)
BDP	*Battaillon de Dragons Portés* (French Army light mechanized infantry battalion)
BEF	British Expeditionary Force
BfSB	battlefield surveillance brigade
BLT	battalion landing team
BMP	Soviet armored fighting vehicle
BRDM	Soviet wheeled armored vehicle
BRT	brigade reconnaissance troop
Bundeswehr	Name of the modern (West) German Army

C

Capitaine	French Army grade equivalent to US Army captain
C	cuirassiers (French heavy cavalry)
CARL	Combined Arms Research Library
cal	caliber
cav	cavalry
cbt	combat
CD	cavalry division
CFV	cavalry fighting vehicle (M3 Bradley)
CH	*chasseurs* (French light cavalry)
cmd	command
COL	colonial (French corps)
COLT	combat observation and lasing team
Commandant	French Army grade equivalent to US Army major
CCR	Combat Command Reserve
CRP	combat reconnaissance patrol

D

D	dragoons (French) medium cavalry)
DAK	*Deutsches Afrika Korps* (German Africa Corps—usually in English, Afrika Korps)
DC	*Division de Cavalerie* (French Army cavalry division)
DCR	*Division Cuirassée de Réserve* (French Army armored division, 1939–40)
div	division
DL	*Division Légère* (French Army interwar light (cavalry) division)
DLB	*Division Légère Blindée* (French Army modern light armored division)
DLC	*Division Légère de Cavalerie* (French Army light cavalry division that was a combined horse-mechanized unit)
DLM	*Division Légère Mécanique* (French Army light armored (literally mechanized) division)

E

EK	*Eingreifkräfte* (German Army Intervention Force)
engr	engineer

EMF	Experimental Mechanized Force
ETO	European Theater of Operations
EW	electronic warfare

F

F or fus	fusilier (German honorific title)
FA	field artillery
FB	*Führerbegreit* (literally leader escort; name of a late war elite German Army panzer brigade)
FFV	Field Force, Vietnam

G

GAM	*Groupe d'Autos-Mitrailleuses* (French Army armored car battalion)
GC	*Groups Cycliste* (French Army light infantry mounted on bicycles)
GD	*Général de Division* (see definition below)
GD	guards (German corps)
GdI	*General der Infanterie*
Général	the second highest French Army general officer rank equivalent to US general
Général de Brigade	literally brigade general; the lowest French Army general officer rank equivalent to US brigadier general
Général de Division	literally division general; the second lowest French Army general officer rank equivalent to US major general
General der Infanterie	literally infantry general; the third highest German Army grade of general in World War I and World War II; rank includes the holder's specific branch, usually the grade of a corps or army commander
General der Panzertruppen	literally panzer general; the third highest German Army grade of general in World War I and World War II; rank includes the holder's specific branch, usually the grade of a corps or army commander
Generalleutnant	literally lieutenant general; the second lowest German Army general officer rank in World War I and World War II, usually the grade of a division or corps commander

Generalmajor	literally major general; the lowest German Army general officer rank in World War I and World War II, usually the grade of a brigade or division commander
Generaloberst	literally colonel general; the second highest German Army general officer rank in World War I and World War II, usually the grade of an army, army group, or theater commander
GHQ	general headquarters
GM	*Generalmajor*
GR	*Groupe de Reconnaissance* (French Army reconnaissance battalion)
GRCA	*Groupe de Reconnaissance de Corps d'Armée* (French Army corps reconnaissance battalion)
GRDI	*Groupe de Reconnaissance de Division d'Infanterie* (French Army divisional reconnaissance battalion)
GS	general support

H

H	hussars (French light cavalry)
H-M	horse-mechanized
HMMWV	high-mobility, multipurpose wheeled vehicle
HT	half-track
hvy	heavy

I

ID	infantry division
IDF	Israeli Defense Force
I&R	intelligence and reconnaissance
IR	infantry regiment (German acronym)
ITV	improved TOW vehicle

J

Jäger	light infantry (German)
JFC	Joint Forces Command

K

km	kilometer

L

LACR	light armored cavalry regiment
LCD XXI	Limited Conversion Division XXI

LAR	light armored reconnaissance
LLDR	Lightweight Laser Designator Rangefinder System
LR	long range
LRAS3	Long-Range Advanced Scout Surveillance System
LRRP	long-range reconnaissance and patrol
lt	light
Luftwaffe	name of German Air Force

M

MACV	US Military Assistance Command, Vietnam
MARCENT	Marine Forces, Central Command
mech	mechanized
med	medium
MG	machine gun
mi	mile
MI	military intelligence
mm	millimeter
MMAS	Master of Military Art and Science
mph	miles per hour

N

NA	not applicable
NATO	North Atlantic Treaty Organization
NBC	nuclear, biological, and chemical
NTC	National Training Center

O

obs	observation
OIF	Operation IRAQI FREEDOM
OPFOR	opposing force

R

R&D	research and development
RAC	*Regiment d'Artillerie de Campagne*
RAC	Royal Armoured Corps
recon	reconnaissance
regt	regiment
Reichswehr	interwar German Armed Forces (usually referred specifically to the Army); replaced by the Wehrmacht
REC	*Régiment Étranger de Cavallerie* (French Foreign Legion cavalry regiment)

RGFC	Republican Guard Forces Command
RHP	*Régiment Husards de Parachutistes* (French Army parachute reconnaissance regiment)
RI	infantry regiment (French acronym)
rkt	rocket
ROAD	Reorganization Objective Army Division
RPG	rocket-propelled grenade
RR	radio/radar
RS	*Régiment de Spahis* (French reconnaissance regiment)
RSTA	reconnaissance, surveillance, and target acquisition
RV	reconnaissance vehicle
RVN	Republic of Vietnam

S

SBCT	Stryker Brigade Combat Team
SC	scout car
SdKfz	German *Sonderkraftfahrzeug* (half-tracked or wheeled armored vehicle)
SK	*Stabilisierungskräfte* (German Army Stabilization Force)
spt	support
SPz	*Spähpanzer* (German scout tank or armored car)
SS	*Schutzstaffel* (Nazi party governmental organization; its military element was the *Waffen SS*, a component of the German land forces in World War II)
svc	service

T

tng	training
TOE	table of organization and equipment
TOW	tube-launched, optically tracked, wire-guided [missile]
TPz	*Transportpanzer* (German armored personnel carrier)
trk	truck

U

U	*Uhlan* (German lancer cavalry)
UAV	unmanned aerial vehicle
USFET	US Forces, European Theater

McGuire, Major Edward C. "Armored Cars in the Cavalry Maneuvers." *Cavalry Journal* 39 (July 1930): 386–399.

Mauer, Mauer, ed. *The US Air Service in World War I: Volume I, The Final Report and a Tactical History.* Washington, DC: Office of Air Force History, 1978.

Military Intelligence Service, US War Department. "Information Bulletin Number 1. German Armored Car Reconnaissance." 20 December 1941. http://www.lonesentry.com/manuals/armored-car/index.html (accessed 10 September 2007).

———. "Information Bulletin Number 18. The German Armored Division." 15 June 1942. http://www.lonesentry.com/manuals/german-panzer-division.index.html (accessed 10 September 2007).

Mingus, Lieutenant Colonel James J. "Finding the Enemy: Bigger than Recon." *Infantry* 97 (January–February 2006): 7–10.

Mitchum, Samuel. *Rommel's Desert War: The Life and Death of the Afrika Korps.* New York: Stein and Day, 1982.

Morton, Matthew D. "Men on 'Iron Ponies': The Death and Rebirth of the Modern US Cavalry." PhD diss., Florida State University, 2004.

Moses, Major R.E. "A Study of the Action of the German IV Army Preparatory to the Battle of the Ardennes, August 1914." Second Year Class, US Army Command and General Staff School, Fort Leavenworth, KS, 1931. Archives, Combined Arms Research Library, Fort Leavenworth, KS.

Murray, Williamson. "The German Response to Victory in Poland." *Armed Forces and Society* 7 (Winter 1981): 285–298.

Myers, David, compiler and ed. *Unit Organizations of World War II: Tables of Organization and Equipment (T.O.E.).* Milwaukee, WI: Z & M Publishing Enterprises, 1983.

Nafziger, George. *The German Order of Battle: Infantry in World War II.* Mechanicsburg, PA: Stackpole, 2000.

Necker, Wilhelm. *The German Army of To-Day.* London: Lindsay Drummond, 1943.

"New Scout Platoon Concept Will Test HMMWVs as 'Stealthy' Scouts." *Armor* 98 (March–April 1998): 51.

Niehorster, Leo. "British Army Authorized Organization Infantry Division Divisional Cavalry Regiment (RAC), 3 September 1939." *World War II Armed Forces—Orders of Battle and Organizations.* 2006. http://niehorster.orbat.com/017_britain/39_org/div_inf_rac.html (accessed 24 September 2007).

———. "British Army Authorized Organization Light Armoured Brigade, 3 September 1939." *World War II Armed Forces—Orders of Battle and Organizations.* 2006. http://niehorster.orbat.com/017_britain/39_org/div_inf_rac.html (accessed 24 September 2007).

———. *German Army Panzer and Panzergrenadier Divisions, 1943–1944.* World War II Organization and Equipment—Book 1. Brooklyn: Enola Games, 1982.

King, Major Marc A. "2x2: The Regimental Cavalry Troop." *Armor* 90 (March–April 1981): 12–13.

Klages, Ron, and John Mulholland. "Number of German Divisions by Front in World War II." http://www.axishistory.com/index.php?id=728 (accessed 12 October 2007).

Kozlik, Captain Michael. "Making a Case for Brigade Reconnaissance Elements." *Armor* 99 (September–October 1990): 12–14.

Lacey, Major A.T. "The Effect of the German Cavalry on the Rumanian Campaign in November 1916." Individual Research Paper, US Army Command and General Staff School, Fort Leavenworth, KS, 1930. Archives, Combined Arms Research Library, Fort Leavenworth, KS.

Lehman, David. "The French Cavalry Corps in 1940." 2005. http://www.militaryphotos.net/forums/archive/index.php/t-43179.html (accessed 21 September 2007).

Leulliot, N. "The Divisions Légères de Cavalerie (DLC-Light Cavalry Divisions) Part 1: Organisations." *France 1940*. http://france1940.free.fr/oob/oob.html (accessed 24 September 2007).

———. "French Army Order of Battle, 10 May 1940." *France 1940*. http://france1940.free.fr/armee/dlc/html (accessed 24 September 2007).

Lightsey, Captain Ross F. "Establishing and Using the Brigade Reconnaissance Troop." *Infantry* 90 (January–April 2000): 10–12.

Little, Major Mark. "The Light Armored Cavalry Regiment—Reconnaissance Force of the Future." Monograph, School of Advanced Military Studies, US Army Command and General Staff College, 1993.

Luck, Hans von. *Panzer Commander: The Memoirs of Colonel Hans von Luck*. New York: Dell, 1991.

Luttwak, Edward, and Daniel Horowitz. *The Israeli Army, 1948–1973*. Lanham, MD: University Press of America, 1983.

Malaguti, Charles J. *Historique du 87e régiment d'infanterie de ligne 1690–1892*. Extract provided to author by Service Historique de l'Armée de Terre, Republique Française, 1984.

Marshall, S.L.A. *Sinai Victory*. Nashville, TN: Battery Press, 1985.

May, Ernest. *Strange Victory: Hitler's Conquest of France*. New York: Hill and Wang, 2000.

McCarthy, Peter, and Mike Syron. *Panzerkrieg: The Rise and Fall of Hitler's Tank Divisions*. New York: Carroll & Graff, 2002.

McGrath, John J. *The Brigade: A History: Its Organization and Employment in the United States Army*. Fort Leavenworth, KS: Combat Studies Institute Press, 2004.

———. *Crossing the Line of Departure: Battle Command on the Move: A Historical Perspective*. Fort Leavenworth, KS: Combat Studies Institute Press, 2006.

———. "Sinai 1973: Israeli Maneuver Organization and the Battle of the Chinese Farm." *An Army at War: Change in the Midst of Conflict: The Proceedings of the Combat Studies Institute 2005 Military History Symposium*. Fort Leavenworth, KS: Combat Studies Institute Press, 2005, 63–109.

Proceedings of the Fourth Art of War Symposium, Garmisch, FRG, October 1987. Edited by Colonel David Glantz. London: Frank Cass, 1993.

Holmes, Terence M. "'One Throw of the Gambler's Dice': A Comment on Holger Herwig's View of the Schlieffen Plan." *Journal of Military History* 67 (April 2003): 513–516.

Holt, Captain Harold G. "The 1st Armored Car Troop." *Cavalry Journal* 37 (October 1928), 599–602.

House, Jonathan M. *Toward Combined Arms Warfare: A Survey of 20th-Century Tactics, Doctrine, and Organization.* Research Survey Number 2. Fort Leavenworth, KS: Combat Studies Institute, US Army Command and General Staff College, 1984.

Hunnicut, R.P. *Bradley: A History of American Fighting and Support Vehicles.* Novato, CA: Presidio, 1999.

Infantry in Battle. 2d ed. Washington, DC: Infantry Journal, 1939.

Isby, David. *Weapons and Tactics of the Soviet Army.* New ed. London: Jane's, 1988.

Jackman, Steven D. "Shoulder to Shoulder: Close Control and 'Old Prussian Drill' in German Offensive Infantry Tactics, 1871–1914." *Journal of Military History* 68 (January 2004): 73–104.

Jackson, Colonel Frederick E. "Tannenberg: The First Use of Signals Intelligence in Modern Warfare." Strategy Research Project, US Army War College, Carlisle Barracks, PA, 2002.

Johnson, Andy, and Pat Callahan. "NATO Order of Battle 1989." http://www.scribd.com/doc/37695/NATO-Order-of-Battle-1989 (accessed 26 October 2007).

Kane, Major Paul V. "A Study of the Preliminary Steps of the Development of the Third and Fourth French Armies in the Battle of the Ardennes." Second Year Class, U.S. Army Command and General Staff School, Fort Leavenworth, KS, 1931. Archives, Combined Arms Research Library, Fort Leavenworth, KS.

Katz, Samuel M. *Fire and Steel: Israel's 7th Armored Brigade.* New York: Pocket Books, 1996.

Kelly, Lieutenant Colonel John F. "Redesigning Recon." *Marine Corps Gazette* 78 (April 1994): 46–49.

Kennedy, Robert M. *The German Campaign in Poland (1939).* Washington, DC: US Army Center of Military History, 1988.

Khoi, Tran Quang. "Fighting to the Finish: The Role of South Viet Nam's III Armor Brigade and III Corps Assault Force in the War's Final Days. *Armor* 105 (March–April 1996): 19–25.

Kim, Kap. "Scout Learns Arabic To Help Platoon, Mission." Army News Service, 4 December 2007, press release. http://www.army.mil/-news/2007/12/04/6426-scout-learns-arabic-to-help-platoon-mission/ (accessed 19 December 2007).

King, Captain (P) Mark A. "The Battalion Scout Platoon Is Alive and Well." *Armor* 87 (September–October 1978): 35–37.

Gudmundsson, Bruce I. *Stormtroop Tactics: Innovation in the German Army, 1914–1918.* New York: Praeger, 1989.

———. "Unexpected Encounter at Bertrix." *Military History Quarterly* 13 (Autumn 2000): 20–27.

———. "Encounter at Bertrix." *Tactical Notebook* (October 1993): 1–11.

Gunsburg, Jeffrey. "The Battle of the Belgian Plain, 12–14 May 1940: The First Great Tank Battle." *Journal of Military History* 56 (April 1992): 207–244.

Habeck, Mary R. *Storm of Steel: The Development of Armor Doctrine in Germany and the Soviet Union, 1919–1939.* Ithaca, NY: Cornell University Press, 2003.

Haldeman, Major William T. "Operations of the Provisional Cavalry Corps Abonneau (4th and 9th Cavalry Divisions) in Belgium, the 18th, 19th, and 20th August 1914—Review of Cavalry, 1927." Group Research Project, Second Year Class, US Army Command and General Staff School, Fort Leavenworth, KS, 1932. Archives, Combined Arms Research Library, Fort Leavenworth, KS.

Harmon, Captain Ernest. "The Second Cavalry in the St. Mihiel Offensive." *Cavalry Journal* (April 1927): 282–289.

Harmon, Major Ernest. "A Critical Analysis of the German Cavalry Operations in the Lodz Campaign to Include the Breakthrough at Brzeziny, With Particular Reference to the I Cavalry Corps." Individual Research Paper, Second Year Class, US Army Command and General Staff School, Fort Leavenworth, KS, 1933. Archives, Combined Arms Research Library, Fort Leavenworth, KS.

Haugh, David R. "Organization and Development of the US Cavalry Division in the 1920s." *Armored Car* 21 (January 1994): 1–3.

Herzog, Chaim. *The Arab-Israeli Wars: War and Peace in the Middle East.* New York: Vintage Books, 1984.

Hillen, First Lieutenant John. "2d Armored Cavalry: The Campaign to Liberate Kuwait." *Armor* 100 (July–August 1991): 8–11.

Historical Inscription at the Battlefield of Hamipré, Belgium. Copy of the inscription available in author's files (from a site visit) and at "1914–18 , Nos Héros & Leur Guerre > 1- Bataille des Ardennes les Combats d'Hamipré–Longlier." *La Guerre de nos Héros, 1914–1918.* http://www.google.com/search?q=cache:3HbsAo-dmKgJ:www.1914-18mibb.com/index.php%3Ffile%3DGallery%26op%3Dcategorie%26cat%3D116%26orderby%3Dnews%26p%3D3+Cussac+commandant+87&hl=en&ct=clnk&cd=6&gl=us (accessed 27 August 2007).

Hobson, Major Richard G. "Effectiveness of Current Mechanized Scout Platoon." MMAS thesis, US Army Command and General Staff College, 2000.

Hoffgarten H.J. von, and Edel Lingenthal. "11th Panzer Division Operations." *The Initial Period of War on the Eastern Front, 22 June–August 1941:*

———. "Abu Ageila, Two Battles—Part 2: 1967." *Armor* 83 (July–August 1974): 16–20.
Gardner, Nikolas. "Command and Control in the 'Great Retreat' of 1914: The Disintegration of the British Cavalry Division." *The Journal of Military History* 63 (January 1999): 29–54.
Gawrych, George W. *Key to the Sinai: The Battles for Abu Ageila in the 1956 and 1967 Arab-Israeli Wars*. Research Survey No. 7. Fort Leavenworth, KS: Combat Studies Institute, US Army Command and General Staff College, 1990.
Gazin, F. *La Cavalerie Française dans la Guerre Mondiale, 1914–1918*. Paris: Payot, 1930.
Gebhardt, James F. *Eyes Behind the Lines: US Army Long-Range Reconnaissance and Surveillance Units*. Global War on Terrorism Occasional Paper No.10. Revised ed. Fort Leavenworth, KS: Combat Studies Institute Press, 2005.
General Staff, War Office [UK]. *Handbook of the French Army, 1914*. Nashville, TN: Battery Press, 1998.
General Staff, War Office [UK]. *Handbook of the German Army in War, April 1918*. Nashville, TN: Battery Press, 1996.
Gepanzerte Kampftruppen, Panzeraufklärer und Panzertruppenschule Sacchstand und Perspektiven." Presentation by the *Bundeswehr*'s Armored Branch Chief on 12 November 2004. www.panzertruppe.com/pdf/pdf%20s-b/struktur_nh.pdf (accessed 29 October 2007).
Glantz, Colonel David. *The Motor-Mechanization Program of the Red Army During the Interwar Years*. Fort Leavenworth, KS: Soviet Army Studies Office, 1990. http://stinet.dtic.mil/cgi-bin/GetTRDoc?AD=ADA232707&Location=U2&doc=GetTRDoc.pdf (accessed 24 September 2007).
———. *The Fundamentals of Soviet Razvedka*. Fort Leavenworth, KS: US Army Soviet Foreign Studies Office, 1989.
Goerlitz, Walter. *History of the German General Staff, 1657–1945*. Translated by Brian Battershaw. New York: Praeger, 1957.
Goldsmith, Martin, with James Hodges. *Applying the National Training Center Experience: Tactical Reconnaissance*. A Rand Note (N-2628-A). Santa Monica, CA: Rand Corporation, 1987.
Guderian, Major General Heinz. *Achtung-Panzer: The Development of Armoured Forces, Their Tactics and Operational Potential*. Translated by Christopher Duffy. London: Arms and Armour Press, 1995.
———. *Panzer Leader*. Translated by Constantine Fitzgibbon. Washington, DC: Zenger, 1952.
———. "III Panzer Corps Operations." *The Initial Period of War on the Eastern Front, 22 June–August 1941: Proceedings of the Fourth Art of War Symposium, Garmisch, FRG, October 1987*. Edited by Colonel David Glantz. London: Frank Cass, 1993.

Dooley, Matthew A. "Ignoring History: The Flawed Effort to Divorce Reconnaissance From Security in Modern Cavalry Transformation." MMAS thesis, US Army Command and General Staff College, 2006.
Doughty, Robert A. *The Breaking Point, Sedan and the Fall of France, 1940.* Hamden, CT: Archon Books, 1990.
———. "French Strategy in 1914: Joffre's Own." *Journal of Military History* 67 (April 2003): 427–454.
Duncan, Major Stephen C. "Seven Years After—Has Task Force Ground Reconnaissance Improved Since the Rand Study?" Monograph, School of Advanced Military Studies, US Army Command and General Staff College, 1994.
The Dupuy Institute. "The Historical Combat Effectiveness of Lighter-Weight Armored Forces." Final Report. McLean, VA: Dupuy Institute, 2001.
Dupuy, R. Ernest, and Trevor N. Dupuy. *The Encyclopedia of Military History From 3500 B.C. to the Present.* Rev. ed. New York: Harper & Row, 1977.
Dupuy, Trevor. *Elusive Victory: The Arab-Israeli Wars, 1947–1974.* Fairfax, VA: HERO Books, 1984.
Ellis, Chris, and Peter Chamberlain, eds. *Handbook on the British Army, 1943.* New York: Hippocrene Books, 1976.
Fisher, Major Paul M., and Captain George C. Hoffmaster Jr. "Armored Division Organization and Doctrine." *Armor* 67 (September–October 1958): 6–13.
Fontenot, Gregory, E.J. Degen, and David Tohn. *On Point: The United States Army in Operation Iraqi Freedom.* Fort Leavenworth, KS: Combat Studies Institute Press, 2004.
Forty, George. *British Army Handbook, 1939–1945.* Stroud, Gloucestershire: Sutton, 2002.
Frieser, Karl-Heinz, with John T. Greenwood. *The Blitzkrieg Legend: The 1940 Campaign in the West.* Annapolis, MD: Naval Institute Press, 2005.
Futrell, Robert F. *Ideas, Concepts, Doctrine: Basic Thinking in the United States Air Force, 1907–1960.* Vol. 1. Maxwell Air Force Base, AL: Air University Press, 1989.
Gabel, Christopher R. *Seek, Strike, and Destroy: U.S. Army Tank Destroyer Doctrine in World War II.* Leavenworth Papers No. 12. Fort Leavenworth, KS: Combat Studies Institute, US Army Command and General Staff College, 1985.
Gameros, First Lieutenant (P) Charles W. Jr. "Scout HMMWVs and Bradley CFVs: Gulf War Provides a Comparison of Scout Vehicles and MTOEs." *Armor* 100 (September–October 1991): 21–25.
Gander, Terry. *Encyclopedia of the Modern British Army.* 2d ed. Cambridge, England: Patrick Stephens, 1982.
Ganz, A. Harding. "Abu Ageila, Two Battles—Part 1: 1956." *Armor* 83 (May–June 1974): 35–41.

Corum, James S. *The Roots of Blitzkrieg: Hans von Seeckt and German Military Reform.* Lawrence: University Press of Kansas, 1992.

Cron, Hermann. *Imperial German Army, 1914–18: Organisation, Structure, Orders of Battle.* Translated by C.F. Coltron. London: Helion & Company, 2002.

Cunningham, J.W. "The French 9th Cavalry Division: Ardennes." Group Research Monograph. Second Year Class, US Army Command and General Staff School, 1933. Archives, Combined Arms Research Library, Fort Leavenworth, KS.

Dahlquist, Captain John. "A Study of the Operations of the Fourth German Army in the Battle of the Ardennes, August 22d–23d, 1914, Based on the Account Contained in Volume I, *Der Weltkrieg* (Official History of the World War)." Second Year Class, US Army Command and General Staff School, Fort Leavenworth, KS, 1931. Archives, Combined Arms Research Library, Fort Leavenworth, KS.

Day, Thomas L. *Along the Tigris: The 101st Airborne Division in Operation Iraqi Freedom, February 2003 to March 2004.* Atglen, PA: Schiffer, 2007.

Dick, C.J. "Soviet Battle Drills: Vulnerability or Strength?" *International Defense Review* 18 (May 1985): 663–665.

"Die Geschichte des Panzeraufklärungslehrbataillons 3." *Freudeskreis der Panzeraufklärer.* http://www.panzeraufklaerungstruppe.de/truppengtg/bataillone/PAB03L/gescchichte.html (accessed 26 October 2007).

"Die Gliederung des Panzeraufklärungsbataillon 12 im Wandel der Heersstrukturen." *KameradschaftPanzeraufklärungsbataillon 12 e.V.* http://www.pzaufklbtl12.de/Geschichte/heeres.htm (accessed 28 October 2007).

"Die Panzeraufklärer der Bundeswehr." *Die Panzeraufklärer im Internet.* http://www.pzaufkl.de/include.php?path=content/articles.php&contentid=2&PHPKITSID=d868e33dcb939f55858d768008fb07f4 (accessed 29 October 2007).

Diehl, Major James G. "Who Is Out There? Tactical Reconnaissance for the Heavy Division." Monograph, School of Advanced Military Studies, US Army Command and General Staff College, 1988.

DiMarco, Major Louis A. "The U.S. Army's Mechanized Cavalry Doctrine in World War II." MMAS thesis, US Army Command and General Staff College, 1995.

Dinackus, Thomas. *Order of Battle: Allied Ground Forces of Operation Desert Storm.* Central Point, OR: Hellgate, 2000.

DiNardo, Richard. "Germany's Panzer Arm: Anatomy and Performance." PhD diss., City University of New York, 1988.

Donnelly, William M. *Transforming an Army at War: Designing the Modular Force, 1991–2005.* Washington, DC: US Army Center of Military History, 2007.

Burke, Lieutenant Colonel James T. "Armored Infantry and Recon Unit Organization." *Armor* 65 (July–August 1956): 15–17.

Burton, Colonel James G. "Pushing Them Out the Back Door." *Proceedings* (June 1993): 37–42.

Carmoy, Phillippe, and Evgeniy Drig. "Soviet Armed Forces: Organization Rifle Division, 22 June 1941." *World War II Armed Forces—Orders of Battle and Organizations*. 2006. http://niehordster.orbat.com/012_ussr/41_organ/41_rifle_div_00.html (accessed 25 September 2007).

Caron, Seth. "The Arab-Israeli Wars, Armies in Conflict, TO&E: Anatomy of a War." *The General* 14 (September–October 1977): 3–9.

Carrell, Paul. *Hitler Moves East, 1941–1943: The Nazis' Surprise Attack on the Russo-German Border*. Translated by Ewald Osers. New York: Ballantine, 1971.

Cason, Lieutenant Colonel Duane S. "Introduction to the New Armored Division." *Armor* 66 (November–December 1957): 4–11.

Chamberlain, Peter, and Hilary Doyle. *Encyclopedia of German Tanks of World War Two: A Complete Illustrated Directory of German Battle Tanks, Armoured Cars, Self-Propelled Guns, and Semi-Tracked Vehicles, 1933–1945*. London: Arms and Armour Press, 1993.

Childers, Erskine. *German Influence on British Cavalry*. London: Edward Arnold, 1911.

Citino, Robert M. *Armored Forces: History and Source Book*. Westport, CT: Greenwood Press, 1994.

———. *The Evolution of Blitzkrieg Tactics, Germany Defends Herself Against Poland, 1918–1933*. Westport, CT: Greenwood Press, 1987.

———. *The Path to Blitzkrieg: Doctrine and Training in the German Army, 1920–1939*. Boulder, CO: Lynee Rienner, 1999.

Clancy, Tom. *Armored Cav: A Guided Tour of an Armored Cavalry Regiment*. New York: Berkley, 1994.

Clancy, Tom, with General (Ret) Fred Franks Jr. *Into the Storm: A Study in Command*. New York: Putnam, 1997.

Clayton, Anthony. *Paths of Glory: The French Army, 1914–18*. London: Cassell, 2003.

Cole, Hugh. *The Ardennes: Battle of the Bulge*. United States Army in World War II: The European Theater of Operations. Washington, DC: US Army Center of Military History, 1965.

Coles, Michael H. "Pershing's Eyes in the Sky." *Military History Quarterly* 13 (Winter 2001): 30–41.

Commans, Stephane. "GRCA and GRDI." *French Orders of Battle*. http://france1940.free.fr/armee/gr.html (accessed 24 September 2007).

———. "Order of Battle Division Infanterie (1940) (Infantry Division)." *French Orders of Battle*. http://enpointe.chez-alice.fr/di.html (accessed 24 September 2007).

Corson, Neal A. "Combat Effectiveness of the Combined Arms Battalion Scout Platoon." MMAS thesis, US Army Command and General Staff College, 2005.

"Army Announces Reconfiguration of Fourth Stryker Brigade." Army News Release, 14 May 2004. http://www.globalsecurity.org/military/library/news/2004/05/mil-040514-usar01.htm (accessed 6 November 2007).

Atkinson, Rick. *In the Company of Soldiers: A Chronicle of Combat.* New York: Henry Holt and Company, 2004.

Avidor, Gideon. "From Brigade to Division." *Military Review* 58 (October 1978): 64–71.

Bahnsen, Captain John C. Jr. "Troop D, Armored Cavalry Squadron, ROAD Armored Division." *Armor* 72 (March–April 1963): 33–37.

Barto, Major Joseph C. III. *Task Force 2-4 Cav—"First In, Last Out": The History of the 2d Squadron, 4th Cavalry Regiment, During Operation Desert Storm.* Fort Leavenworth, KS: Combat Studies Institute, 1993.

Battistelli, Pier Paolo. *Rommel's Afrika Korps: Tobruk to El Alamein.* Battle Orders No. 20. London: Osprey, 2006.

Beall, Colonel John. "Revisions to ROCAD." *Armor* 68 (March–April 1959): 48–51.

Behrendt, Hans-Otto. *Rommel's Intelligence in the Desert Campaign, 1941–1943.* London: William Kimber, 1985.

Bell, Captain Raymond E. Jr. "A New Role for the ACRV." *Armor* 72 (March–April 1963): 49–52.

Benson, Lieutenant Colonel Kevin. "Whither the 2d Cavalry." *Armor* 106 (January–February 1997): 20–21.

Boeglen, Kenneth L. "Does the Heavy Maneuver Brigade Commander Need an Organic Reconnaissance/Security Organization?" MMAS thesis, US Army Command and General Staff College, 1992.

Bolté, Brigadier General (Ret) Phillip L. "Full Circle: The Armored Cavalry Platoon." *Armor* 103 (September–October 1994): 35–37.

Bou, Jean. "Cavalry, Firepower, and Swords: The Australian Light Horse and the Tactical Lessons of Cavalry Operations in Palestine, 1916–1918." *Journal of Military History* (January 2007): 99–126.

Boucherie, Colonel [nfn]. *Historique du Corps de Cavalerie Sordet.* 2d ed. Paris: Charles-Lavauelle, 1924.

Bourque, Stephen A. *Jayhawk!: The VII Corps in the Persian Gulf War.* Washington, DC: US Army Center of Military History, 2002.

Bourque, Stephen A., and John W. Burdan III. *The Road to Safwan: The 1st Squadron, 4th Cavalry in the 1991 Persian Gulf War.* Denton: University of North Texas Press, 2007.

Boyle, Captain William O. "M114: The Scout's New Vehicle." *Armor* 72 (November–December 1963): 43–46.

Brennan, Matthew. *Headhunters: Stories From the 1st Squadron, 9th Cavalry in Vietnam, 1965–1971.* Novato, CA: Presidio, 1987.

———. *Hunter-Killer Squadron: Aero-Weapons, Aero-Scouts, Aero-Rifles, Vietnam 1965–1972.* Novato, CA: Presidio, 1990.

Brinkmann, Kay. "German Observations of the U.S. Civil War: A Study in Lessons Not Learned." MMAS thesis, US Army Command and General Staff College, 2000.

———. "Organization, Equipment and Tactical Employment of the Armored Division." Study Number 48. Bad Nauheim, GE, 1945-46.

———. "Organization, Equipment, and Tactical Employment of the Infantry Division." Study Number 15. Bad Nauheim, GE, 1945.

———. "Tactics, Employment, Technique, Organization, and Equipment of Mechanized Cavalry Units." Study Number 49. Bad Nauheim, GE, 1945–46.

US War Department. FM 100-5, *Field Service Regulations, Operations*. Washington, DC: US War Department, 1941.

———. FM 100-5, *Field Service Regulations, Operations*. Washington, DC: US War Department, 1944.

———. *Revised United States Army Regulations of 1861*. Washington, DC: Government Printing Office, 1863.

———. Table of Organization and Equipment No. 5-15, *Headquarters and Headquarters and Service Company, Engineer Combat Battalion*. Washington, DC: War Department, 13 March 1944.

———. Technical Manual (TM-E) 30-451, *Handbook on German Military Forces*. Washington, DC: War Department, 1945.

US War Department, Office of the Chief of Staff. *Reorganization of the French Cavalry: Extract From the Report of the Military Committee of the Chamber of Deputies, Session of 1912*. Washington, DC: Government Printing Office, 1913.

Secondary Sources

24th Infantry Division (Mechanized). *The Victory Book: A Desert Storm Chronicle*. Fort Stewart, GA: 24th Infantry Division (Mechanized), 1991.

"The 87th Armored Recon Battalion [IDF]." http://www.87th.org.il/enhistory.html (accessed 3 August 2005).

"1940 Population Estimates for European Countries." *Population Index* 8 (April 1942).

"The 1980s." *Armored and Cavalry Units in the European Theater*, http://www.usarmygermany.com/Units/ArmoredCav/USAREUR_Armd%20Cav.htm (accessed 26 October 2007).

Abenheim, Donald. *Reforging the Iron Cross: The Search for Tradition in the West German Armed Forces*. Princeton, NJ: Princeton University Press, 1988.

Allen, Major R.C. "A Study of the Initial Operations of the French Fourth Army in the Battle of the Ardennes." Second Year Class, US Army Command and General Staff School, Fort Leavenworth, KS, 1931. Archives, Combined Arms Research Library, Fort Leavenworth, KS.

The American Arsenal: The World War II Official Standard Ordnance Catalog of Artillery, Small Arms, Tanks, Armored Cars, Artillery, Antiaircraft Guns, Ammunition, Grenades, Mines, Et Cetera. Mechanicsburg, PA: Stackpole, 1996.

———. Field Manual 3-21.31, *The Stryker Brigade Combat Team*. Washington, DC: Department of the Army, 2003.

———. Field Manual 17-98, *Scout Platoon*. Washington, DC: Department of the Army, 1994.

———. Field Manual 100-2-3, *The Soviet Army: Troops, Organization, Equipment*. Washington, DC: Department of the Army, 1984.

———. Table of Organization and Equipment (T/O-E) 17-57N, *Reconnaissance Company*. Washington, DC: Department of the Army, 23 January 1948.

———. TOE 1-65A, *Air Reconnaissance Squadron (OH-58D), Division Aviation Brigade, Airborne Division*. Washington, DC: Department of the Army, 1998.

———. TOE 1-167A, *Air Reconnaissance Troop (AH-1/OH-58D), Cavalry Squadron, Division Aviation Brigade, Infantry Division (Light)*. Washington, DC: Department of the Army, 1997.

———. TOE 17-87F, *Brigade Reconnaissance Troop (HMMWV Mounted)*. Washington, DC: Department of the Army, 1999.

———. TOE 17-105, *Armored Cavalry Squadron, Armored Division, Armored Cavalry Squadron, Infantry Division, Armored Cavalry Squadron, Infantry Division (Mechanized)*. Washington, DC: Department of the Army, 15 July 1963.

———. TOE 17-107G, *Armored Cavalry Troop, Armored Cavalry Squadron, Armored Division, Armored Cavalry Squadron, Infantry Division, Armored Cavalry Squadron, Infantry Division (Mechanized), Separate Armored Brigade, Infantry Brigade, Infantry Brigade (Mechanized)*. Washington, DC: Department of the Army, 15 July 1963.

———. TOE 17-108G, *Air Cavalry Troop, Armored Cavalry Squadron, Armored Division, Armored Cavalry Squadron, Infantry Division, Armored Cavalry Squadron, Infantry Division (Mechanized), Separate Armored Brigade, Infantry Brigade, Infantry Brigade (Mechanized)*. Washington, DC: Department of the Army, 31 March 1966.

———. TOE 17-185L, *Cavalry Squadron, Light Infantry Division*. Washington, DC: Department of the Army, 1997.

———. TOE 17-187L, *Cavalry Troop, Cavalry Squadron, Infantry Division (Light)*. Washington, DC: Department of the Army, 1996.

———. TOE 17-285L, *Air Reconnaissance Squadron (OH-58D), Division Aviation Brigade, Air Assault Division*. Washington, DC: Department of the Army, 1993.

———. TOE 17-285L100, *Cavalry Squadron (AH-1)*/TOE 17-285L200, *Cavalry Squadron (OH-58D) Cavalry Squadron, Division Aviation Brigade, Heavy Division*. Washington, DC: Department of the Army, 1995.

———. TOE 17-376L, *Headquarters and Headquarters Company, Tank Battalion, Heavy Division*. Washington, DC: Department of the Army, 1997.

US Forces, European Theater, General Board. "Army Tactical Information Service." Study Number 18, Bad Nauheim, GE, 1945.

Selected Bibliography

Primary Sources

"2d Bde 3 AD History (1st Edition) Operation Desert Shield December 1990 thru 27 February 1991." 3d Brigade, 1st Armored Division, 1991.

3d Infantry Division (Mechanized). *Operation Iraqi Freedom After Action Report*, Final Draft, 12 May 2003.

101st Airborne Division (Air Assault). *Lessons Learned Part I, Operation Iraqi Freedom*, 30 May 2003.

Adan, Avraham. *On the Banks of the Suez: An Israeli General's Personal Account of the Yom Kippur War*. London: Arms and Armour Press, 1980.

C., *Feldwebel*, 1st Sergeant. 88th Infantry Regiment, 21st Division, 18th Army Corps [German Army]. *The Diary of a German Soldier*. New York: Alfred A. Knopf, 1919.

Command and General Staff School, Fort Leavenworth, KS, 1931. Archives, Combined Arms Research Library, Fort Leavenworth, KS.

Condell, Bruce, and David Zabecki, trans. and ed. *On the German Art of War: Truppenführung*, Boulder, CO: Lynee Rienner Publications, 2001.

French Army *Grand Quartier Général (G.O.G.)* General Order No. 1, 8 August 1914.

French Fourth Army Order Number 426, dated 2000 hours, 17 August 1914.

Gott, Kendall D. *In Glory's Shadow: In Service With the 2d Armored Cavalry Regiment During the Persian Gulf War, 1990–1991*. Unpublished manuscript, 1997. Copy in the archives of the Combined Arms Research Library, Fort Leavenworth, KS.

Harmon, Captain Ernest. "The Second Cavalry in the St. Mihiel Offensive." *Cavalry Journal* (April 1927): 282–289.

L'Armée deTerre. *Les'Armées Françaises dans la Grande Guerre*. Tome I, Volume 1-Annexes.

Le 9e Division Cavalerie. *Historique des Faits les 5-25 août 1914*. Service Historique de l'Armée deTerre, Republique Française, Paris.

Le 87e Régiment Infanterie. *Historique des Faits, les 5, 14-22 août 1914*. Service Historique de l'Armée de Terre, Republique Française, Paris.

Office of the Theater Historian, European Theater of Operations. *Order of Battle of the United States Army, World War II: European Theater of Operations, Divisions*. Paris, December 1945.

US Army Force Management Support Agency. "United States Army Force Structure." PowerPoint briefing, 31 January 2006.

US Army Training and Doctrine Command, Task Force Modularity. *Army Comprehensive Guide to Modularity*. Version 1.0. Fort Monroe, VA: US Army Training and Doctrine Command, 8 October 2004.

US Department of the Army. Field Manual 3-20.96, *Cavalry Squadron (RSTA)*. Washington, DC: Department of the Army, 2002.

———. Field Manual 3-21.21, *The Stryker Brigade Combat Team Infantry Battalion*. Washington, DC: Department of the Army, 2003.

———."Soviet Armed Forces Organization Soviet Mechanized Corps, 22 June 1941." *World War II Armed Forces—Orders of Battle and Organizations*. 2006. http://niehorster.orbat.com/012_ussr/41_organ/40_mech-corps.html (accessed 25 September 2007).

———. "Soviet Armed Forces Organization Soviet Mechanized Division, 22 June 1941." *World War II Armed Forces—Orders of Battle and Organizations*. 2006. http://niehorster.orbat.com/012_ussr/41_organ/40_mech-div.html (accessed 24 September 2007).

———. "Soviet Armed Forces Organization Soviet Tank Division, 22 June 1941." *World War II Armed Forces—Orders of Battle and Organizations*. 2006. http://niehorster.orbat.com/012_ussr/41_organ/40_tank-div.html (accessed 25 September 2007).

Niepold, Gerd. "Conclusions From the German Perspective." *The Initial Period of War on the Eastern Front, 22 June–August 1941: Proceedings of the Fourth Art of War Symposium, Garmisch, FRG, October 1987*. Edited by Colonel David Glantz. London: Frank Cass, 1993.

Ogorkiewicz, Richard. *Armor: A History of Mechanized Forces*. New York: Praeger, 1960.

Ohrloff, Horst. "XXXIX Motorized Corps Operations." *The Initial Period of War on the Eastern Front, 22 June–August 1941: Proceedings of the Fourth Art of War Symposium, Garmisch, FRG, October 1987*. Edited by Colonel David Glantz. London: Frank Cass, 1993.

Oliver, Major Bryan. "The Combat Reconnaissance Detachment in the Meeting Engagement and Defense." *Armor* 99 (July–August 1990): 7–11.

Orr, Ori. "Bloody Gaza." *Jerusalem Post Supplement, The Six Day War—30th Anniversary*. 4 June 1997. http://info.jpost.com/1998/Supplements/30years/orr.html (accessed 17 October 2003).

Pallud, Jean-Paul. *Battle of the Bulge: Then and Now*. London: After the Battle Magazine, 1984.

———. *Blitzkrieg in the West: Then and Now*. London: After the Battle, 1991.

"Panzerbrigade 18—Holstein, 1956–1994." http://www.bundesarchiv.de/php/bestaende_findmittel/bestaendeuebersicht/druckansicht.php?id_bestand=3778 (accessed 29 October 2007).

Perett, Bryan. *German Armoured Cars and Reconnaissance Half-Tracks, 1939–45*. London: Osprey, 1982.

Phelps, Lieutenant Colonel William, Major James Ellingsworth, Captain William C. Jones, Captain Sidney Haszard, and Captain Dandridge Hering. "A Standard Reconnaissance Battalion." Committee 6, Armored Officer Advance Course, 1952–1953. Fort Knox, KY: US Army Armored School, 1953.

Pigg, Jim. "Why Cav Changed in the '70s." *Armor* 104 (January–February 1995): 3, 50.

Plato, A.D. von, and R.O. Stoves. "1st Panzer Division Operations." *The Initial Period of War on the Eastern Front, 22 June–August 1941: Proceedings* of the Fourth Art of War Symposium, Garmisch, FRG, October 1987. Edited by Colonel David Glantz. London: Frank Cass, 1993.

Poseck, M. von. *The German Cavalry: 1914 in Belgium and France*. Edited by Jerome Howe. Translated by Alexander Strecker, Oscar Koch, Gordon Gordon-Smith, and Anton Hesse. Berlin: E.S. Mittler & Sohn, 1923.

Posen, Barry R. *The Sources of Military Doctrine: France, Britain, and Germany Between the World Wars*. Ithaca, NY: Cornell, 1984.

Quarrie, Bruce. *The Ardennes Offensive V US Corps & XVIII US (Airborne) Corps Northern Sector*. Order of Battle Series No. 5. London: Osprey, 1999.

———. *The Ardennes Offensive VI Panzer Armee Northern Sector*. Order of Battle Series No. 4. London: Osprey, 1999.

Quinlan, Major Kenneth J. "The Army-of-Excellence Division Cavalry Squadron. Monograph, School of Advanced Military Studies, US Army Command and General Staff College, 1986.

"R&S Lessons Learned—Brigade Reconnaissance Troop Employment—Reconnaissance and Surveillance." *Military Intelligence Professional Bulletin* 26 (October–December 2000): 62–63.

Raines, Edgar Jr. *Eyes of the Artillery: The Origins of Modern US Army Aviation*. Washington, DC: US Army Center of Military History, 2000.

Reardon, Mark J., and Jeffrey A. Charlston. *From Transformation to Combat: The First Stryker Brigade at War*. Washington, DC: US Army Center of Military History, 2007.

Ritgen, Helmut. *The 6th Panzer Division, 1937–45*. London: Osprey, 1982.

Romjue, John L. *The Army of Excellence: The Development of the 1980s Army*. Fort Monroe, VA: US Army Training and Doctrine Command, 1993.

———. *A History of Army 86, Volume II: The Development of the Light Division, the Corps, and Echelons Above Corps, November 1979—December 1980*. Fort Monroe, VA: US Army Training and Doctrine Command, 1982.

Rothbrust, Florian K. *Guderian's XIXth Panzer Corps and the Battle of France: Breakthrough in the Ardennes, May 1940*. Westport, CT: Praeger, 1990.

Rothe, Hermann, and H. Ohrloff. "7th Panzer Division Operations." *The Initial Period of War on the Eastern Front, 22 June–August 1941: Proceedings of the Fourth Art of War Symposium, Garmisch, FRG, October 1987*. Edited by Colonel David Glantz. London: Frank Cass, 1993.

Rothenberg, Gunther. *The Anatomy of the Israeli Army: The Israel Defence Force, 1948–78*. New York: Hippocrene, 1979.

Rottman, Gordon. *US Marine Corps World War II Order of Battle: Ground and Air Units in the Pacific War, 1939–1945*. Westport, CT: Greenwood Press, 2002.

Runde, Richard J. Jr. "The Intelligence and Reconnaissance Platoon, 1935–1965: Lost in Time." MMAS thesis, US Army Command and General Staff College, 1994.

Salerno, Captain George "Repairing the Broken Sabre: Overview of L-Series Divisional Cavalry." *Armor* 103 (January–February 1994): 29–34.

Sawicki, James. *Cavalry Regiments of the US Army.* Dumfries, VA: Wyvern Publications, 1985.

———. *Tank Battalions of the US Army.* Dumfries, VA: Wyvern, 1983.

"Sayeret Matkal." http://www.militaryphotos.net/forums/showthread.php?t+4006 (accessed 21 October 2007).

Scheibert, Horst. *Panzer Grenadier Division Grossdeutschland,* Edited by Bruce Culver. Translated by Gisele Hockenberry. Warren, MI: Squadron/ Signal, 1977.

Schneider, Wolfgang. *Panzer Tactics: German Small-Unit Armor Tactics in World War II.* Mechanicsburg, PA: Stackpole, 2005.

Schultz, Kurt S. "The Revolution Rearmed: Development of Soviet Mobile Warfare Doctrine, 1920–1941." *Historical Analysis of the Use of Mobile Forces by Russia and the USSR.* Edited by Jacob W. Kipp et al. Occasional Paper No. 10. College Park: Center for Strategic Technology, The Texas Engineering Experiment Station, Texas A&M University System, 1985.

Schulz, Thomas Koch. *Das deutsche Heer Heute.* Bonn, GE: Mittler, 1987.

Scribner, Major Barry. "HMMWVs and Scouts: Do They Mix?" *Armor* 98 (July–August 1989): 33–38.

Seaton, Albert. *The German Army: 1933–1945.* New York: St. Martin's Press, 1982.

Senger und Etterlin, Frido von. *Neither Fear Nor Hope.* Translated by George Malcolm. Novato, CA: Presidio, 1989.

Sepp, Kalev I. "The Pentomic Puzzle: The Influence of Personality and Nuclear Weapons on US Army Organization, 1952–1958." *Army History* 51 (Winter 2001): 1–13.

Service Historique de l'Armée de Terre, Republique Française. "Notes on French Army Operations in the Ardennes, 1914." Provided to author, 25 June1984. These notes include "Niveau GQG" and "Niveau 4e Armee."

Sheftick, Gary. "Army to Reset into Modular Brigade-Centric Force. Army News Service, 24 February 2004. http://www4.army.mil/ocpa/read.php?story_ id_key+5703 (accessed 9 November 2007).

Showalter, Dennis E. *Tannenberg: Clash of Empires, 1914.* Washington, DC: Brassey's, 2004.

Smith, Leonard V. *Between Mutiny and Obedience: The Case of the French Fifth Infantry Division During World War I.* Princeton, NJ: Princeton University Press, 1994.

Stacy, William E. *US Army Border Operations in Germany, 1945–1983.* Heidelberg, GE: US Army, Europe, 1984.

Stanton, Shelby L. *Order of Battle, U.S. Army, World War II.* Novato, CA: Presidio, 1984.

———. *Vietnam Order of Battle.* Washington, DC: US News Books, 1981.

Starry, General Donn A. *Mounted Combat in Vietnam.* Vietnam Studies. Washington, DC: Department of the Army, 1978.

Stubbs, Mary Lee, and Stanley R. Connor. *Armor-Cavalry, Part I: Regular Army and Army Reserve.* Washington, DC: US Army Center of Military History, 1969.

Summerall, General Charles P. "Cavalry in Modern Combat." *Cavalry Journal* 39 (October 1930): 491–493.

Taylor, Curtis D. *Trading the Saber for Stealth: Can Surveillance Technology Replace Traditional Aggressive Reconnaissance?* Arlington, VA: Institute of Land Warfare, Association of the United States Army, 2005.

Tessin, Georg. *Vergände und Truppen der deutschen Wehrmacht und der Waffen-SS im Zweiten Weltkrieg 1939–1945, Band 2: Die Landstreitkräfte. Nrn. 1–5.* Osnabrück, GE: Biblio Verlag, 1973.

Teveth, Shabtai. *The Tanks of Tammuz.* New York: Viking, 1969.

Third Cavalry Museum. *Blood and Steel: The History, Customs, and Traditions of the 3d Armored Cavalry Regiment.* Fort Carson, CO: Third Cavalry Museum, 2006. http://www.hood.army.mil/3d_ACR/docs/history_2.pdf (accessed 6 November 2007).

Tolson, Lieutenant General John J. *Airmobility, 1961–1971.* Vietnam Studies. Washington, DC: Department of the Army, 1973.

Toomey, Charles Lane. *XVIII Airborne Corps in Desert Storm: From Planning to Victory.* Central Point, OR: Hellgate Press, 2004.

Tosh, Captain Vernie G., and Captain James B. Hobson, "Pentomic Infantry Division: Mobility." *Infantry* 47 (July 1957): 35–39.

"Tradition." *KameradschaftPanzeraufklärungsbataillon 12 e.V.* http://www.pzaufklbtl12.de/Tradition/tradition.htm (accessed 29 October 2007).

"Unit Designations in the Army Modular Force." US Army Center of Military History presentation to the Association of the US Army (AUSA) Conference, 26 September 2005. www.cascom.army.mil/odct/Documents/AUSA_Briefing_26_Sep_05.ppt (accessed 6 November 2007).

Unterseher, Lutz. "Europe's Armed Forces at the Millennium: A Case Study of Change in France, the United Kingdom, and Germany." Project on Defense Alternatives Briefing Report No. 11, November 1999. http://www.comw.org/pda/9911eur.html (accessed 26 October 2007).

US Bureau of the Census. "Statistical Abstract of the United States, 1940." http://www2.census.gov/prod2/statcomp/documents/1941-02.pdf (accessed 12 October 2007).

Veller, Lawrence C. Jr. *Never Without Heroes: Marine Third Reconnaissance Battalion in Vietnam, 1965–70.* New York: Ivy, 1996.

Wagner, Major General Robert E. "Division Cavalry: The Broken Sabre." *Armor* 98 (September–October 1989): 35–41.

Welsch, Major O. "Cavalry in the Palestine Campaign." [British] *Cavalry Journal* 17 (April 1927): 293–301.

"Why Five?" *Infantry* 47 (April 1957): 6–11.

Wilson, John B. *Armies, Corps, Divisions, Separate Brigades.* Army Lineage Series. Washington, DC: US Army Center of Military History, 1987.

———. *Maneuver and Firepower: The Evolution of Divisions and Separate Brigades.* Washington, DC: US Army Center of Military History, 1998.

———. "Mobility Versus Firepower: The Post-World War I Infantry Division." *Parameters* 13 (September 1983): 47–52.

Windrow, Martin, and Richard Hook. *The Panzer Division*. Rev ed. London: Osprey, 1982.

Witsken, Captain Jeff, and Captain Lee MacTaggart, "Light Cavalry in the 10th Mountain Division, *Armor* 99 (July–August 1990): 36–40.

Zetterling, Niklas. *Normandy 1944: German Military Organization, Combat Power and Organizational Effectiveness*. Winnipeg, ON: J.J. Fedorowicz, 2000.

Ziemke, Earl F., and Magna E. Bauer. *Moscow to Stalingrad: Decision in the East*. Washington, DC: US Army Center of Military History, 1989.

———. *Stalingrad to Berlin: The German Defeat in the East*. Washington, DC: US Army Center of Military History, 1983.

Zinsmeister, Karl. *Boots on the Ground: A Month With the 82d Airborne in the Battle for Iraq*. New York: Truman Tally Books, St. Martin's Press, 2003.

Zobel, Horst. "3rd Panzer Division Operations." *The Initial Period of War on the Eastern Front, 22 June–August 1941: Proceedings of the Fourth Art of War Symposium, Garmisch, FRG, October 1987*. Edited by Colonel David Glantz. London: Frank Cass, 1993.

Appendix
Selective Comparative Reconnaissance Platforms

Platform (Nations)	Year Made	Weight (tons)	Range (miles)	Max Road Speed (mph)	Characteristics/ Armament	Remarks
T-1 Pontiac Lt Armd Car (US)	1927	1.25	150	70	4 wheels Crew: 3 2 .30-cal MGs	
T-2 LaSalle Med Armd Car (US)	1928	2.75	150	60	4 wheels Crew: 4 1 .30-cal MG	4 produced
T-3 Dodge Med Armd Car (US)	1930	5.00	NA	NA		
M1 (T4) Armd Car (US)	1931		NA	55		
Carden-Lloyd Mark VI Tankette (UK)	1930s	1.50	NA	28	Crew: 2 .303-cal MG	
M3 Half-Track APC (US)	1940–45	9.30	175	40	Crew: 3 Various configurations	
Truck, Utility, Jeep (US)	1941–45	0.25	300	65	4 wheels Various configurations	Scout vehicle
SdKfz 250 (Germany)	1941–43	5.80	130	35	Half-track Crew: 2 Various configurations	Recon bns Designed to carry half a section (squad)
M3/M5 Stuart Lt Tank (US)	1941–43	14.70	100	36	37-mm gun	
M8 Lt Armd Car (US)	1943–45	7.80	350	55	6 wheels Crew: 4 37-mm gun	
M24 Chaffee Lt Tank (US)	1944–53	18.40	175	35	Crew: 5 75-mm gun	Replaced by M41
M41 Walker Bulldog Lt Tank (US) (RVN)	1953–65 1961–75	23.50	100	43	Crew: 4 76-mm gun	Replaced by M551
AMX-13 Lt Tank (France) (Israel)	1953–75 1956–73	13.70	240	36	Crew: 5 75-/90-105-mm gun	Standard Soviet recon tank replaced by BMP/T-62 tank

Platform (Nations)	Year Made	Weight (tons)	Range (miles)	Max Road Speed (mph)	Characteristics/ Armament	Remarks
PT-76 Lt Amphibious Tank (USSR)	1953–present	14.00	156	26	Crew: 3 76.2-mm gun	
BRDM Cbt Recon Patrol Vehicle (USSR)	1957–present	7.00	450	57	4 wheels Crew: 4 14.5-mm MG	
M113 APC (US and many other countries)	1960–present	12.30	300	41	Crew: 2 Various configurations	
M114 Cmd and Recon Vehicle (US)	1963–71	5.90	266	35	Crew: 3 .50-cal MG	
M551 Sheridan Lt Tank (US)	1967–78 (1996 in abn role)	15.20	336	40	Crew: 4 152-mm gun/ missile launcher	
FV107 Scimitar Lt Armd Recon Vehicle (Lt Tank) (UK)	1971–present	7.80	386	50	Crew: 3 30-mm gun	Used in formation recon regiments
FV101 Scorpion Lt Tank (UK)	1973–96	8.70	386	57	Crew: 6 76-mm gun	
AMX-10RC Armd Car (France)	1976–present	14.20	360	40	6 wheels Crew: 4 105-mm gun in turret	
ERC-90 Panhard Armd Car (France)	1977–present	8.30	438	55	6 wheels Crew: 3 90-mm gun	
FV103 Spartan APC (UK)	1978–present	8.10	290	48	Crew: 2 7.62-mm MG Milan ATGM	
Luchs *Spähpanzer* Armd Car (Germany)	1978–present	19.50	438	55	8 wheels Crew: 4 20-mm gun in turret	
M3 Bradley CFV (US)	1981–present	30.40	300	41	Crew: 3 25-mm gun TOW ATGM	
Fenneck *Leichte Gepanzerte Spähwagen* (Armd Car) (Germany/ Netherlands)	2003–present	9.70	516	70	4 wheels Crew: 3 12.7-mm MG	Replacing the Luchs

Index

73 Easting, Battle of (1991), 172–173
106-mm recoilless rifles, 127, 154
Abonneau, *Général de Division* Pierre, 22, 25–26, 34
Abu Ageila, Egypt, 124–125, 127, 129
Adam, *Generaloberst* Wilhelm, 62
Adan, Major General Avraham, 130–132
aerial reconnaissance, 15, 35–36, 145
Afst, Belgium 102–104
air assault division, 166–167, 172, 177, 183
airmobile division (see air assault division), 152, 154, 159
Allenby, General Sir Edmund, 39–40, 51, 65
American Civil War, 3, 8
Arab-Israeli War, 1973, 123, 130–131
Ardennes, 16–27, 35–36, 45, 47, 78, 81, 83–85, 95–96, 101, 111, 200
Argonne Offensive, 40–41
Arlon, Belgium, 29
armored cars, 51–55, 60–66, 68, 70–71, 77, 80–81, 84, 86–87, 89–91, 93, 96, 99, 105–106, 110, 112, 114, 134, 138, 141–145, 147, 150, 154, 159, 182, 183
    troop (US), 52–53
artillery, 1, 2, 3, 8, 10, 18, 26–28, 30, 32, 37–39, 42–43, 51–53, 66, 68, 70, 85, 87, 96, 98–100, 103, 106, 109, 129, 141, 151, 162–163, 170, 173, 175, 177–178, 180, 200, 202

Baker, Colonel Chauncey, 40
Bastogne, Belgium, 18–19, 23, 27, 29–30, 34, 46
Beersheba, Battle of (1917), 39
Belgium
    1914 campaign, 5, 7, 14–36 passim
    1940 campaign, 79–87 passim
    1944 campaign, 101–104 passim
Berlin Blockade, 147
Berlin crisis (1961), 151
Bertrix, Belgium, 17, 29–30, 34–35, 47
bicycles, military use of, 7, 9–11, 26, 30–31, 33, 56–57, 62, 68, 74, 78, 94–95, 117
Bossut, *Capitaine*, 27, 29–30, 46
Bouillon, Belgium, 19, 23, 29–30, 85–86
British and Commonwealth Forces, 35, 37, 39, 41, 43, 47, 52, 64–67, 71, 77–78, 81, 86–87, 91–92, 111–115, 118, 138–139, 145, 182, 188
    25-pdr guns, 91
    armored cars, 64–66, 112
    armored personnel carriers, 77, 140, 182
        Spartan, 140, 234

235

armored scout carriers, 64
ATGMs
    Swingfire, 140
Bren armored personnel carrier, 111–112, 114
British Expeditionary Force (BEF), 65–66
close reconnaissance squadron, 139–140
divisional reconnaissance, 141
Household Cavalry, 139
Long Range Desert Group, 112, 118
medium reconnaissance squadron, 140
reconnaissance regiment, 139, 141
Royal Armoured Corps (RAC), 64, 66, 139
tanks
    Centurion, 126
    heavy (infantry), 65
    light, 65–67, 111–112
    light cruiser, 65
    Scorpion, 139–140, 234
    Scimitar, 139–140, 234
units
    Desert Mounted Corps, 39
    1st Armoured Division, 66, 140–141
    16/15 Queen's Royal Lancers, 140
Brom, Major Yoav, 132, 186

Cambodia, 158–159
Caucasus, 93
cavalry, horse, 1–5, 11, 39, 49, 51, 53–54, 56, 58, 60, 62, 65, 69–71, 84, 109, 113, 116–117, 133, 197, 201–202, 205
    American, 2, 3, 40, 50–52, 54–55, 71–73, 98, 109
    converted to mechanized cavalry, 2, 49, 51–55, 57, 64, 69–70, 98, 113–114, 133
    dismounted, 3, 9, 18, 36, 38–41, 43
    divisional, 2, 9–10, 12–14, 24, 27–28, 35, 40, 56–57, 60–61, 69, 79, 81
    divorced from reconnaissance role, 56, 98
    French, 7–13, 15–36
    German, 7–38, 56–58, 60, 62, 64–65, 68, 71, 87, 94, 117
    in the American Civil War, 3, 8
    mounted, 3, 7, 9, 11, 15, 20, 36–37, 39, 41–42
    regimental organization, 4, 10, 27
    Russian/Soviets, 37, 47, 69, 70, 133
    tactics, 13, 14
        dismounted, 39–42
    shock, 2, 7–8, 22, 25, 39
        versus cavalry, 3, 8
Chinese Farm, Battle of (1973), 131, 183

counterinsurgency operations, 138, 155–156, 182
counterreconnaissance, 1, 2, 7, 51, 54, 100, 106–107, 110–112, 161, 197, 201, 204
cuirassiers, 8–9, 15, 25–26, 43
Cussac, *Commandant* Antoine, 26–27, 30–33, 35
cyclist (bicycle) troops, 7, 9–11, 26, 30–33, 46, 56, 62, 64, 68, 74

Daika Pass, operations at (1956), 125
De Cugnac, Colonel Gaspard-Jean-Marie-René, 26, 30
De Langle de Cary, *Général* Ferdinand Louis Armand, 22, 25, 35
De Sailly, *Général de Brigade* Emmanuel-Philibert-Henri, 26, 29
De Séréville, *Général de Brigade* Gombau, 26, 30
deep battle, 69, 113
DESERT STORM, Operation, 140–141, 160, 162, 166, 168–172, 174–175, 183, 192, 195, 200, 202
Deversoir, Egypt, 124, 131–132
Devine, Colonel Mark, 102–103
Dinant, Belgium, 19–21, 23, 25, 29–30, 34
dragoons, 8–9, 25–26, 29–33
Dyle River, 80–82, 111

Eastern Front, World War I, 37–38
echelonment, 5, 197, 201
Egyptian Army
    engineers, 125
    units, 127–132
        Second Army, 132
El Alamein, 92
El Arish, Egypt, 124, 128–129
Elista, Russia, 93, 100
Euphrates River, 176–177
    valley, 175
European Theater of Operations (ETO) (World War II), 98, 100, 105–108
exploitation, 1, 2

France
    1914 campaign, 5, 7, 14–36
    1940 campaign, 77–87
Franks, Lieutenant General Frederick, 173
French Army
    armies
        World War I
            Fourth, 16–17, 22–23, 25–26, 34–35, 47
            Fifth, 16, 22–23, 47
    armored cars
        AMX-10RC, 141–142, 234
        ERC-90, 141–142, 234

artillery, 10, 26, 30, 32, 68
ATGMs
    HOT, 141, 187
    Milan, 143
battalions
    World War I
        1st Battalion, 87th Infantry Regiment, 26, 29–33, 35
brigades
    World War I
        1st Cuirassier, 26, 30, 32–33
        9th Dragoon, 26, 29–31, 33
        16th Dragoon, 26–27, 30–31, 33
cavalry, 7–37, 41, 43–47, 67–69, 71, 78–88, 111, 116
chasseurs, 9, 13, 26
chasseurs à pied, 9
corps
    World War I
        I Cavalry (Cavalry Corps Sordet), 16, 18–22
        Corps Abonneau, 22–23, 25–26, 34
    World War II
        Cavalry Corps, 80–81, 111
deployment, 1940, 81, 111
deployment, August 1914, 12–14, 16, 25
divisions
    World War I
        1st Cavalry, 20
        3d Cavalry, 20–21
        4th Cavalry, 18–19, 22–23, 25, 33–34, 41, 45
        5th Cavalry, 18, 20–21
        5th Infantry, 47
        9th Cavalry, 22–23, 25–26, 30, 34–35
    World War II
        1st *DCR*, 82, 86
        1st *DLC*, 82
        2d *DLC*, 82
        4th *DLC*, 22
        5th *DLC*, 82, 84
        2d *DLM*, 82
        3d *DLM*, 82, 87
        5th *DLM*, 85
    since 1945
        6th *DLB*, 141
groupe, 10, 26
groupe cycliste, 9, 26
prewar (1914) organization, 7–14

reconnaissance units, World War II, 78–88, 111, 113
regiments
    World War I
        1st Dragoons, 26, 29–32
        3d Dragoons, 26, 30–31
        24th Dragoons, 26, 29–30
    since 1945
        1 *REC*, 141
squadrons
    since 1945
        1/*RHP*, 142
        2/*RHP*, 142
types of units
    Bataillon de Dragons Portés (BDP), 68
    Brigade de Cavalerie (BC), 68
    Division Cuirassée de Rèserve (DCR), 67, 82
    Division de Cavalerie (DC), 68
    Division Légère (DL), 68
    Division Légère Mècanique (DLM), 67, 79–81, 111
    Division Légère de Cavalerie (DLC), 67, 79, 81–82, 86, 111
    Groupe d'Autos-Mitrailleuses (GAM), 68
    Groupe de Reconnaissance (GR), 69
    Groupe de Reconnaissance de Corps d'Armée (GRCA), 69, 79
    Groupe de Reconnaissance de Division d'Infanterie (GRDI), 69, 79–81
use of reservists, 11–13, 44
Gaza Strip, 124–125, 127–128
Gaza, Third Battle of, 39
Gembloux, Battle of (1940), 82
German Army
    Abteilung, 10–11, 74
    armies
        World War I
            First, 16, 18, 22
            Second, 16, 18, 22, 23
            Third, 16, 20, 23–25
            Fourth, 16–17, 20, 22–25, 33–34
            Fifth, 20, 23
        World War II
            Fifth Panzer, 101
            Sixth Panzer, 95, 101
    army groups
        World War II
            A, 93
            B, 93
    artillery, 8, 10–11, 27, 32, 37–38, 43, 85, 96, 103

battalions
  World War I
    1st Battalion, 3d Foot Artillery, 28
  World War II
    3d Armored Reconnaissance, 91
brigades
  World War I
    21st Artillery, 28
    41st, 28, 30, 32–34
    42d, 28, 32–34
  World War II
    Führer Escort, 101
    1st Cavalry, 60, 62
Bundeswehr (since 1955)
  armored cars
    Fuchs, 142–144
    Luchs, 142–144, 234
  armored personnel carriers
    Hotchkiss *SPz kurz*, 143
    Marder, 143
  armored reconnaissance battalion, 62, 71, 83–84, 88–89, 90–91, 95, 116–117, 142, 144
  Intervention Force, 144
  scout platoon, 83, 144
  Stabilization Force, 144
  tanks
    Leopard I/II, 143–144
cavalry
  organization, 8–11, 16, 94
    wartime reorganization, 11–12, 94–95
corps
  World War I
    I Cavalry, 16, 18–21, 44
    II Cavalry, 16, 18
    III Cavalry, 16
    IV Cavalry, 20, 25, 27, 44
    VI, 23, 28
    XVIII, 23–24, 27, 33–34
  World War II
    XIV, 78, 82
    XV, 82, 85–86
    XVI, 80, 82
    XIX, 82, 84, 86
    XXXXI, 82
    Deutsches Afrika Korps (*DAK*), 91–92

deployment, August 1914, 16, 18
divisions
    World War I
        3d Cavalry, 27
        12th, 28
        21st, 25, 27–30, 32–33
        25th, 25, 28, 34
        Guards Cavalry, 12
    interwar
        3d Cavalry, 58
    World War II
        1st Light, 78, 115
        1st Panzer, 82–85, 117
        2d Panzer, 85
        5th Panzer, 82, 84–85
        7th Panzer, 85–86, 91, 118
        10th Panzer, 83–85, 100
        15th Panzer, 91
        16th Motorized, 93, 100
        18th *Volksgrenadier*, 101–104
        21st Panzer, 91–92, 117
        90th Light Africa, 91
        164th Light Africa, 91
groups
    World War II
        Panzergruppe Kleist, 81–82
*Jäger*s, 9, 11, 18, 36
light divisions, 58–60, 68, 71, 78, 91
motorized infantry divisions, 62–63, 71, 81, 85, 90–100
Motorized Troops Combat Directorate, 58
panzer divisions, 56, 58, 61–62, 69, 71, 77–85, 88, 90–95, 97, 100–101, 103, 115–118
panzergrenadier divisions, 77, 90, 96–97
regiments
    World War I
        6th *Uhlan*, 28
        27th Artillery, 28
        63d Artillery, 28
        80th Fusiliers, 28, 31–32
        81st Infantry (1st Hessian), 28, 31
        87th Infantry (1st Nassau), 26, 28, 31–32
        88th Infantry (2d Nassau), 28, 31
    World War II
        Grossdeutschland motorized infantry, 83

Reichswehr (1919–35), 56, 58, 60–62
    cavalry organization, 56, 58, 60
    field service regulations, 1921, 1923, 56
    field service regulations, 1933, 57
    squadrons, 12, 37, 47, 56, 60, 63, 82, 84, 87–88, 93–94, 115
    use of reservists, 11, 12
    Wehrmacht (1935–45), 60, 62, 77–78
        armored cars (*Panzerspähwagen*)
            Kfz 13, 61–62
            SdKfz 221, 61–62
            SdKfz 231, 77
            SdKfz 234/4, 77, 90
        cavalry designations, 88
        cavalry organization, 60–61
        divisional reconnaissance, 58–64, 79, 82–84, 86–89, 90–96
        fusilier battalions, 94–95
        half-tracks
            SdKfz 250/251, 89, 117, 233
        motorcycle units, 60–64, 74, 77, 83–85, 87–88, 91, 93–94, 114, 116, 118
    Volksgrenadier Divisions, 95, 101–104
Gette River, 18
Gonen, Major General Shmuel, 127, 129
Great Bitter Lake, 131–132
Guadalcanal, 109
Guderian *Generaloberst* Heinz, 56, 58, 60–61, 63–64, 69, 78, 82–86, 116
    Achtung Panzer, 63, 73

Haelen, Battle of (1914), 18
Hamipré, Battle of (1914), 16–36, 46, 64
Hamipré, Belgium, 16–17, 29–35
Harel, Lieutenant Colonel Baruch, 128
Henry, Major General Guy, 53
high-mobility, multipurpose wheeled vehicle (HMMWV), 144, 162–163, 166, 168–170, 174, 178,–181, 183, 199
Hillah, Iraq, 176–177
Holder, Colonel Leonard "Don," 173
hussars, 8–9, 13, 26
hybrid organizations, 54–55, 205
hybrid units, 68, 71, 81, 94, 98, 111, 157, 167, 183, 197, 200–201

Ia Drang campaign (1965), 159
infantry
    versus horse cavalry, 3, 39–40
    light, 9–11, 26, 71, 166, 168, 172, 180, 198
    augmenting cavalry, 9–11

Intra-German border, 151
Iraqi Army
    Republican Guard, 173–174
        Republican Guard Forces Command, 173
        Tawakalna Mechanized Division, 173
IRAQI FREEDOM (OIF), Operation, 171, 175, 177
Israeli Defense Force (IDF)
    armored brigades, 124–125, 127–130, 132
    armored corps, 126
    infantry brigades, 124–125
    paratrooper brigades, 125
    reconnaissance units, 123–133
    tanks
        AMX-13, 126, 233
        Centurion, 126
        M48 Patton, 126
    units
        Granit Force, 127, 129, 185
        Steel Division (*Ugdat ha'Plada*), 127, 185
        4th Infantry Brigade, 125
        7th Armored Brigade, 125, 127–130
        14th Armored Brigade, 130
        27th Armored Brigade, 125
        87th Armored Reconnaissance Battalion, 131–133
        643d Reconnaissance Company, 127–128
jeeps, 99, 105–111, 114, 123–125, 127–130, 133, 146, 149, 152, 154–155, 183
Jiradi, Battle of (1967), 128–129
Joffre, General Joseph, 13, 15–17, 21–22, 25, 35, 45, 47

Kalmyk Steppe, 93
Kantara, Egypt, 124, 127, 129
Karbala, Iraq, 176–177
Kasserine Pass, 92
Khan Yunis, Palestine, 124, 127–128, 186
Kleist, *General der Kavallerie* Ewald von, 83
Korea/Korean War, 123, 146–147, 149, 154, 156, 159
Kraftfahrkampftruppe, 61
Kraftfahrtruppe, 60
Krag, *SS-Sturmbannführer* Ernst-August, 96
Krewinkel, Belgium, 102–104
Kubelwagen, 90
Kursk, Battle of (1943), 94
Kusseima, Egypt, 124–125

L'Espée, *Général de Division* Jean-François de, 25, 27, 29–32
lance, use of, 3, 8–9, 43, 56
Lanzerath, Belgium, 102–104
Léglise, Belgium, 29
Lesse River, 19, 21, 23
Libya, 91–92
Liege, 16–19, 21–23, 45
Łodz, Battle of (1915), 38, 47
long-range reconnaissance units, 91, 133–134, 136–137, 160
Longlier, Belgium, 29–33
Losheim Gap, 101–102, 104
Luftwaffe (German)
    air reconnaissance squadron, 78, 82, 115
    units
        3d Parachute (*Fallschirmjäger*) Division, 101, 103
Luxembourg, 16, 18–20, 22–23, 25, 82–83, 101

MacArthur, General Douglas, 53
machine guns, 8, 10–11, 38, 51–52, 62–63, 65, 69–70, 77, 88, 110, 114, 125, 127, 135, 154–156, 163, 166, 168
    in German cavalry, 1914, 8
Manderfeld, Belgium, 102–104
Marne Campaign (1914), 35, 43
Marshall, General George, 98
Martelange, Belgium, 19, 23, 25, 27, 29
Meuse River, 16, 18–20, 22–23, 25, 45, 80–82, 84–86, 111
Mitchell, Brigadier General William, 50
Montgomery, Field Marshal Bernard, 112
Moscow, 112
motorcycle units, 51, 54, 60, 61, 63, 66–70, 77, 83–84, 87–88, 93–94, 112, 116, 118, 134–135

Najaf, Iraq, 176–177
Nakhl, Egypt, 125
Namoussart, Belgium, 29–31, 33
Neufchâteau, Belgium, 16, 19–25, 27, 29–35, 46–47, 84–85
North Africa, 73, 90–91, 93, 100, 112–113
North Atlantic Treaty Organization (NATO), 123, 138, 182, 188

Orr, Captain Ori, 127–129

Palestine campaign (1917–18), 39–40, 42
Pastouiel, Lieutenant, 27, 29–30, 46
Patrick, Major General Mason, 50
pickets, 4
Plan XVII, 15–16, 44

Polish campaign (1939), 55, 58, 74, 78
pursuit, 38–39, 42, 49–51, 64, 86

Rafah Junction, Egypt, 127, 129
Rafah, Palestine, 124–125, 127
reconnaissance
 defined, 2
 operational, 1, 2, 4, 10, 13, 64, 68, 78–80, 82–83, 91–93, 97, 113, 145, 161–162, 202
 tactical, 2, 4, 10, 13–14, 36, 79–80, 82
reconnaissance paradox, 198–200, 202–203, 205
reconnaissance units
 echelonment, 2, 5
 equipment debate, 5
Richthofen, *Generalleutnant* Baron Manfred von, 18, 20–21, 24
Romanian campaign (1917), 38
Rommel, *Generalfeldmarschall* Erwin, 86–87, 91–92, 112
Russian Army (World War I)
 cavalry forces, 37–38, 47
Russian campaign, 1941–45, 88, 90, 92–94, 112–113

sabers, 3, 8, 9
Samawah, Iraq, 176–177
Salmchâteau, Belgium, 96
Sambre River, 19, 23, 47
Saudi Arabia, 140
Schenck, *General der Infanterie* Freiherr von, 24–25, 27
Schlieffen Plan, 11, 13, 17–18, 22
Schnee Eifel, 101
security, 1–4, 7–8, 18, 38, 40, 49, 51, 64, 100, 106–107, 110, 113, 120, 136, 141, 145, 151, 157–160, 172, 174–175, 177, 182–183, 200–203
Semois River, 19, 23, 30, 34, 81, 84–85
Sharon, Major General Ariel, 126–127, 129, 131–132, 185
Sinai, 123–127, 129–133
Sinai campaign (1956), 125
Sinai campaign (1967), 127, 129
skirmishers, 4
Snuol, Cambodia, 158
Sordet, *Général de Division* Jean-François, 20–22, 44–45, 68
Southeast Asia, 155–156
Soviet (Red) Army
 Afghan War, 1979–89, 133, 138
 armored cars
  BRDM, 134–135, 234
 cavalry, 69–70, 133

245

Cold War
    reconnaissance units, 133–135, 138
    invasion of Czechoslovakia, 1968, 133, 138
combat reconnaissance patrol (CRP), 137
divisional reconnaissance, 92, 134, 137
doctrine, 69, 136–138
fighting vehicles
    BMP, 134–135
mechanized brigades, 70
mechanized corps, 70
motorized rifle divisions, 70, 133–134
tank division, 70
tanks, light
    PT-76, 135, 234
St. Mihiel Offensive (1918), 40–41
Stavelot, Belgium, 96
Suez Canal,126–127, 129, 132
surveillance, 161, 178, 180–182, 184, 191

Tal, Major General Yisrael, 127–129, 185
Targu Jiu, Battle of, 38
Thoma, *General der Panzertruppen* Wilhelm Ritter von, 92
TOW missile system, 133, 154, 163–164, 166, 168
Tukhachevsky, Marshal Mikhail, 69–70
Tunisia, 92, 112
Turkish Army (World War I)
    divisions
        27th Infantry, 39

US Air Force
    Army Air Corps, 50
    Army Air Force, 50
        divisional observation squadron, 50
US Army
    Air Service, 41, 50
        observation group, 41
    armored cars
        M1 (T4), 53
        M8, 110, 159
    armored cavalry regiments, 145, 148–150, 156, 158, 160–163, 165, 171, 183, 190
    Armored Force, 54, 72, 97, 106, 147
    armored personnel carriers
        armored cavalry assault vehicle (ACAV), 154–156, 158
        half-track, M3, 106, 114, 233
        M113, 130, 144, 152–156, 158–159, 162–164, 168, 234
        Stryker, 178–179

armored command and reconnaissance vehicle
M114, 145–146, 152–155, 159, 234
armored gun system (AGS), 163
ATGMs
    Shillelagh 152-mm gun/missile, 155–156
    TOW, 133, 154, 163, 166, 168
battalion scout platoon, 154–155, 169–170–171, 174
battlefield surveillance brigade (BfSB), 182
brigade combat team (BCT) concept, 169, 180
brigade reconnaissance troop (BRT), 169–170
cavalry
    air cavalry units, 152, 154, 156–158, 160, 166, 177, 183, 190, 192
        aeroscout platoon (white team), 152
        aeroweapons platoon (red team), 152
        aerorifle platoon (blue team), 152
    armored cavalry units, 145, 147–167, 171–173, 179, 183, 190
    in World War I, 40–42
    mechanized, 51–55
Cavalry branch, 51–52, 54–55, 72, 98, 147
Experimental Mechanized Force (EMF), 52–54
field service regulation, 1941, 99
fighting vehicle
    M2/M3 cavalry fighting vehicle (CFV), Bradley, 161–168, 174, 180–181, 234
General Board, ETO, 100, 104, 106–108
heavy divisions, 120, 151–152, 163
helicopters
    AH-1, 168
    AH-1G Cobra, 152
    AH-64 Apache, 161–162, 165, 167
    OH-6A Cayuse, 152–153
    OH-58/OH-58D Kiowa, 152, 161–162, 164–165, 167–168, 175, 177
    UH-1B Huey, 152–153
    UH-1D Huey, 152
    UH-60 Blackhawk, 161–162, 164
improved TOW vehicle (ITV), 168
Infantry branch, 72, 108
interwar period, 49, 50
    cavalry division organization, 51
    horse-mechanized cavalry regiment, 54–55, 58, 71, 73
light armored cavalry regiment (LACR), 163, 166, 178
light versus heavy debate, 5, 197–198, 203
Lightweight Laser Designator Rangefinder (LLDR), 180–181
Long-Range Advanced Scout Surveillance System (LRAS3), 180–181
long-range reconnaissance and patrol (LRRP) units, 160, 191

maneuvers, 1940, 107
maneuvers, 1941, 107
military intelligence units, 162, 178, 180, 182, 184
MK-19 automatic grenade launcher, 168
National Training Center (NTC), 168–170, 183
organizational structures
    Army of Excellence (AOE), 160–163, 166–171, 175, 181
    Division 86, 162–163, 166, 170
    Division-centric versus brigade-centric, 180
    Force XXI, 168–170, 177–178
    H-series tables of organization and equipment, 162
    J-series tables of organization and equipment, 165, 192
    Limited Conversion Division XXI (LCD XXI), 170
    L-series tables of organization and equipment, 166–167, 175, 192
    Modular Army, 163, 166, 170, 177–182
        heavy brigade, 180
        light brigade, 181
    ROAD reorganization, 151–154, 156, 160, 162, 164, 168–169
Pentomic division, 145, 147–149, 151
rangers, 133, 160
reconnaissance surveillance and target acquisition (RSTA), 178
    brigade, 182
    squadron, 178–182, 184, 194
reconnaissance units, postwar critiques of, 100, 106–110, 145
scout cars
    M3, 110
Stryker brigade combat team, 163, 177–179, 184
tanks
    M1 Abrams, 161–163, 167
    M48 Patton, 126, 143, 146, 157–158, 190
    M60 Patton, 152, 155–156
tank destroyers, 98, 100–102, 108, 120
tanks, light
    M3/M5 Stuart, 110, 146, 233
    M24 Chaffee, 146, 149, 159, 233
    M41 Walker Bulldog, 142, 146, 159, 233
    M551 Sheridan, 146, 152, 154–156, 234
units
    commands and headquarters
        World War I
            American Expeditionary Force (AEF), 7, 40–42, 48, 50–51, 197, 203
        since 1945
            US Forces, European Theater, 145
            US Military Assistance Command, Vietnam (MACV), 158

armies
- World War II
  - Third, 101, 119

brigades
- since 1945
  - 1st Brigade, 1st Infantry Division, 174
  - 2d Brigade, 82d Airborne Division, 175–177

companies
- since 1945
  - D Company, 52d Infantry, 179

corps
- World War II
  - V, 101
  - VIII, 101
- since 1945
  - II Field Force, Vietnam (II FFV), 158
  - VII, 171–174, 195
  - XVIII Airborne, 172, 174

divisions
- interwar
  - 1st Cavalry Division, 52, 54–55
  - 1st Cavalry Regiment (Mechanized), 53
  - 7th Cavalry Brigade (Mechanized), 53–54
  - 13th Cavalry Regiment (Mechanized), 53
- World War II
  - 2d Infantry, 96, 101
  - 75th Infantry, 96
  - 99th Infantry, 96, 101, 103
  - 106th Infantry, 101, 103
- since 1945
  - 1st Armored, 54, 173–174, 193
  - 2d Armored, 147
  - 1st Infantry, 158, 173, 174
  - 1st Cavalry 154, 158–159, 189
  - 3d Armored, 120, 173–174, 189
  - 3d Infantry, 175–177
  - 11th Air Assault, 154
  - 24th Infantry, 172–174
  - 25th Infantry, 158
  - 82d Airborne, 173–177
  - 101st Airborne, 154, 174–177

groups
- World War II
  - 14th Cavalry, 101–104

regiments
- since 1945
  - 2d Armored Cavalry, 151, 172–175, 178, 194
  - 3d Armored Cavalry149, 172, 181, 193
  - 6th Armored Cavalry, 151
  - 11th Armored Cavalry, 155, 158, 190
  - 14th Armored Cavalry, 151
  - 2d Cavalry (Light), 163
- squadrons/battalions
  - World War II
    - 18th Cavalry Squadron, 101–103
    - 32d Cavalry Squadron, 102
    - 820th Tank Destroyer Battalion, 101–102
  - since 1945
    - 2d Squadron, 4th Cavalry, 172, 174
    - 2d Squadron, 14th Cavalry, 179
    - 3d Squadron, 7th Cavalry, 175–176
    - 1st Squadron, 4th Cavalry, 174
    - 1st Squadron, 9th Cavalry, 158–159
    - 1st Squadron, 17th Cavalry, 174–175, 177
    - 2d Squadron, 17th Cavalry, 174–175, 177

US Constabulary, 146

utility vehicles
- jeep, 97, 99, 105, 107–108, 110, 112, 114, 145, 148–150, 154, 233
- HMMWV, 144, 162–164, 166, 168–170, 174, 178, 180–181, 183

World War II
- armored division, 97, 104–106, 108, 119–120
- armored reconnaissance battalions, 97, 106
- combat commands, 105–106
- force structure, 97–100
- mechanized cavalry squadron, 98–99, 105
- reconnaissance troop (infantry division), 98–99, 103, 105, 107–108, 110, 114, 119

US Marine Corps
- divisional reconnaissance units, 108–109
- LAV-25 light amphibious vehicle, 171
  - light armored reconnaissance (LAR) battalions, 171
- units
  - Amphibious Reconnaissance Company, Fleet Marine Force, Pacific, 108
  - V Amphibious Corps, 108
  - 1st Marine Division, 109, 171
  - 3d Marine Division, 171
  - 3d Battalion, 2d Marines, 109

Verdun, 20, 37
Vietnam, 123, 145, 154–160, 183, 202
Vietnam, Republic of (South Vietnam), 159
  Army of the Republic of Vietnam (ARVN), 159
Vistula River, 78
Von Oven, *Generalmajor* Ernst, 27, 32
Von Seeckt, *Generaloberst* Hans, 56–57, 60

Waffen SS (German)
  units
    Sixth Panzer Army, 95, 101
    1st SS Panzer Division, 95, 103, 119
    2d SS Panzer Division, 96
    12th SS Panzer Division, 96, 101
Wallace, General William, 197
Weckerath, Belgium, 102–104
World War I, 1, 2, 4–5, 7–8, 12, 37, 40, 42–43, 49–52, 55–56, 65, 180, 197, 202, 203

About the Author

Boston native John J. McGrath has worked for the United States Army in one capacity or another since 1978. A retired Army Reserve officer, Mr. McGrath served in infantry, field artillery, and logistics units, both on active duty and as a reservist. Before coming to work at the Combat Studies Institute, he worked for 4 years at the US Army Center of Military History in Washington, DC, as a historian and archivist. Before that, Mr. McGrath worked full-time for the United States Army Reserve in Massachusetts for more than 15 years, both as an active duty reservist and as a civilian military technician. He also served as a mobilized reservist in 1991 in Saudi Arabia with the 22d Support Command during Operation DESERT STORM as the Command Historian and in 1992 at the US Army Center of Military History as a researcher/writer.

Mr. McGrath is a graduate of Boston College and holds an MA in history from the University of Massachusetts at Boston. He is the author of numerous articles and military history publications. In 1994, the Army Material Command published his book *Theater Logistics in the Gulf War*. The US Army Combined Arms Center Combat Studies Institute Press has published the following books written by Mr. McGrath: *The Brigade: A History* (2005), *Crossing the Line of Departure: Battle Command on the Move* (2006), *Boots on the Ground: Troop Density in Contingency Operations* (2006), and *The Other End of the Spear: The Tooth-to-Tail Ratio (T3R) in Modern Military Operations* (2007). Mr. McGrath was also the general editor of the proceedings of the Combat Studies Institute's 2005 Military History Symposium, *An Army at War: Change in the Midst of Conflict*, and contributed to CSI's anthology *In Contact! Case Studies From the Long War*. Aside from a general interest in things military and historical, his areas of particular interest include modern military operations, the German Army in World War II, August 1914, and the Union Army in the Civil War. He has a keen interest in ancient history, historical linguistics, the city of Boston, and baseball. He is also a PhD candidate at Kansas State University.